"A Soldiers Dying Heart"

About the Gulf War and the After Effects

Written By: Randy L. Stamm

Sergeant First Class US Army (Retired) 1980-1995

ISBN: 1-4033-6486-9 (e-book)
ISBN: 1-4033-6487-7 (Paperback)

This book is printed on acid free paper.

1stBooks – rev. 10/21/02

"A Soldiers Dying Heart"

About the Gulf War

From the time I enlisted until now, and the way the Government has treated the Gulf War Veterans. This has been a 7-year challenge with the Veterans Administration so this includes research to help other Gulf War Veterans.

Dedication to **Specialist Roy T. Damien, Jr.** of California, of the 121st Signal Battalion in the "The Big Red One" 1st Infantry Division. Loosing his life at 21 years old after the invasion of Kuwait.

To my dear daughter I live every day for you, **Brittni Lynn Stamm born at Fort Hood Texas in 1986.**

To **Larry & Wanda Logan** of Gun Barrel City, Texas. Mom and Dad. I still love you both.

And to all my brothers and sisters, I love you too, Wendy Townzen, Tommy Stamm, Pandora Browning, Larry A. Logan JR, Gary Logan, Charles Logan, Michael Logan, Lori Logan, Elizabeth Logan.

To the Officers and Non-Commissioned Officers that have helped me mentally to better myself during my military career.

Lieutenant General Thomas Rhame	**Commander 1st Infantry Division (Retired)**
Brigadier General Dennis C. Moran	**Commander 5th Signal Command**
Colonel Jeffrey W. Foley	**Chief of Staff, Ft. Gordon Georgia**
Colonel Elwood (Bud) Jones	**Commander 51st Signal Battalion (Retired)**
Lieutenant Colonel Beth Foley	**Army Doctor Pentagon (Retired)**
Lieutenant Colonel William Hedges	**Germany**
Major Kenneth Evans	**2nd Battalion 75th Field Artillery XO**
Captain Rob Campbell	**1/10th Special Forces Group - Friend**
Captain John J. Wheelan Jr.	**Tac Sat Platoon Leader Gulf War**
Chief WO2 Brian D. Hubbs	**2nd Ranger Battalion (Ft. Lewis Wash)**
Command Sergeant Major Michel Pagano	**Somewhere in Oklahoma/Ohio (Retired)**
Command Sergeant Major Tom Edmundson	**Division Artillery Sergeant Major, 1st Infantry Fort Riley Kansas (Retired I think)**
Command Sergeant Major Bobby J. Payne	**3rd Signal Brigade Sergeant Major (Retired)**
Command Sergeant Major John S. Acock	**CSM DISA (Retired)**
Command Sergeant Major Luis Lopez	**Fort Bragg North Carolina**
Command Sergeant Major Thomas J. Clark	**440th Signal Battalion CSM Germany**
Sergeant Major Gerald Williams	**5th Signal Command Germany**

First Sergeant James Bell   First Sergeant Desert Storm (Retired)
Master Sergeant Billy L. Thetford   G-2 Central Command (Retired)
Sergeant First Class Frank Charles   D. Co. 57th Signal Bn (Retired)

To soldiers that I served with during this tough time in life, SGT David Kagels Medically Retired, SSG Marlon Tomera Fort Hood Texas, and Specialist Jason Jones of the Headquarters and Headquarters Company 51st Signal Battalion, Stuttgart Germany. Guys we made it back to Germany due to a TEAM EFFORT.

Preface

The one SOLDIER that I want to thank more than all is Command Sergeant Major Thomas J. Clark for showing me early in my career of what a soldier is all about, being a soldier and friend for the last 18 years And being there through thick and thin, good and bad. I'm one of those guys that only knows how to read one publication and that is the Army Times. To this day I still order it to see what is going on in the Army since I am a soldier at heart and still praise to soldiers still putting their lives on the line for all of us each and every day. This all started in late 1991 after arriving back to Germany after Desert Shield/Storm. I was a normal aggressive soldier and family man that had a whole career ahead of him until one day when it all started falling apart. Now I take medications to wake up to go to sleep and anything in between to function semi normally on a daily basis. But guess what the only people that understand are the other soldier just like me that are having the same problem that I am currently having and some of the time I have to look and see what is going on in the real world. The secret is the Government does not care about you unless you are under the ground and then they don't care what you have done for them.

Chapter I

Being a dedicated, professional soldier does not come overnight

For someone that went into the army at the age of 19 and spent his 20th birthday in Basic Training at Fort Sill, Oklahoma as a Cannon Crewmember a 13 Bravo as a career field. One thing I learned later on during the training the word that said "FIELD" I should have figured that out but no stupid me. This was something that I always dreamed about was being a Soldier. Some soldiers do it to escape things in their lives and I was one trying to turn my life around. When I joined the Army in 1980 and went through (OSUT) One Station Unit Training and never getting the chance to leave Fort Sill until Graduation Day if that would ever happen. I thought that I was mature enough to endure what ever was thrown at me. Well just imagine your worst nightmare and I was living it knowing if I could finish this part of life it may help me become something that my parents would be proud of just like all other men that I was serving with in 1st Platoon, Delta Battery 2d Cannon Training Battalion. And yes the part of Fort Sill I was at was all BOYS wanting to be MEN. We even had some guys that were in during Vietnam and decided for one reason or another that they wanted to come back into the Army. Someone forgot to open our eyes and tell us that it was not a dream. I can remember the first time I called home I was so depressed especially after getting just about thrown off of the bus at the reception station.

One thing that they did prepare me for was what was to come way in the future. For the first three years in the army while assigned to the 1st Battalion 78th Field Artillery in Alpha Battery, driving A howitzer which was not 25 tons of fun. It was harder than working in the oil field in East Texas. Breaking tracks was not the hardest task in the world but DIRTY, NASTY, FILTHY work. That was when soldiers wore their fatigues to Physical Training and then went to work. Not like the soldiers of today they to be pampered from the time they get up to the time they go to bed. And they have rights now from what I hear from the soldiers of today. I think I was as wild as anyone else that is single and did not have a life. Going from Bar to Bar playing pool without a care in the world. Until one day in 1992 and Sergeant

1

Major Michel F. Pagano called me into his office in Germany while assigned to the Headquarters & Headquarters 2nd Battalion 75th Field Artillery in Hanau just outside of Frankfurt. He told me just like my father did when I arrived to the United States and was going to Fort Gordon Georgia and that was since I was getting married that I had to grow up. "He always told me like it was and no lines in between" The sergeant major was a Frenchman and was hard as hell to put it nicely. One thing about him when I went to the first promotion board and failed he told me I was too cocky. To get my head out of my A _ _. Well a little time went by and I took to heart what he told me and it was to get my GED and go to college when ever I could and if I was a quitter I would not make the Army a career especially since I had just reenlisted for the MOS 26 Quebec 3 more years and the job title there was Tactical Satellite Microwave Systems Operator. Dummy me I still did not learn anything; I'm going back to the Field for 3 long years. After busting my butt in Fort Gordon Georgia and winning the Soldier of the Quarter Board and yes I still have the only plaque I would get in the army except for 2 others that came in 1992 in Stuttgart Germany from the 51st Signal Battalion S-3 during a move back to the states and in 1995 while having to accept early retirement for having all kinds of problems, mentally and physically.

To give you a little insight about me was that I had long hair when going into the Army and my older brother Tommy used to introduce me a sister. Me I was all of 125lbs when I entered the Army and began to see what it was all about. Not a Cakewalk and all of the older guys were Vietnam Veterans and hard core to the bone. They did not give an inch no matter if it was a duty roster or a picnic. You bust your butt from the time you get there until the time you finish then you can set back and relax and see if you had fun? In the Civilian world you have a mentor in the army you have a SERGEANT and during that time frame all of them earned them as well. You did not complete any school and get a ribbon on your uniform just to say I made it, but I was in the Army for 3 years and finally earned the Army Achievement Medal and I was on top of the world. I have not only one ribbon to wear home nut now I have 2 an Overseas ribbon. And I though that I was hot Shit but when arriving to Fort Gordon Georgia in 1993 everyone there was just like me either a Specialist or Sergeant or Staff Sergeant. Then the Army got tougher on promotions. But coming from a Combat Arms MOS I knew what that Sergeant Major told me in Germany and that was study and set you education because that was going to make the difference. And the OLD GUYS KNOW TOO. He was associated with the guy that was someday to become the USAREUR, United States Army Europe Command Sergeant Major George L. Horvath III. With whom I had met while attending a Soldier of the Quarter board at Fort Hood, Texas some 2 years later. These two went to the Sergeants Major Academy together when the dinosaurs were there, I think? There are a lot of War stories to tell but that will come later when the SHIT hits the Fan. During my second term of service I had the pleasure to work with some of the best Soldiers in the United States Army and some still serve today in Key Leadership positions throughout the World. And these guys still put their hearts and souls into it every day to keep us from people like Suddam Hussein and President Milosivich in Yugoslavia. And one thing that you cannot take away from a real soldier is his pride. Today I still have all of my medals that I received while serving in positions all over the world from Korea, Alaska, Germany and The Persian Gulf War. Like I said in the beginning of this book was that I wanted to thank the soldiers that helped me get what I had on my chest because without quality soldier no soldier would survive. The medals that I earned belong to all of the Marlon Tomera's and David Kagel's of the world.

The Awards that I earned while in are as follows: Bronze Star Medal, Meritorious Service Medal 3rd Award, Army Commendation Medal 4th Award, Army Achievement Medal 7th Award, Good Conduct Medal 4th Award, National Defense Service Medal, Armed Forces Expeditionary Medal, South West Asia Service Medal with 3 Service Stars, NCO Professional Development Ribbon with Number 3, Army Service Ribbon, Overseas Ribbon with number 3, Kuwait Liberation Medal, US Air Force Master Space Badge, Drivers Badge for wheeled & Tracked Vehicles, Expert Marksmanship Badge, Sharpshooter Grenade.

And one thing that I can say is I am proud of is the hard work and dedication that I gave during my 15 years 2 months and 17 days of active military service. To this day if I was healthy I have no doubt in my military mind that I would be promoted to Sergeant Major but due to the Medical problems after returning to Germany and later to Fort Leavenworth Kansas serving in a leadership position as well since that's what all good soldiers do is try to excel and compete for the next higher position. I chose to leave the Army on my terms and not theirs and that was the Early Retirement which has plagued me every since. One thing is I still have friends in the Army… "Once a Soldier always a Soldier" but GOD someone raise their pay and allowances equal to the civilian sector. This is for all of the soldiers defending whatever in the middle of the night all over the world. And the pay for the Senate and Congress is outrageous since they do nothing but make decisions. On June 30, 2002 I went out with my girlfriend and had a few drinks and met this young man who was in Uniform and was wearing a Ranger Tab for the 75th Regiment and was just called to active duty and that tells me that something is getting ready to start all over again because that is the first Soldiers that are called with the exception on the Special Operations Guys. I bought him and his wife a drink and wished him well in whatever happens and he saluted me and walked away with the feeling of someone respecting him and just talking to him. During something like that you feel alone and I know because I was there and not knowing what was around the corner during the Gulf War!

Chapter II

Preparation for Deployment

One thing that the army preached was practice, practice and more practice. But no matter how much you do its still not enough or even to get you ready for deployment. Especially to some place that you have never been and what to expect when you get there. At the time that we were told about Saudi Arabia a group of guys that were in the TAC-SAT Platoon were told that we were on standby to go somewhere else in the world from Germany. A new Captain was going to be the detachment commander for this deployment. And I was asked to be the NCOIC for this deployment. The Battalion Commander was Lieutenant Colonel BUD JONES. I was called in and told about very little of this mission but was told to prepare the troops on this mission to get ready and we don't know what is there. Captain Kenneth Woodburn was a very aggressive person and was a good Officer. So I figured that he was a good choice for this position and was always told to do what the officers over me were competent for the challenge. Some of the people looked at it just as a combat patch. A few weeks later I told my wife about what we were told and said that everything would be OK and we would be all right. And about the same time the things with Saddam Hussain was on the loose and had just invaded Kuwait. At the time I lived on the Germany economy and lived in a 3rd floor apartment the size of a portion of a house just to get my wife and daughter to Germany since I went to school before leaving for Germany. But the saddest thing that I have ever experienced was the Vietnam Memorial in Washington DC, while visiting Ken and Myra Evans. Ken was a old boss and friend since going to Germany the first time in 1981, he was the Battalion XO and a real screamer but he knew how to get things done no matter what the case was. He was the man to go to and he really taught me a lot and I thought that he understood me as a young man and he was the one that made me the way that I thought all about the army from day light to dark. Since you are a soldier 24 hours a day 365 days a year. To this day Ken and I are good friends and I would still do anything for him. Ken finally got out of the Army over a position of a General Officer and his own views about where money was suppose to go for the soldiers in Ken's eyes and the General was working on a Business venture after he retired from the Army. So since Ken opened a can of worms on this General he was forced to resign but we still need more officers like him even today. That is what the military lacks in today's officers. A little information about Ken he was my boss in Hanau Germany from 1981 to 1992 when he left to go back to the states. Well at one point in his military career he was a Major and one hell of an Officer, but damn he was hard to figure out. I tried and finally succeeded and just when you get to know someone its time for either you or them to move somewhere else in the world. We Ken got sent to Washington, DC and was doing some kind of work and decided to resign his commission sometime in the early 90's. That was one of the biggest losses for the army because he was for the soldiers since that was where he started early in his career as an enlisted soldier. We worked for Lieutenant Colonel James H. Chapman of the Special Forces and he was an excellent commander in my book but other people had their doubts but he knew his stuff. He was in the show GREEN BERET with John Wayne when he was a Captain and detachment Commander. Our unit in Germany spent a lot of time in Grafenwohr Germany. I think the entire 41st Field Artillery Brigade lived there but that was part of being a field soldier we did rotations of 45 days in and out of the woods. The unit was so rough from living in the woods all of the time the philosophy was we work hard and we play hard. One guy names Specialist Peterson we called him peety, came in one night with a little to much to drink and we tied him up with Commo wire in his sleeping bag and then put shaving cream in his boots and hands and started tickling him and he got shaving cream all over everything but did not know until the next day when he finally woke up and has to use the Latrine. We would use the mess hall in garrison as a movie theater to keep most of the guys in the area without causing problem. There was another guy named Jothan Berryman and he was the Colonels driver but he had a whole 8th grade education and but was good as gold. Boy could we get into trouble, I was always told I was wilder than a March Hair but I could not hold a candle to Jon he was a country boy from someplace like Kentucky or Alabama or somewhere in one of those hick places. I was so wild during this time and my room mate and some of the other enlisted guys that were Administrative clerks decided since the Warrant Officer in the S-4 (supply) Section all way messed with all of the enlisted so we did a 4187 and requested this office Jump School just to get even to Mr. Stamey. Well he finally got orders and could not figure out how a veteran of 20 plus years would ever get orders to attend jump school at Fort Benning Georgia. Come to find out later about 5 years later he came to Fort Hood as a civilian working the Department of Defense, he never had a clue. He was there to do an inspection and it was like finding a needle in the haystack, he came to the 3rd Signal Brigade for this inspection. I never found out how the inspection went. This was called the school of hard knock without that you really expect what the soldiers now a days expect for someone to do nothing and expect everything.

Stage I

During the preparation phase in Germany it was like a big mess to put it nicely. Trying to get soldiers to volunteer to ride on the ship from Holland to Saudi Arabia... Well I had a friend volunteer his name was Sergeant Paul Walker. He had an accident and fell into the hole of the ship and broke his neck then spent allot of time in the hospital and never completely recovered. The last time I saw Paul he was stationed at Fort Bragg North Carolina and he was still missing part of his ear but that did not stop him from anything after he recovered. At this point in time I haven't got a clue to where he is today. And another friend of mine Master Sergeant Claude A. Perrea nickname CAP lives in Colorado with his wife and the last time we talked he was going back to College. CAP was the only person that I ever knew that did not even look athletic and could out do allot of the Jocks in the unit. Never figured that one out, but I asked a few time but never got an answer from him...

As for Staff Sergeant Brian Hubbs he is not Stationed at Fort Lewis Washington with the Ranger Battalion there and is currently a Chief Warrant Officer 3. And doing great... This is right up Brian's alley to go for something like this especially after serving in the 10th Mountain Division before coming to Germany in 1989. We arrived about the same time to the 51st Signal Battalion in Ludwigsburg Germany just right outside of Stuttgart. Brian Hubbs and I became very good friends over the time we arrived and waited on our wives to arrive in Germany.

Stage II

Before the deployment about 2 days before we were leaving and not knowing when we were or if we would return to Germany we had a lot of doubt since a lot of us had never been in this situation before. And very few were in the Unit that were in Vietnam but this was a different scenario for all of us since this was a Desert Condition. The difference in climate and temperatures and the magnitude of what was presently happening in Kuwait. Cable TV was hard to come by living on the economy in Germany so there was very little that we knew about what was happening on a daily basis. My self and 1LT Wheelan sat the night before in my quarters and we sat on the floor since I had just moved there luckily having my family stable and we watched the Texas A&M Football game that night and left the next morning and to this day I cant remember who won the football game that night maybe I had a few too many cokes since we were ordered not to drink. And as a Team Chief for a Satellite team and having soldiers that I will be responsible for and still am to this day and it is 10 years later. I vowed for all of us to come back to Germany all in one piece and as A group.

Chapter III
Deployment from Europe

In December 1989 while preparing to head to Saudi Arabia from Stuttgart Germany the first problem was driving to Frankfurt in the snow that was falling at the time. We left on the 2d of December and arrived on the 2d of December, but there was one catch and that was only half of my equipment could get on the C5A Galaxy Air Force Plane according to the loadmaster. So My Platoon Leader 1st Lieutenant John J. Wheelan Jr. and myself on the first plane and we were told that our other equipment would follow. When we arrived at Dhahran Airfield in Saudi Arabia we were without any bags because they were in our other truck in Stuttgart. In fact our equipment was more than a few day late it was over 2 weeks late and it seemed like no body cared since their clothes and equipment was there for them. Until our equipment arrived we were just SOL and I don't need to define this for anyone since it is a common phrase in the Army.

Chapter IV

Ground War

A total of 27,243 Bronze Stars were awarded to Army soldiers for their actions in the Gulf War out of almost 700,000 service members from all branches of service that served. A Bronze Star medal represents "heroic or meritorious achievement or service in connection with military operations against an armed enemy."

Friendly fire is believed to have accounted for about 15 percent of all casualties in 20th century wars.

In the Gulf War, 24 percent of the Americans killed in action (35 of 146) and 15 percent of those wounded (72 of 467) fell victim to their own comrades in arms.

The Marines and the U.S. Army organize their infantry troops similarly:

4 MARINES = 1 FIRE TEAM
3 FIRE TEAMS = 1 SQUAD
(13 MARINES OR ARMY)
3 SQUADS = 1 PLATOON
(43 MARINES OR ARMY)
3 PLATOONS = 1 COMPANY
(182 MARINES OR ARMY)
3 COMPANIES = 1 BATTALION
(905 MARINES OR ARMY)
3 BATTALIONS = 1 REGIMENT (ARMY EQUIVALENT IS BRIGADE)
(3,037 MARINES OR ARMY)
3 REGIMENTS = 1 DIVISION
(9, 111 MARINES OR ARMY)

(From: Coyne, James P. Airpower in the Gulf Washington: Air Force Association, 1992.)

(From: "Gulf War Air Power Survey Summary Report" by Thomas A. Keaney and Eliot A. Cohen, Washington, 1993)

Notes: The selected munitions were those most often employed in the Kuwait theater. Other types of laser-guided bombs and air-to-surface missiles were used in the war, but not, principally, in the Kuwait theater.

The Navy and Marine Corps also fired a total of 283 BGM-71 TOW munitions from helicopters.

In the inevitable confrontation between the military and the media to control the flow of war news, it was the Pentagon, which won in the Gulf War.

Many in the U.S. military had blamed the media for the United States' defeat in the Vietnam War. Resolving never to let it happen again, the U.S. Department of Defense devised by the 1970s a system of prior review and pool coverage. The pool system required that a military escort accompany every reporter in the field.

By the time of the Gulf War, the Pentagon had this pool reporting firmly in place; the press had begun submitting incrementally to Pentagon controls after being excluded altogether from the front lines in the 1983 invasion of Grenada.

Strengthening the Pentagon's ability to set ground rules in the Gulf War were two other factors: the Gulf War's theater of operation was in country generally hostile to the Western press and, the war took place in desert terrain that limited the possibilities for independent maneuver.

Many American reporters protested the Pentagon rules in the Gulf War as an unreasonable infringement on press freedom. Some disguised themselves in GI uniforms and hid among troops. Many were arrested. Bob Simon and his CBS-TV crew broke away from the military escorts, leading to their capture by the Iraqis in Kuwait.

The debate has continued as to whether or not the Pentagon's ground rules distorted the reporting in the Gulf War.

- Arnett, Peter *Live From The Battlefield*
- Browne, Malcolm *New York Times Magazine*, March 3, 1991, "The Military vs. The Press: A Correspondent's Account."
- DeParle, Jason *New York Times*, two-part series, May 5, 1991, "Covering the War," and May 6, 1991, "After the War: An Uneasy American Press Corps."
- Fialka, John *Hotel Warriors: Covering the Gulf War*, Washington: Woodrow Wilson Center Press, 1992.

- Gannett Foundation Report, *The Media at War: The Press and the Persian Gulf,* Freedom Forum, June 1991.
- MacArthur, John R. *Second Front: Censorship and Propaganda in the Gulf War*, Hill and Wang, 1992.
- Moore, Molly *A Woman at War: Storming Kuwait with the U.S. Marines*, Scribners, 1993.

ATTENTION ALL VETERANS:

I have just been given a heads-up on 38 U.S. Code §1118(c) Determination of Service Connection Regarding Presumed Sarin Exposure. If we don't get their attention we will lose again, so get it together and contact all who are interested in helping our cause. We need these letters, faxes, and e-mails sent to our government officials to let them know about this, and if you don't think this concerns you, your wrong.

I was tested and was found to have been exposed to chemical/bio-chemical agents to include Sarin. I am one of tens of thousands who will be tested, and the results will be just as mine showed - Trust me on this, this is no joke!

Please get the word out - time is short, and the only ones who will lose is us...

God Bless you all,

Ken Rogers, Sr.

Suggested Letter For You to Send To The VA Secretary, Your U.S. Representative and Senators, and The White House If you will, please write another letter that could do a lot of good for yourself and other ill Gulf War veterans. The suggested letter follows. Please add your own words to it, if you would like to. Time is important in getting it out however. According the law (38 U.S. Code §1118(c)), the Secretary of Veterans Affairs has 60 days from the Institute of Medicine's September 7, 2000 report to "determine whether or not a presumption of service connection is warranted." The Institute of Medicine will probably not do another report on Sarin for five years, according to its leader, Dr. Harold Sox, who I spoke with on September 15, 2000. So the time to encourage is now.

The Honorable Hershel W. Gober
Secretary of Veterans Affairs
Department of Veterans Affairs
810 Vermont Ave. NW
Washington, D.C. 20420

Re: 38 U.S. Code §1118(c) Determination of Service Connection
Regarding Presumed Sarin Exposure

Dear Secretary Gober:

All Gulf War veterans are presumed exposed to Sarin nerve agent
by Public Law 105-277 (Oct. 21, 1998). The National Academy of
Science's Institute of Medicine report of September 7, 2000 shows a
positive association between exposure to Sarin and the health
problems that Gulf War veterans have suffered. This positive
association crosses the statutory threshold, which is set out in 38 U.S.
Code §1118(b)(3): "The credible evidence of the association is equal
to or outweighs the credible evidence against the association." The
standard is not the criminal standard of "proof beyond a reasonable
doubt," or the civil litigation standard of "preponderance of the
evidence." The reason the legal standard is essentially an "as likely as
not" standard is the remedial intent of the law.

Since Gulf War Illness is a chronic long-standing multi-symptom
illness, connections to transient acute local effects like redness and
swelling at an inoculation site can be disregarded. Concerning long-
term effect, there was only one compound that rose above the "we
don't know" category: that was exposure to Sarin sufficient to cause
acute signs and symptoms. They held that probably did cause long-
term health effects like the kind the vets suffer. They based this on
studies of industrial workers exposed to Sarin in the U.S. and Japanese
civilians exposed to Sarin terrorist attacks. In regard to low-level Sarin
exposure, they made this positive association (p. E5-8):

"On the basis of positive findings in studies of nonhuman primates
and humans exposed to organophosphate insecticides, it is reasonable
to hypothesize that long-term adverse health effects can occur after

13

exposure to low levels of Sarin. Studies of industrial workers exposed to low levels of organophosphate insecticides consistently show a higher prevalence of neurological and/or psychiatric symptom reporting."

The chronic multi-symptom illness that was described by the Centers for Disease Control and Prevention ("CDC") in its case definition of Gulf War Illness is the same kind of chronic multi-symptom illness that Sarin exposure produces. Compare the CDC definition published in the Journal of the American Medical Association (JAMA), September 16, 1998, Vol. 280, pp. 981-88, with the following finding by the Institute of Medicine (p. E5-8):

"After sarin exposure, many health effects are reported to persist (e.g., fatigue; headache; visual disturbances such as asthenopia, blurred vision, and narrowing of the visual field; asthenia; shoulder stiffness; and symptoms of posttraumatic stress disorder; and abnormal test results, of unknown clinical significance, on the digit symbol test of psychomotor performance, electroencephalogram (EEG) records of sleep, event-related potential, visual evoked potential, and computerized posturography."

Sufficient evidence exists to meet the legal standard of 38 U.S. Code §1118. Thus, a determination of service connection with illness regarding the presumed Sarin exposure is warranted. It is almost the 10th anniversary of the Gulf War. It will be fair and just to make this determination.

[Any additional text you would like to add, including that you are a veteran of the Gulf War]

Thank you for your attention and service to our nation's veterans.

Respectfully submitted,

[type or print your name, and then sign above it]

The same letter should be sent to your U.S. Representative, each of your Senators and the White House. Their addresses are as follows:

[Your U.S. Representative's name]

[Your 1st Senator's name]
Member of Congress
United States Senator
House Office Building
State Office Building
Washington, D.C. 20515
Washington, D.C. 20510

[Your 2nd Senator's name]
President William Jefferson Clinton
United States Senator
President of the United States
Senate Office Building
The White House
Washington, D.C. 20510
1600 Pennsylvania Ave., NW
Washington, D.C. 20500
Attn: Veterans Affairs Policy Advisor

CIA says it told FBI of two hijackers' meeting with al-Qaida in early 2000

Tue Jun 4, 4:49 AM ET By PETE YOST, Associated Press Writer WASHINGTON - Both the CIA and FBI knew as early as January 2000 that one of the eventual Sept. 11 hijackers would be attending a meeting of suspected al-Qaida members, a CIA official said in the latest revelation amid growing evidence of intelligence failures.

Word that the agencies had reason to be suspicious of Khalid Almihdhar emerged as the Senate and House intelligence committees vowed to dig into what went wrong before the terrorist attacks. Meeting in soundproofed, secure rooms at the Capitol, lawmakers will take stock of an intelligence community that overlooked clues and didn't always share information it had about the hijackers. The closed door hearings begin Tuesday before going public June 25. The intense scrutiny has led to fingerpointing between the CIA and FBI. Over the weekend, government sources said the CIA had important information in early 2000 about two of the future hijackers, Almihdhar and Nawaf Alhazmi, both of whom attended a mid-January 2000 meeting in Malaysia. Responding to the disclosure, a CIA official, speaking

15

Monday on condition of anonymity, disputed reports that the agency had kept that information from the FBI. The CIA official said two FBI officials were briefed on Almihdhar. Neither agency gave the information enough significance to alert authorities to watch for Almihdhar or Alhazmi at U.S. points of entry until three weeks before the attacks, when the CIA, alerted to a large al-Qaida operation in the offing, added the two men to a watch list that INS and State officials use. By this time, however, they were already in the country. Almihdhar, in fact, already had been in and out of the United States several times. The U.S. government had given him a multiple entry visa enabling him the freedom to come and go as he pleased. Both hijackers were aboard American Airlines Flight 77 that crashed into the Pentagon FBI officials declined comment Monday night, saying Director Robert Mueller was not interested in engaging in fingerpointing. In other developments: _Egyptian President Hosni Mubarak said in a New York Times interview for Tuesday editions that his country's intelligence service warned U.S. officials about a week before the Sept. 11 attacks that al-Qaida was in the advance stages of an attack on an unspecified American target. The Times quoted a senior U.S. intelligence official, however, as denying any such information was passed on to the CIA. The White House press office declined comment when contacted by The Associated Press. _Defense Secretary Donald H. Rumsfeld said Osama bin Laden does not seem to be formally directing al-Qaida, although the terror organization remains active worldwide. "My guess is, if he were active, we would know it—we would have some visible sense of it," he said in Tuesday editions of The Washington Post. Rumsfeld was leaving Tuesday for Europe and the Gulf to discuss the war on terrorism and other issues. He also planned to visit India and Pakistan. "What we want to learn is all the information that the agencies had or didn't have and whether they disseminated it," said Sen. Richard Shelby the ranking Republican on the Senate Intelligence Committee. Despite the array of problems that have already come to light, "this is just the beginning," said Shelby, the committee's vice chairman. Another early clue pointing to one of the hijackers' alleged accomplices emerged on the eve of the congressional hearings. The CIA received vague intelligence about Zacarias Moussaoui in the spring of 2001, but from an informant who knew the Frenchman only by an alias and the CIA didn't link the two names until well after Sept. 11. Moussaoui was arrested at a Minnesota flight school the month before the Sept. 11 suicide attacks. An intelligence official said that in April 2001 a CIA informant mentioned a man he had met in 1997 during a gathering of Islamic extremists. In early 2002, the source recognized Moussaoui from pictures he had seen on television. The FBI's handling of Moussaoui will be the focus of a hearing Thursday by the Senate Judiciary Committee when Minnesota FBI agent Coleen Rowley testifies. The FBI whistleblower says FBI headquarters ignored her office's pleas to aggressively investigate Moussaoui following his arrest last August. In addition, the FBI has been criticized for failing to link Moussaoui and the warnings of a Phoenix field agent that Middle Eastern men were training at American flight schools. The former head of CIA counterterrorism, Cofer Black, probably will be the first witness of the intelligence hearings, this Thursday. The CIA's counterterrorism center will be an early focus of the intelligence panels' inquiry. Set up in the mid-1980s, the No. 2 official at the CIA's counterterrorism center, located at CIA headquarters in Langley, Virginia, is an FBI official. The No. 2 official at the FBI's counterterrorism operation at Washington headquarters is a CIA official. "Turf jurisdiction has always been a problem, but we were led to believe as far as the FBI and CIA were concerned, that had been resolved," said Rep. Saxby Chambliss a Georgia Republican.

Defense secretary to visit Europe and Persian Gulf to consult on terror war

Tue Jun 4, 2:30 AM ET By ROBERT BURNS, AP Military Writer WASHINGTON - The dangers posed by Iraq's nuclear ambitions will be a topic of discussion when Defense Secretary Donald H. Rumsfeld visits allied nations in the Persian Gulf, but he will not be seeking support for a U.S. invasion, a defense official said. "We're not at the stage where we're going around soliciting allies for something like that," the official, who discussed aspects of Rumsfeld's trip on condition that he not be identified, said Monday. The secretary, meanwhile, said Osama bin Laden does not seem to be formally directing the al-Qaida terror network, although the organization remains active worldwide. "My guess is, if he were active, we would know it—we would have some visible sense of it, which we haven't

17

seem to have had, for some reason," he told The Washington Post in a story for Tuesday editions. He added he did not know whether bin Laden was simply lying low or was ill or dead. Rumsfeld will leave Tuesday on an extended trip to Europe and the Gulf to discuss the war on terrorism and other issues. He also plans to visit India and Pakistan but the timing has not been set, the official said. He will be preceded in New Delhi and Islamabad by Richard Armitage, the deputy secretary of state, as the Bush administration presses for a diplomatic resolution of the tensions over cross-border attacks by militants in the Indian portion of the disputed Kashmir region. The official would not discuss any specifics of Rumsfeld's intended message to the Indians and Pakistanis, but it is likely to include mention of the Pentagon 's estimate of the casualties a nuclear exchange could cause. A recent Defense Intelligence Agency study concluded that, in the worst case, a nuclear exchange between India and Pakistan could kill as many as 12 million people on both sides, with another 2 million to 6 million injured. Rumsfeld will begin his trip in Britain on Wednesday, where he is scheduled to meet with Defense Minister Geoffrey Hoon. Later he flies to Brussels, Belgium, for meetings at NATO headquarters on Thursday and Friday, including the first meeting of the NATO-Russia Council, which was created last month to make former Cold War foe Russia a limited partner in the Western alliance. The NATO meeting is intended, in part, to set the stage for a summit meeting of alliance leaders in November in Prague, where as many as nine European countries may be invited to become NATO members. After a stop at Geilenkirchen Air Base in Germany to thank NATO airborne warning aircraft crews and commanders for their help in patrolling U.S. skies in the months after the Sept. 11 attacks, Rumsfeld will fly to Estonia for a meeting with defense ministers from the Baltic and Nordic nations. The sequence of visits after Estonia has not been set, the defense officials said, but they will include stops in Kuwait, Qatar and Bahrain. The United States has troops in each of the three Gulf countries, including thousands at Camp Doha in Kuwait and the Navy's 5th Fleet headquarters in Bahrain. Whether the Pakistan and India visits are before or after the Gulf tour is still open, one official said. It is unusual for a U.S. defense secretary to visit the Gulf without stopping in Saudi Arabia. The U.S. official who discussed this portion of Rumsfeld's trip said there was no political message in leaving Saudi Arabia off the itinerary. He noted that Rumsfeld had stopped there on his last Gulf tour in October 2001 and had yet to visit Kuwait, Qatar and Bahrain during his 17 months in office.

Geneva Convention relative to the Treatment of Prisoners of War Adopted on 12 August 1949 by the Diplomatic Conference for the Establishment of International Conventions for the Protection of Victims of War, held in Geneva from 21 April to 12 August, 1949 *entry into force* 21 October 1950

PART I
GENERAL PROVISIONS
Article 1
The High Contracting Parties undertake to respect and to ensure respect for the present Convention in all circumstances.
Article 2
In addition to the provisions which shall be implemented in peace time, the present Convention shall apply to all cases of declared war or of any other armed conflict which may arise between two or more of the High Contracting Parties, even if the state of war is not recognized by one of them.

The Convention shall also apply to all cases of partial or total occupation of the territory of a High Contracting Party, even if the said occupation meets with no armed resistance.

Although one of the Powers in conflict may not be a party to the present Convention, the Powers who are parties thereto shall remain bound by it in their mutual relations. They shall furthermore be bound by the Convention in relation to the said Power, if the latter accepts and applies the provisions thereof.
Article 3
In the case of armed conflict not of an international character occurring in the territory of one of the High Contracting Parties, each party to the conflict shall be bound to apply, as a minimum, the following provisions:

1. Persons taking no active part in the hostilities, including members of armed forces who have laid down their arms and those placed hors de combat by sickness, wounds, detention, or any other

cause, shall in all circumstances be treated humanely, without any adverse distinction founded on race, colour, religion or faith, sex, birth or wealth, or any other similar criteria.

To this end the following acts are and shall remain prohibited at any time and in any place whatsoever with respect to the above-mentioned persons:

(a) Violence to life and person, in particular murder of all kinds, mutilation, cruel treatment and torture;

(b) Taking of hostages;

(c) Outrages upon personal dignity, in particular, humiliating and degrading treatment;

(d) The passing of sentences and the carrying out of executions without previous judgment pronounced by a regularly constituted court affording all the judicial guarantees which are recognized as indispensable by civilized peoples.

2. The wounded and sick shall be collected and cared for.

An impartial humanitarian body, such as the International Committee of the Red Cross, may offer its services to the Parties to the conflict.

The Parties to the conflict should further endeavour to bring into force, by means of special agreements, all or part of the other provisions of the present Convention.

The application of the preceding provisions shall not affect the legal status of the Parties to the conflict.

Article 4

A. Prisoners of war, in the sense of the present Convention, are persons belonging to one of the following categories, who have fallen into the power of the enemy:

1. Members of the armed forces of a Party to the conflict as well as members of militias or volunteer corps forming part of such armed forces.

2. Members of other militias and members of other volunteer corps, including those of organized resistance movements, belonging to a Party to the conflict and operating in or outside their own territory, even if this territory is occupied, provided that such militias or

volunteer corps, including such organized resistance movements, fulfil the following conditions:

(a) That of being commanded by a person responsible for his subordinates;
(b) That of having a fixed distinctive sign recognizable at a distance;
(c) That of carrying arms openly;
(d) That of conducting their operations in accordance with the laws and customs of war.
3. Members of regular armed forces who profess allegiance to a government or an authority not recognized by the Detaining Power.
4. Persons who accompany the armed forces without actually being members thereof, such as civilian members of military aircraft crews, war correspondents, supply contractors, members of labour units or of services responsible for the welfare of the armed forces, provided that they have received authorization from the armed forces which they accompany, who shall provide them for that purpose with an identity card similar to the annexed model.
5. Members of crews, including masters, pilots and apprentices, of the merchant marine and the crews of civil aircraft of the Parties to the conflict, who do not benefit by more favourable treatment under any other provisions of international law.
6. Inhabitants of a non-occupied territory, who on the approach of the enemy spontaneously take up arms to resist the invading forces, without having had time to form themselves into regular armed units, provided they carry arms openly and respect the laws and customs of war.
B. The following shall likewise be treated as prisoners of war under the present Convention:

1. Persons belonging, or having belonged, to the armed forces of the occupied country, if the occupying Power considers it necessary by reason of such allegiance to intern them, even though it has originally liberated them while hostilities were going on outside the territory it occupies, in particular where such persons have made an unsuccessful attempt to rejoin the armed forces to which they belong and which are

engaged in combat, or where they fail to comply with a summons made to them with a view to internment.

2. The persons belonging to one of the categories enumerated in the present Article, who have been received by neutral or non-belligerent Powers on their territory and whom these Powers are required to intern under international law, without prejudice to any more favourable treatment which these Powers may choose to give and with the exception of Articles 8, 10, 15, 30, fifth paragraph, 58-67, 92, 126 and, where diplomatic relations exist between the Parties to the conflict and the neutral or non-belligerent Power concerned, those Articles concerning the Protecting Power. Where such diplomatic relations exist, the Parties to a conflict on whom these persons depend shall be allowed to perform towards them the functions of a Protecting Power as provided in the present Convention, without prejudice to the functions which these Parties normally exercise in conformity with diplomatic and consular usage and treaties.

C. This Article shall in no way affect the status of medical personnel and chaplains as provided for in Article 33 of the present Convention.

Article 5

The present Convention shall apply to the persons referred to in Article 4 from the time they fall into the power of the enemy and until their final release and repatriation.

Should any doubt arise as to whether persons, having committed a belligerent act and having fallen into the hands of the enemy, belong to any of the categories enumerated in Article 4, such persons shall enjoy the protection of the present Convention until such time as their status has been determined by a competent tribunal.

Article 6

In addition to the agreements expressly provided for in Articles 10, 23, 28, 33, 60, 65, 66, 67, 72, 73, 75, 109, 110, 118, 119, 122 and 132, the High Contracting Parties may conclude other special agreements for all matters concerning which they may deem it suitable to make separate provision. No special agreement shall adversely affect the situation of prisoners of war, as defined by the present Convention, nor restrict the rights which it confers upon them.

Prisoners of war shall continue to have the benefit of such agreements as long as the Convention is applicable to them, except where express provisions to the contrary are contained in the aforesaid or in subsequent agreements, or where more favourable measures have been taken with regard to them by one or other of the Parties to the conflict.

Article 7

Prisoners of war may in no circumstances renounce in part or in entirety the rights secured to them by the present Convention, and by the special agreements referred to in the foregoing Article, if such there be.

Article 8

The present Convention shall be applied with the cooperation and under the scrutiny of the Protecting Powers whose duty it is to safeguard the interests of the Parties to the conflict. For this purpose, the Protecting Powers may appoint, apart from their diplomatic or consular staff, delegates from amongst their own nationals or the nationals of other neutral Powers. The said delegates shall be subject to the approval of the Power with which they are to carry out their duties.

The Parties to the conflict shall facilitate to the greatest extent possible the task of the representatives or delegates of the Protecting Powers.

The representatives or delegates of the Protecting Powers shall not in any case exceed their mission under the present Convention. They shall, in particular, take account of the imperative necessities of security of the State wherein they carry out their duties.

Article 9

The provisions of the present Convention constitute no obstacle to the humanitarian activities which the International Committee of the Red Cross or any other impartial humanitarian organization may, subject to the consent of the Parties to the conflict concerned, undertake for the protection of prisoners of war and for their relief.

Article 10

The High Contracting Parties may at any time agree to entrust to an organization which offers all guarantees of impartiality and efficacy the duties incumbent on the Protecting Powers by virtue of the present Convention.

When prisoners of war do not benefit or cease to benefit, no matter for what reason, by the activities of a Protecting Power or of an organization provided for in the first paragraph above, the Detaining Power shall request a neutral State, or such an organization, to undertake the functions performed under the present Convention by a Protecting Power designated by the Parties to a conflict.

If protection cannot be arranged accordingly, the Detaining Power shall request or shall accept, subject to the provisions of this Article, the offer of the services of a humanitarian organization, such as the International Committee of the Red Cross, to assume the humanitarian functions performed by Protecting Powers under the present Convention.

Any neutral Power or any organization invited by the Power concerned or offering itself for these purposes, shall be required to act with a sense of responsibility towards the Party to the conflict on which persons protected by the present Convention depend, and shall be required to furnish sufficient assurances that it is in a position to undertake the appropriate functions and to discharge them impartially.

No derogation from the preceding provisions shall be made by special agreements between Powers one of which is restricted, even temporarily, in its freedom to negotiate with the other Power or its allies by reason of military events, more particularly where the whole, or a substantial part, of the territory of the said Power is occupied.

Whenever in the present Convention mention is made of a Protecting Power, such mention applies to substitute organizations in the sense of the present Article.

Article 11

In cases where they deem it advisable in the interest of protected persons, particularly in cases of disagreement between the Parties to the conflict as to the application or interpretation of the provisions of the present Convention, the Protecting Powers shall lend their good offices with a view to settling the disagreement.

For this purpose, each of the Protecting Powers may, either at the invitation of one Party or on its own initiative, propose to the Parties to the conflict a meeting of their representatives, and in particular of the authorities responsible for prisoners of war, possibly on neutral territory suitably chosen. The Parties to the conflict shall be bound to give effect to the proposals made to them for this purpose. The Protecting Powers may, if necessary, propose for approval by the Parties to the conflict a person belonging to a neutral Power, or delegated by the International Committee of the Red Cross, who shall be invited to take part in such a meeting.

PART II
GENERAL PROTECTION OF PRISONERS OF WAR

Article 12

Prisoners of war are in the hands of the enemy Power, but not of the individuals or military units who have captured them. Irrespective of the individual responsibilities that may exist, the Detaining Power is responsible for the treatment given them.

Prisoners of war may only be transferred by the Detaining Power to a Power which is a party to the Convention and after the Detaining Power has satisfied itself of the willingness and ability of such transferee Power to apply the Convention. When prisoners of war are transferred under such circumstances, responsibility for the application of the Convention rests on the Power accepting them while they are in its custody.

Nevertheless if that Power fails to carry out the provisions of the Convention in any important respect, the Power by whom the prisoners of war were transferred shall, upon being notified by the Protecting Power, take effective measures to correct the situation or shall request the return of the prisoners of war. Such requests must be complied with.

Article 13

Prisoners of war must at all times be humanely treated. Any unlawful act or omission by the Detaining Power causing death or seriously endangering the health of a prisoner of war in its custody is prohibited, and will be regarded as a serious breach of the present Convention. In particular, no prisoner of war may be subjected to physical mutilation or to medical or scientific experiments of any kind which are not justified by the medical, dental or hospital treatment of the prisoner concerned and carried out in his interest.

Likewise, prisoners of war must at all times be protected, particularly against acts of violence or intimidation and against insults and public curiosity.

Measures of reprisal against prisoners of war are prohibited.

Article 14

Prisoners of war are entitled in all circumstances to respect for their persons and their honour. Women shall be treated with all the regard due to their sex and shall in all cases benefit by treatment as favourable as that granted to men. Prisoners of war shall retain the full civil capacity which they enjoyed at the time of their capture. The Detaining Power may not restrict the exercise, either within or without its own territory, of the rights such capacity confers except in so far as the captivity requires.

Article 15

The Power detaining prisoners of war shall be bound to provide free of charge for their maintenance and for the medical attention required by their state of health.

Article 16

Taking into consideration the provisions of the present Convention relating to rank and sex, and subject to any privileged treatment which may be accorded to them by reason of their state of health, age or professional qualifications, all prisoners of war shall be treated alike by the Detaining Power, without any adverse distinction based on race, nationality, religious belief or political opinions, or any other distinction founded on similar criteria.

PART III
CAPTIVITY
SECTION I
BEGINNING OF CAPTIVITY

Article 17

Every prisoner of war, when questioned on the subject, is bound to give only his surname, first names and rank, date of birth, and army, regimental, personal or serial number, or failing this, equivalent information. If he wilfully infringes this rule, he may render himself liable to a restriction of the privileges accorded to his rank or status.

Each Party to a conflict is required to furnish the persons under its jurisdiction who are liable to become prisoners of war, with an identity card showing the owner's surname, first names, rank, army, regimental, personal or serial number or equivalent information, and date of birth. The identity card may, furthermore, bear the signature or the fingerprints, or both, of the owner, and may bear, as well, any other information the Party to the conflict may wish to add concerning persons belonging to its armed forces. As far as possible the card shall measure 6.5 x 10 cm. and shall be issued in duplicate. The identity card shall be shown by the prisoner of war upon demand, but may in no case be taken away from him.

No physical or mental torture, nor any other form of coercion, may be inflicted on prisoners of war to secure from them information of any kind whatever. Prisoners of war who refuse to answer may not be threatened, insulted, or exposed to any unpleasant or disadvantageous treatment of any kind.

Prisoners of war who, owing to their physical or mental condition, are unable to state their identity, shall be handed over to the medical service. The identity of such prisoners shall be established by all possible means, subject to the provisions of the preceding paragraph.

The questioning of prisoners of war shall be carried out in a language which they understand.

Article 18

All effects and articles of personal use, except arms, horses, military equipment and military documents shall remain in the possession of prisoners of war, likewise their metal helmets and gas masks and like articles issued for personal protection. Effects and articles used for their clothing or feeding shall likewise remain in their possession, even if such effects and articles belong to their regulation military equipment.

At no time should prisoners of war be without identity documents. The Detaining Power shall supply such documents to prisoners of war who possess none.

Badges of rank and nationality, decorations and articles having above all a personal or sentimental value may not be taken from prisoners of war.

Sums of money carried by prisoners of war may not be taken away from them except by order of an officer, and after the amount and particulars of the owner have been recorded in a special register and an itemized receipt has been given, legibly inscribed with the name, rank and unit of the person issuing the said receipt. Sums in the currency of the Detaining Power, or which are changed into such currency at the prisoner's request, shall be placed to the credit of the prisoner's account as provided in Article 64.

The Detaining Power may withdraw articles of value from prisoners of war only for reasons of security; when such articles are withdrawn, the procedure laid down for sums of money impounded shall apply.

Such objects, likewise the sums taken away in any currency other than that of the Detaining Power and the conversion of which has not been asked for by the owners, shall be kept in the custody of the Detaining Power and shall be returned in their initial shape to prisoners of war at the end of their captivity.

Article 19

Prisoners of war shall be evacuated, as soon as possible after their capture, to camps situated in an area far enough from the combat zone for them to be out of danger.

Only those prisoners of war who, owing to wounds or sickness, would run greater risks by being evacuated than by remaining where they are, may be temporarily kept back in a danger zone.

Prisoners of war shall not be unnecessarily exposed to danger while awaiting evacuation from a fighting zone.

Article 20

The evacuation of prisoners of war shall always be effected humanely and in conditions similar to those for the forces of the Detaining Power in their changes of station.

The Detaining Power shall supply prisoners of war who are being evacuated with sufficient food and potable water, and with the necessary clothing and medical attention. The Detaining Power shall take all suitable precautions to ensure their safety during evacuation, and shall establish as soon as possible a list of the prisoners of war who are evacuated.

If prisoners of war must, during evacuation, pass through transit camps, their stay in such camps shall be as brief as possible.

SECTION II

INTERNMENT OF PRISONERS OF WAR

Chapter I

GENERAL OBSERVATIONS

Article 21

The Detaining Power may subject prisoners of war to internment. It may impose on them the obligation of not leaving, beyond certain limits, the camp where they are interned, or if the said camp is fenced in, of not going outside its perimeter. Subject to the provisions of the present Convention relative to penal and disciplinary sanctions, prisoners of war may not be held in close confinement except where necessary to safeguard their health and then only during the continuation of the circumstances which make such confinement necessary.

Prisoners of war may be partially or wholly released on parole or promise, in so far as is allowed by the laws of the Power on which they depend. Such measures shall be taken particularly in cases where this may contribute to the improvement of their state of health. No prisoner of war shall be compelled to accept liberty on parole or promise.

Upon the outbreak of hostilities, each Party to the conflict shall notify the adverse Party of the laws and regulations allowing or forbidding its own nationals to accept liberty on parole or promise. Prisoners of war who are paroled or who have given their promise in conformity with the laws and regulations so notified, are bound on their personal honour scrupulously to fulfil, both towards the Power on which they depend and towards the Power which has captured them, the engagements of their paroles or promises. In such cases, the Power on which they depend is bound neither to require nor to accept from them any service incompatible with the parole or promise given.

Article 22

Prisoners of war may be interned only in premises located on land and affording every guarantee of hygiene and healthfulness. Except in particular cases which are justified by the interest of the prisoners themselves, they shall not be interned in penitentiaries.

Prisoners of war interned in unhealthy areas, or where the climate is injurious for them, shall be removed as soon as possible to a more favourable climate.

The Detaining Power shall assemble prisoners of war in camps or camp compounds according to their nationality, language and customs, provided that such prisoners shall not be separated from prisoners of war belonging to the armed forces with which they were serving at the time of their capture, except with their consent.

Article 23

No prisoner of war may at any time be sent to or detained in areas where he may be exposed to the fire of the combat zone, nor may his presence be used to render certain points or areas immune from military operations.

Prisoners of war shall have shelters against air bombardment and other hazards of war, to the same extent as the local civilian population. With the exception of those engaged in the protection of their quarters against the aforesaid hazards, they may enter such shelters as soon as possible after the giving of the alarm. Any other protective measure taken in favour of the population shall also apply to them.

Detaining Powers shall give the Powers concerned, through the intermediary of the Protecting Powers, all useful information regarding the geographical location of prisoner of war camps.

Whenever military considerations permit, prisoner of war camps shall be indicated in the day-time by the letters PW or PG, placed so as to be clearly visible from the air. The Powers concerned may, however, agree upon any other system of marking. Only prisoner of war camps shall be marked as such.

Article 24

Transit or screening camps of a permanent kind shall be fitted out under conditions similar to those described in the present Section, and the prisoners therein shall have the same treatment as in other camps.

Chapter II
QUARTERS, FOOD AND CLOTHING OF PRISONERS OF WAR

Article 25

Prisoners of war shall be quartered under conditions as favourable as those for the forces of the Detaining Power who are billeted in the same area. The said conditions shall make allowance for the habits and customs of the prisoners and shall in no case be prejudicial to their health.

The foregoing provisions shall apply in particular to the dormitories of prisoners of war as regards both total surface and minimum cubic space, and the general installations, bedding and blankets.

The premises provided for the use of prisoners of war individually or collectively, shall be entirely protected from dampness and adequately heated and lighted, in particular between dusk and lights out. All precautions must be taken against the danger of fire.

In any camps in which women prisoners of war, as well as men, are accommodated, separate dormitories shall be provided for them.

Article 26

The basic daily food rations shall be sufficient in quantity, quality and variety to keep prisoners of war in good health and to prevent loss of weight or the development of nutritional deficiencies. Account shall also be taken of the habitual diet of the prisoners.

The Detaining Power shall supply prisoners of war who work with such additional rations as are necessary for the labour on which they are employed.

Sufficient drinking water shall be supplied to prisoners of war. The use of tobacco shall be permitted.

Prisoners of war shall, as far as possible, be associated with the preparation of their meals; they may be employed for that purpose in the kitchens. Furthermore, they shall be given the means of preparing, themselves, the additional food in their possession.

Adequate premises shall be provided for messing.

Collective disciplinary measures affecting food are prohibited.

Article 27

Clothing, underwear and footwear shall be supplied to prisoners of war in sufficient quantities by the Detaining Power, which shall make allowance for the climate of the region where the prisoners are detained. Uniforms of enemy armed forces captured by the Detaining Power should, if suitable for the climate, be made available to clothe prisoners of war.

The regular replacement and repair of the above articles shall be assured by the Detaining Power. In addition, prisoners of war who work shall receive appropriate clothing, wherever the nature of the work demands.

Article 28

Canteens shall be installed in all camps, where prisoners of war may procure foodstuffs, soap and tobacco and ordinary articles in daily use. The tariff shall never be in excess of local market prices. The profits made by camp canteens shall be used for the benefit of the prisoners; a special fund shall be created for this purpose. The prisoners' representative shall have the right to collaborate in the management of the canteen and of this fund.

When a camp is closed down, the credit balance of the special fund shall be handed to an international welfare organization, to be employed for the benefit of prisoners of war of the same nationality as those who have contributed to the fund. In case of a general repatriation, such profits shall be kept by the Detaining Power, subject to any agreement to the contrary between the Powers concerned.

Chapter III
HYGIENE AND MEDICAL ATTENTION

Article 29

The Detaining Power shall be bound to take all sanitary measures necessary to ensure the cleanliness and healthfulness of camps and to prevent epidemics.

Prisoners of war shall have for their use, day and night, conveniences which conform to the rules of hygiene and are maintained in a constant state of cleanliness. In any camps in which women prisoners of war are accommodated, separate conveniences shall be provided for them.

Also, apart from the baths and showers with which the camps shall be furnished, prisoners of war shall be provided with sufficient water and soap for their personal toilet and for washing their personal laundry; the necessary installations, facilities and time shall be granted them for that purpose.

Article 30

Every camp shall have an adequate infirmary where prisoners of war may have the attention they require, as well as appropriate diet. Isolation wards shall, if necessary, be set aside for cases of contagious or mental disease.

Prisoners of war suffering from serious disease, or whose condition necessitates special treatment, a surgical operation or hospital care, must be admitted to any military or civilian medical unit where such treatment can be given, even if their repatriation is contemplated in the near future. Special facilities shall be afforded for the care to be given to the disabled, in particular to the blind, and for their rehabilitation, pending repatriation.

Prisoners of war shall have the attention, preferably, of medical personnel of the Power on which they depend and, if possible, of their nationality.

Prisoners of war may not be prevented from presenting themselves to the medical authorities for examination. The detaining authorities shall, upon request, issue to every prisoner who has undergone treatment, an official certificate indicating the nature of his illness or injury, and the duration and kind of treatment received. A duplicate of this certificate shall be forwarded to the Central Prisoners of War Agency.

The costs of treatment, including those of any apparatus necessary for the maintenance of prisoners of war in good health, particularly dentures and other artificial appliances, and spectacles, shall be borne by the Detaining Power.

Article 31

Medical inspections of prisoners of war shall be held at least once a month. They shall include the checking and the recording of the weight of each prisoner of war. Their purpose shall be, in particular, to supervise the general state of health, nutrition and cleanliness of prisoners and to detect contagious diseases, especially tuberculosis, malaria and venereal disease. For this purpose the most efficient methods available shall be employed, e.g. periodic mass miniature radiography for the early detection of tuberculosis.

Article 32

Prisoners of war who, though not attached to the medical service of their armed forces, are physicians, surgeons, dentists, nurses or medical orderlies, may be required by the Detaining Power to exercise their medical functions in the interests of prisoners of war dependent on the same Power. In that case they shall continue to be prisoners of war, but shall receive the same treatment as corresponding medical personnel retained by the Detaining Power. They shall be exempted from any other work under Article 49.

Chapter IV

MEDICAL PERSONNEL AND CHAPLAINS RETAINED TO ASSIST PRISONERS OF WAR

Article 33

Members of the medical personnel and chaplains while retained by the Detaining Power with a view to assisting prisoners of war, shall not be considered as prisoners of war. They shall, however, receive as a minimum the benefits and protection of the present Convention, and shall also be granted all facilities necessary to provide for the medical care of, and religious inistration to, prisoners of war.

They shall continue to exercise their medical and spiritual functions for the benefit of prisoners of war, preferably those belonging to the armed forces upon which they depend, within the scope of the military laws and regulations of the Detaining Power and under the control of its competent services, in accordance with their professional etiquette. They shall also benefit by the following facilities in the exercise of their medical or spiritual functions:

(a) They shall be authorized to visit periodically prisoners of war situated in working detachments or in hospitals outside the camp. For this purpose, the Detaining Power shall place at their disposal the necessary means of transport.

(b) The senior medical officer in each camp shall be responsible to the camp military authorities for everything connected with the activities of retained medical personnel. For this purpose, Parties to the conflict shall agree at the outbreak of hostilities on the subject of the corresponding ranks of the medical personnel, including that of societies mentioned in Article 26 of the Geneva Convention for the Amelioration of the Condition of the Wounded and Sick in Armed Forces in the Field of August 12, 1949. This senior medical officer, as well as chaplains, shall have the right to deal with the competent authorities of the camp on all questions relating to their duties. Such authorities shall afford them all necessary facilities for correspondence relating to these questions.

(c) Although they shall be subject to the internal discipline of the camp in which they are retained, such personnel may not be compelled to carry out any work other than that concerned with their medical or religious duties.

During hostilities, the Parties to the conflict shall agree concerning the possible relief of retained personnel and shall settle the procedure to be followed.

None of the preceding provisions shall relieve the Detaining Power of its obligations with regard to prisoners of war from the medical or spiritual point of view.

Chapter V
RELIGIOUS, INTELLECTUAL AND PHYSICAL ACTIVITIES
Article 34

Prisoners of war shall enjoy complete latitude in the exercise of their religious duties, including attendance at the service of their faith, on condition that they comply with the disciplinary routine prescribed by the military authorities.

Adequate premises shall be provided where religious services may be held.

Article 35

Chaplains who fall into the hands of the enemy Power and who remain or are retained with a view to assisting prisoners of war, shall be allowed to minister to them and to exercise freely their ministry amongst prisoners of war of the same religion, in accordance with their religious conscience. They shall be allocated among the various camps and labour detachments containing prisoners of war belonging to the same forces, speaking the same language or practising the same religion. They shall enjoy the necessary facilities, including the means of transport provided for in Article 33, for visiting the prisoners of war outside their camp. They shall be free to correspond, subject to censorship, on matters concerning their religious duties with the ecclesiastical authorities in the country of detention and with international religious organizations. Letters and cards which they may send for this purpose shall be in addition to the quota provided for in Article 71.

Article 36

Prisoners of war who are ministers of religion, without having officiated as chaplains to their own forces, shall be at liberty, whatever their denomination, to minister freely to the members of their community. For this purpose, they shall receive the same treatment as the chaplains retained by the Detaining Power. They shall not be obliged to do any other work.

Article 37

When prisoners of war have not the assistance of a retained chaplain or of a prisoner of war minister of their faith, a minister belonging to the prisoners' or a similar denomination, or in his absence a qualified layman, if such a course is feasible from a confessional point of view, shall be appointed, at the request of the prisoners concerned, to fill this office. This appointment, subject to the approval of the Detaining Power, shall take place with the agreement of the community of prisoners concerned and, wherever necessary, with the approval of the local religious authorities of the same faith. The person thus appointed shall comply with all regulations established by the Detaining Power in the interests of discipline and military security.

Article 38

While respecting the individual preferences of every prisoner, the Detaining Power shall encourage the practice of intellectual, educational, and recreational pursuits, sports and games amongst prisoners, and shall take the measures necessary to ensure the exercise thereof by providing them with adequate premises and necessary equipment.

Prisoners shall have opportunities for taking physical exercise, including sports and games, and for being out of doors. Sufficient open spaces shall be provided for this purpose in all camps.

Chapter VI
DISCIPLINE
Article 39

Every prisoner of war camp shall be put under the immediate authority of a responsible commissioned officer belonging to the regular armed forces of the Detaining Power. Such officer shall have in his possession a copy of the present Convention; he shall ensure that its provisions are known to the camp staff and the guard and shall be responsible, under the direction of his government, for its application.

Prisoners of war, with the exception of officers, must salute and show to all officers of the Detaining Power the external marks of respect provided for by the regulations applying in their own forces.

Officer prisoners of war are bound to salute only officers of a higher rank of the Detaining Power; they must, however, salute the camp commander regardless of his rank.

Article 40

The wearing of badges of rank and nationality, as well as of decorations, shall be permitted.

Article 41

In every camp the text of the present Convention and its Annexes and the contents of any special agreement provided for in Article 6, shall be posted, in the prisoners' own language, at places where all may read them. Copies shall be supplied, on request, to the prisoners who cannot have access to the copy which has been posted.

Regulations, orders, notices and publications of every kind relating to the conduct of prisoners of war shall be issued to them in a language which they understand. Such regulations, orders and publications shall be posted in the manner described above and copies shall be handed to the prisoners' representative. Every order and command addressed to prisoners of war individually must likewise be given in a language which they understand.

Article 42

The use of weapons against prisoners of war, especially against those who are escaping or attempting to escape, shall constitute an extreme measure, which shall always be preceded by warnings appropriate to the circumstances.

Chapter VII

RANK OF PRISONERS OF WAR

Article 43

Upon the outbreak of hostilities, the Parties to the conflict shall communicate to one another the titles and ranks of all the persons mentioned in Article 4 of the present Convention, in order to ensure equality of treatment between prisoners of equivalent rank. Titles and ranks which are subsequently created shall form the subject of similar communications.

The Detaining Power shall recognize promotions in rank which have been accorded to prisoners of war and which have been duly notified by the Power on which these prisoners depend.

Article 44

Officers and prisoners of equivalent status shall be treated with the regard due to their rank and age.

In order to ensure service in officers' camps, other ranks of the same armed forces who, as far as possible, speak the same language, shall be assigned in sufficient numbers, account being taken of the rank of officers and prisoners of equivalent status. Such orderlies shall not be required to perform any other work.

Supervision of the mess by the officers themselves shall be facilitated in every way.

Article 45

Prisoners of war other than officers and prisoners of equivalent status shall be treated with the regard due to their rank and age.

Supervision of the mess by the prisoners themselves shall be facilitated in every way.

Chapter VIII

TRANSFER OF PRISONERS OF WAR AFTER THEIR ARRIVAL IN CAMP

Article 46

The Detaining Power, when deciding upon the transfer of prisoners of war, shall take into account the interests of the prisoners themselves, more especially so as not to increase the difficulty of their repatriation.

The transfer of prisoners of war shall always be effected humanely and in conditions not less favourable than those under which the forces of the Detaining Power are transferred. Account shall always be taken of the climatic conditions to which the prisoners of war are accustomed and the conditions of transfer shall in no case be prejudicial to their health.

The Detaining Power shall supply prisoners of war during transfer with sufficient food and drinking water to keep them in good health, likewise with the necessary clothing, shelter and medical attention. The Detaining Power shall take adequate precautions especially in case of transport by sea or by air, to ensure their safety during transfer, and shall draw up a complete list of all transferred prisoners before their departure.

Article 47

Sick or wounded prisoners of war shall not be transferred as long as their recovery may be endangered by the journey, unless their safety imperatively demands it.

If the combat zone draws closer to a camp, the prisoners of war in the said camp shall not be transferred unless their transfer can be carried out in adequate conditions of safety, or if they are exposed to greater risks by remaining on the spot than by being transferred.

Article 48

In the event of transfer, prisoners of war shall be officially advised of their departure and of their new postal address. Such notifications shall be given in time for them to pack their luggage and inform their next of kin.

They shall be allowed to take with them their personal effects, and the correspondence and parcels which have arrived for them. The weight of such baggage may be limited, if the conditions of transfer so require, to what each prisoner can reasonably carry, which shall in no case be more than twenty-five kilograms per head.

Mail and parcels addressed to their former camp shall be forwarded to them without delay. The camp commander shall take, in agreement with the prisoners' representative, any measures needed to ensure the transport of the prisoners' community property and of the luggage they are unable to take with them in consequence of restrictions imposed by virtue of the second paragraph of this Article.

The costs of transfers shall be borne by the Detaining Power.

SECTION III
LABOUR OF PRISONERS OF WAR

Article 49

The Detaining Power may utilize the labour of prisoners of war who are physically fit, taking into account their age, sex, rank and physical aptitude, and with a view particularly to maintaining them in a good state of physical and mental health.

Non-commissioned officers who are prisoners of war shall only be required to do supervisory work. Those not so required may ask for other suitable work which shall, so far as possible, be found for them.

If officers or persons of equivalent status ask for suitable work, it shall be found for them, so far as possible, but they may in no circumstances be compelled to work.

Article 50

Besides work connected with camp administration, installation or maintenance, prisoners of war may be compelled to do only such work as is included in the following classes:

(a) Agriculture;

(b) Industries connected with the production or the extraction of raw materials, and manufacturing industries, with the exception of metallurgical, machinery and chemical industries; public works and building operations which have no military character or purpose;

(c) Transport and handling of stores which are not military in character or purpose;

(d) Commercial business, and arts and crafts;

(e) Domestic service;

(f) Public utility services having no military character or purpose.

Should the above provisions be infringed, prisoners of war shall be allowed to exercise their right of complaint, in conformity with Article 78.

Article 51

Prisoners of war must be granted suitable working conditions, especially as regards accommodation, food, clothing and equipment;

such conditions shall not be inferior to those enjoyed by nationals of the Detaining Power employed in similar work; account shall also be taken of climatic conditions.

The Detaining Power, in utilizing the labour of prisoners of war, shall ensure that in areas in which prisoners are employed, the national legislation concerning the protection of labour, and, more particularly, the regulations for the safety of workers, are duly applied.

Prisoners of war shall receive training and be provided with the means of protection suitable to the work they will have to do and similar to those accorded to the nationals of the Detaining Power. Subject to the provisions of Article 52, prisoners may be submitted to the normal risks run by these civilian workers.

Conditions of labour shall in no case be rendered more arduous by disciplinary measures.

Article 52

Unless he be a volunteer, no prisoner of war may be employed on labour which is of an unhealthy or dangerous nature.

No prisoner of war shall be assigned to labour which would be looked upon as humiliating for a member of the Detaining Power's own forces.

The removal of mines or similar devices shall be considered as dangerous labour.

Article 53

The duration of the daily labour of prisoners of war, including the time of the journey to and fro, shall not be excessive, and must in no case exceed that permitted for civilian workers in the district, who are nationals of the Detaining Power and employed on the same work.

Prisoners of war must be allowed, in the middle of the day's work, a rest of not less than one hour. This rest will be the same as that to which workers of the Detaining Power are entitled, if the latter is of longer duration. They shall be allowed in addition a rest of twenty-four consecutive hours every week, preferably on Sunday or the day of rest in their country of origin. Furthermore, every prisoner who has worked for one year shall be granted a rest of eight consecutive days, during which his working pay shall be paid him.

If methods of labour such as piece-work are employed, the length of the working period shall not be rendered excessive thereby.

Article 54

The working pay due to prisoners of war shall be fixed in accordance with the provisions of Article 62 of the present Convention.

Prisoners of war who sustain accidents in connection with work, or who contract a disease in the course, or in consequence of their work, shall receive all the care their condition may require. The Detaining Power shall furthermore deliver to such prisoners of war a medical certificate enabling them to submit their claims to the Power on which they depend, and shall send a duplicate to the Central Prisoners of War Agency provided for in Article 123.

Article 55

The fitness of prisoners of war for work shall be periodically verified by medical examinations at least once a month. The examinations shall have particular regard to the nature of the work which prisoners of war are required to do.

If any prisoner of war considers himself incapable of working, he shall be permitted to appear before the medical authorities of his camp. Physicians or surgeons may recommend that the prisoners who are, in their opinion, unfit for work, be exempted therefrom.

Article 56

The organization and administration of labour detachments shall be similar to those of prisoner of war camps.

Every labour detachment shall remain under the control of and administratively part of a prisoner of war camp. The military authorities and the commander of the said camp shall be responsible, under the direction of their government, for the observance of the provisions of the present Convention in labour detachments.

The camp commander shall keep an up-to-date record of the labour detachments dependent on his camp, and shall communicate it to the delegates of the Protecting Power, of the International Committee of the Red Cross, or of other agencies giving relief to prisoners of war, who may visit the camp.

Article 57

The treatment of prisoners of war who work for private persons, even if the latter are responsible for guarding and protecting them, shall not be inferior to that which is provided for by the present Convention. The Detaining Power, the military authorities and the commander of the camp to which such prisoners belong shall be entirely responsible for the maintenance, care, treatment, and payment of the working pay of such prisoners of war.

Such prisoners of war shall have the right to remain in communication with the prisoners' representatives in the camps on which they depend.

SECTION IV
FINANCIAL RESOURCES OF PRISONERS OF WAR
Article 58

Upon the outbreak of hostilities, and pending an arrangement on this matter with the Protecting Power, the Detaining Power may determine the maximum amount of money in cash or in any similar form, that prisoners may have in their possession. Any amount in excess, which was properly in their possession and which has been taken or withheld from them, shall be placed to their account, together with any monies deposited by them, and shall not be converted into any other currency without their consent.

If prisoners of war are permitted to purchase services or commodities outside the camp against payment in cash, such payments shall be made by the prisoner himself or by the camp administration who will charge them to the accounts of the prisoners concerned. The Detaining Power will establish the necessary rules in this respect.

Article 59

Cash which was taken from prisoners of war, in accordance with Article 18, at the time of their capture, and which is in the currency of the Detaining Power, shall be placed to their separate accounts, in accordance with the provisions of Article 64 of the present Section.

The amounts, in the currency of the Detaining Power, due to the conversion of sums in other currencies that are taken from the prisoners of war at the same time, shall also be credited to their separate accounts.

Article 60

The Detaining Power shall grant all prisoners of war a monthly advance of pay, the amount of which shall be fixed by conversion, into the currency of the said Power, of the following amounts:

Category I: Prisoners ranking below sergeant: eight Swiss francs.

Category II: Sergeants and other non-commissioned officers, or prisoners of equivalent rank: twelve Swiss francs.

Category III: Warrant officers and commissioned officers below the rank of major or prisoners of equivalent rank: fifty Swiss francs.

Category IV: Majors, lieutenant-colonels, colonels or prisoners of equivalent rank: sixty Swiss francs.

Category V: General officers or prisoners of equivalent rank: seventy-five Swiss francs.

However, the Parties to the conflict concerned may by special agreement modify the amount of advances of pay due to prisoners of the preceding categories.

Furthermore, if the amounts indicated in the first paragraph above would be unduly high compared with the pay of the Detaining Power's armed forces or would, for any reason, seriously embarrass the Detaining Power, then, pending the conclusion of a special agreement with the Power on which the prisoners depend to vary the amounts indicated above, the Detaining Power:

(a) Shall continue to credit the accounts of the prisoners with the amounts indicated in the first paragraph above;

(b) May temporarily limit the amount made available from these advances of pay to prisoners of war for their own use, to sums which are reasonable, but which, for Category I, shall never be inferior to the amount that the Detaining Power gives to the members of its own armed forces.

The reasons for any limitations will be given without delay to the Protecting Power.

Article 61

The Detaining Power shall accept for distribution as supplementary pay to prisoners of war sums which the Power on which the prisoners depend may forward to them, on condition that the sums to be paid shall be the same for each prisoner of the same category, shall be payable to all prisoners of that category depending on that Power, and shall be placed in their separate accounts, at the earliest opportunity, in accordance with the provisions of Article 64. Such supplementary pay shall not relieve the Detaining Power of any obligation under this Convention.

Article 62

Prisoners of war shall be paid a fair working rate of pay by the detaining authorities direct. The rate shall be fixed by the said authorities, but shall at no time be less than one-fourth of one Swiss franc for a full working day. The Detaining Power shall inform prisoners of war, as well as the Power on which they depend, through the intermediary of the Protecting Power, of the rate of daily working pay that it has fixed.

Working pay shall likewise be paid by the detaining authorities to prisoners of war permanently detailed to duties or to a skilled or semi-skilled occupation in connection with the administration, installation or maintenance of camps, and to the prisoners who are required to carry out spiritual or medical duties on behalf of their comrades.

The working pay of the prisoners' representative, of his advisers, if any, and of his assistants, shall be paid out of the fund maintained by canteen profits. The scale of this working pay shall be fixed by the prisoners' representative and approved by the camp commander. If there is no such fund, the detaining authorities shall pay these prisoners a fair working rate of pay.

Article 63

Prisoners of war shall be permitted to receive remittances of money addressed to them individually or collectively.

Every prisoner of war shall have at his disposal the credit balance of his account as provided for in the following Article, within the limits fixed by the Detaining Power, which shall make such payments as are requested. Subject to financial or monetary restrictions which the Detaining Power regards as essential, prisoners of war may also have payments made abroad. In this case payments addressed by prisoners of war to dependants shall be given priority.

In any event, and subject to the consent of the Power on which they depend, prisoners may have payments made in their own country, as follows: the Detaining Power shall send to the aforesaid Power through the Protecting Power a notification giving all the necessary particulars concerning the prisoners of war, the beneficiaries of the payments, and the amount of the sums to be paid, expressed in the Detaining Power's currency. The said notification shall be signed by the prisoners and countersigned by the camp commander. The Detaining Power shall debit the prisoners' account by a corresponding amount; the sums thus debited shall be placed by it to the credit of the Power on which the prisoners depend.

To apply the foregoing provisions, the Detaining Power may usefully consult the Model Regulations in Annex V of the present Convention.

Article 64

The Detaining Power shall hold an account for each prisoner of war, showing at least the following:

1. The amounts due to the prisoner or received by him as advances of pay, as working pay or derived from any other source; the sums in the currency of the Detaining Power which were taken from him; the sums taken from him and converted at his request into the currency of the said Power.

2. The payments made to the prisoner in cash, or in any other similar form; the payments made on his behalf and at his request; the sums transferred under Article 63, third paragraph.

Article 65

Every item entered in the account of a prisoner of war shall be countersigned or initialled by him, or by the prisoners' representative acting on his behalf.

Prisoners of war shall at all times be afforded reasonable facilities for consulting and obtaining copies of their accounts, which may likewise be inspected by the representatives of the Protecting Powers at the time of visits to the camp.

When prisoners of war are transferred from one camp to another, their personal accounts will follow them. In case of transfer from one Detaining Power to another, the monies which are their property and are not in the currency of the Detaining Power will follow them. They shall be given certificates for any other monies standing to the credit of their accounts.

The Parties to the conflict concerned may agree to notify to each other at specific intervals through the Protecting Power, the amount of the accounts of the prisoners of war.

Article 66

On the termination of captivity, through the release of a prisoner of war or his repatriation, the Detaining Power shall give him a statement, signed by an authorized officer of that Power, showing the credit balance then due to him. The Detaining Power shall also send through the Protecting Power to the government upon which the prisoner of war depends, lists giving all appropriate particulars of all prisoners of war whose captivity has been terminated by repatriation, release, escape, death or any other means, and showing the amount of their credit balances. Such lists shall be certified on each sheet by an authorized representative of the Detaining Power.

Any of the above provisions of this Article may be varied by mutual agreement between any two Parties to the conflict.

The Power on which the prisoner of war depends shall be responsible for settling with him any credit balance due to him from the Detaining Power on the termination of his captivity.

Article 67

Advances of pay, issued to prisoners of war in conformity with Article 60, shall be considered as made on behalf of the Power on which they depend. Such advances of pay, as well as all payments made by the said Power under Article 63, third paragraph, and Article 68, shall form the subject of arrangements between the Powers concerned, at the close of hostilities.

Article 68

Any claim by a prisoner of war for compensation in respect of any injury or other disability arising out of work shall be referred to the Power on which he depends, through the Protecting Power. In accordance with Article 54, the Detaining Power will, in all cases, provide the prisoner of war concerned with a statement showing the nature of the injury or disability, the circumstances in which it arose and particulars of medical or hospital treatment given for it. This statement will be signed by a responsible officer of the Detaining Power and the medical particulars certified by a medical officer.

Any claim by a prisoner of war for compensation in respect of personal effects, monies or valuables impounded by the Detaining Power under Article 18 and not forthcoming on his repatriation, or in respect of loss alleged to be due to the fault of the Detaining Power or any of its servants, shall likewise be referred to the Power on which he depends. Nevertheless, any such personal effects required for use by the prisoners of war whilst in captivity shall be replaced at the expense of the Detaining Power. The Detaining Power will, in all cases, provide the prisoner of war with a statement, signed by a responsible officer, showing all available information regarding the reasons why such effects, monies or valuables have not been restored to him. A copy of this statement will be forwarded to the Power on which he depends through the Central Prisoners of War Agency provided for in Article 123.

SECTION V
RELATIONS OF PRISONERS OF WAR WITH THE EXTERIOR

Article 69

Immediately upon prisoners of war falling into its power, the Detaining Power shall inform them and the Powers on which they depend, through the Protecting Power, of the measures taken to carry out the provisions of the present Section. They shall likewise inform the parties concerned of any subsequent modifications of such measures.

Article 70

Immediately upon capture, or not more than one week after arrival at a camp, even if it is a transit camp, likewise in case of sickness or transfer to hospital or another camp, every prisoner of war shall be enabled to write direct to his family, on the one hand, and to the Central Prisoners of War Agency provided for in Article 123, on the other hand, a card similar, if possible, to the model annexed to the present Convention, informing his relatives of his capture, address and state of health. The said cards shall be forwarded as rapidly as possible and may not be delayed in any manner.

Article 71

Prisoners of war shall be allowed to send and receive letters and cards. If the Detaining Power deems it necessary to limit the number of letters and cards sent by each prisoner of war, the said number shall not be less than two letters and four cards monthly, exclusive of the capture cards provided for in Article 70, and conforming as closely as possible to the models annexed to the present Convention. Further limitations may be imposed only if the Protecting Power is satisfied that it would be in the interests of the prisoners of war concerned to do so owing to difficulties of translation caused by the Detaining Power's inability to find sufficient qualified linguists to carry out the necessary censorship. If limitations must be placed on the correspondence addressed to prisoners of war, they may be ordered only by the Power on which the prisoners depend, possibly at the request of the Detaining Power. Such letters and cards must be conveyed by the most rapid method at the disposal of the Detaining Power; they may not be delayed or retained for disciplinary reasons.

Prisoners of war who have been without news for a long period, or who are unable to receive news from their next of kin or to give them news by the ordinary postal route, as well as those who are at a great distance from their homes, shall be permitted to send telegrams, the fees being charged against the prisoners of war's accounts with the Detaining Power or paid in the currency at their disposal. They shall likewise benefit by this measure in cases of urgency.

As a general rule, the correspondence of prisoners of war shall be written in their native language. The Parties to the conflict may allow correspondence in other languages.

Sacks containing prisoner of war mail must be securely sealed and labelled so as clearly to indicate their contents, and must be addressed to offices of destination.

Article 72

Prisoners of war shall be allowed to receive by post or by any other means individual parcels or collective shipments containing, in particular, foodstuffs, clothing, medical supplies and articles of a religious, educational or recreational character which may meet their needs, including books, devotional articles, scientific equipment, examination papers, musical instruments, sports outfits and materials allowing prisoners of war to pursue their studies or their cultural activities.

Such shipments shall in no way free the Detaining Power from the obligations imposed upon it by virtue of the present Convention.

The only limits which may be placed on these shipments shall be those proposed by the Protecting Power in the interest of the prisoners themselves, or by the International Committee of the Red Cross or any other organization giving assistance to the prisoners, in respect of their own shipments only, on account of exceptional strain on transport or communications.

The conditions for the sending of individual parcels and collective relief shall, if necessary, be the subject of special agreements between the Powers concerned, which may in no case delay the receipt by the prisoners of relief supplies. Books may not be included in parcels of clothing and foodstuffs. Medical supplies shall, as a rule, be sent in collective parcels.

Article 73

In the absence of special agreements between the Powers concerned on the conditions for the receipt and distribution of collective relief shipments, the rules and regulations concerning collective shipments, which are annexed to the present Convention, shall be applied.

The special agreements referred to above shall in no case restrict the right of prisoners' representatives to take possession of collective relief shipments intended for prisoners of war, to proceed to their distribution or to dispose of them in the interest of the prisoners.

Nor shall such agreements restrict the right of representatives of the Protecting Power, the International Committee of the Red Cross or any other organization giving assistance to prisoners of war and responsible for the forwarding of collective shipments, to supervise their distribution to the recipients.

Article 74

All relief shipments for prisoners of war shall be exempt from import, customs and other dues.

Correspondence, relief shipments and authorized remittances of money addressed to prisoners of war or despatched by them through the post office, either direct or through the Information Bureaux provided for in Article 122 and the Central Prisoners of War Agency provided for in Article 123, shall be exempt from any postal dues, both in the countries of origin and destination, and in intermediate countries.

If relief shipments intended for prisoners of war cannot be sent through the post office by reason of weight or for any other cause, the cost of transportation shall be borne by the Detaining Power in all the territories under its control. The other Powers party to the Convention shall bear the cost of transport in their respective territories.

In the absence of special agreements between the Parties concerned, the costs connected with transport of such shipments, other than costs covered by the above exemption, shall be charged to the senders.

The High Contracting Parties shall endeavour to reduce, so far as possible, the rates charged for telegrams sent by prisoners of war, or addressed to them.

Article 75

49

Should military operations prevent the Powers concerned from fulfilling their obligation to assure the transport of the shipments referred to in Articles 70, 71, 72 and 77, the Protecting Powers concerned, the International Committee of the Red Cross or any other organization duly approved by the Parties to the conflict may undertake to ensure the conveyance of such shipments by suitable means (railway wagons, motor vehicles, vessels or aircraft, etc.). For this purpose, the High Contracting Parties shall endeavour to supply them with such transport and to allow its circulation, especially by granting the necessary safe-conducts.

Such transport may also be used to convey:

(a) Correspondence, lists and reports exchanged between the Central Information Agency referred to in Article 123 and the National Bureaux referred to in Article 122;

(b) Correspondence and reports relating to prisoners of war which the Protecting Powers, the International Committee of the Red Cross or any other body assisting the prisoners, exchange either with their own delegates or with the Parties to the conflict.

These provisions in no way detract from the right of any Party to the conflict to arrange other means of transport, if it should so prefer, nor preclude the granting of safe-conducts, under mutually agreed conditions, to such means of transport.

In the absence of special agreements, the costs occasioned by the use of such means of transport shall be borne proportionally by the Parties to the conflict whose nationals are benefited thereby.

Article 76

The censoring of correspondence addressed to prisoners of war or despatched by them shall be done as quickly as possible. Mail shall be censored only by the despatching State and the receiving State, and once only by each.

The examination of consignments intended for prisoners of war shall not be carried out under conditions that will expose the goods contained in them to deterioration; except in the case of written or printed matter, it shall be done in the presence of the addressee, or of a fellow-prisoner duly delegated by him. The delivery to prisoners of individual or collective consignments shall not be delayed under the pretext of difficulties of censorship.

Any prohibition of correspondence ordered by Parties to the conflict, either for military or political reasons, shall be only temporary and its duration shall be as short as possible.

Article 77

The Detaining Powers shall provide all facilities for the transmission, through the Protecting Power or the Central Prisoners of War Agency provided for in Article 123, of instruments, papers or documents intended for prisoners of war or despatched by them, especially powers of attorney and wills.

In all cases they shall facilitate the preparation and execution of such documents on behalf of prisoners of war; in particular, they shall allow them to consult a lawyer and shall take what measures are necessary for the authentication of their signatures.

SECTION VI
RELATIONS BETWEEN PRISONERS OF WAR AND THE AUTHORITIES
Chapter I
COMPLAINTS OF PRISONERS OF WAR RESPECTING THE CONDITIONS OF CAPTIVITY

Article 78

Prisoners of war shall have the right to make known to the military authorities in whose power they are, their requests regarding the conditions of captivity to which they are subjected.

They shall also have the unrestricted right to apply to the representatives of the Protecting Powers either through their prisoners' representative or, if they consider it necessary, direct, in order to draw their attention to any points on which they may have complaints to make regarding their conditions of captivity.

These requests and complaints shall not be limited nor considered to be a part of the correspondence quota referred to in Article 71. They must be transmitted immediately. Even if they are recognized to be unfounded, they may not give rise to any punishment.

Prisoners' representatives may send periodic reports on the situation in the camps and the needs of the prisoners of war to the representatives of the Protecting Powers.

Chapter II
PRISONER OF WAR REPRESENTATIVES

Article 79

In all places where there are prisoners of war, except in those where there are officers, the prisoners shall freely elect by secret ballot, every six months, and also in case of vacancies, prisoners' representatives entrusted with representing them before the military authorities, the Protecting Powers, the International Committee of the Red Cross and any other organization which may assist them. These prisoners' representatives shall be eligible for re-election.

In camps for officers and persons of equivalent status or in mixed camps, the senior officer among the prisoners of war shall be recognized as the camp prisoners' representative. In camps for officers, he shall be assisted by one or more advisers chosen by the officers; in mixed camps, his assistants shall be chosen from among the prisoners of war who are not officers and shall be elected by them.

Officer prisoners of war of the same nationality shall be stationed in labour camps for prisoners of war, for the purpose of carrying out the camp administration duties for which the prisoners of war are responsible. These officers may be elected as prisoners' representatives under the first paragraph of this Article. In such a case the assistants to the prisoners' representatives shall be chosen from among those prisoners of war who are not officers.

Every representative elected must be approved by the Detaining Power before he has the right to commence his duties. Where the Detaining Power refuses to approve a prisoner of war elected by his fellow prisoners of war, it must inform the Protecting Power of the reason for such refusal.

In all cases the prisoners' representative must have the same nationality, language and customs as the prisoners of war whom he represents. Thus, prisoners of war distributed in different sections of a camp, according to their nationality, language or customs, shall have for each section their own prisoners' representative, in accordance with the foregoing paragraphs.

Article 80

Prisoners' representatives shall further the physical, spiritual and intellectual well-being of prisoners of war.

In particular, where the prisoners decide to organize amongst themselves a system of mutual assistance, this organization will be within the province of the prisoners' representative, in addition to the special duties entrusted to him by other provisions of the present Convention.

Prisoners' representatives shall not be held responsible, simply by reason of their duties, for any offences committed by prisoners of war.

Article 81

Prisoners' representatives shall not be required to perform any other work, if the accomplishment of their duties is thereby made more difficult.

Prisoners' representatives may appoint from amongst the prisoners such assistants as they may require. All material facilities shall be granted them, particularly a certain freedom of movement necessary for the accomplishment of their duties (inspection of labour detachments, receipt of supplies, etc.).

Prisoners' representatives shall be permitted to visit premises where prisoners of war are detained, and every prisoner of war shall have the right to consult freely his prisoners' representative.

All facilities shall likewise be accorded to the prisoners' representatives for communication by post and telegraph with the detaining authorities, the Protecting Powers, the International Committee of the Red Cross and their delegates, the Mixed Medical Commissions and with the bodies which give assistance to prisoners of war. Prisoners' representatives of labour detachments shall enjoy the same facilities for communication with the prisoners' representatives of the principal camp. Such communications shall not be restricted, nor considered as forming a part of the quota mentioned in Article 71.

Prisoners' representatives who are transferred shall be allowed a reasonable time to acquaint their successors with current affairs.

In case of dismissal, the reasons therefor shall be communicated to the Protecting Power.

Chapter III
PENAL AND DISCIPLINARY SANCTIONS
I. General provisions
Article 82

A prisoner of war shall be subject to the laws, regulations and orders in force in the armed forces of the Detaining Power; the Detaining Power shall be justified in taking judicial or disciplinary measures in respect of any offence committed by a prisoner of war against such laws, regulations or orders. However, no proceedings or punishments contrary to the provisions of this Chapter shall be allowed.

If any law, regulation or order of the Detaining Power shall declare acts committed by a prisoner of war to be punishable, whereas the same acts would not be punishable if committed by a member of the forces of the Detaining Power, such acts shall entail disciplinary punishments only.

Article 83

In deciding whether proceedings in respect of an offence alleged to have been committed by a prisoner of war shall be judicial or disciplinary, the Detaining Power shall ensure that the competent authorities exercise the greatest leniency and adopt, wherever possible, disciplinary rather than judicial measures.

Article 84

A prisoner of war shall be tried only by a military court, unless the existing laws of the Detaining Power expressly permit the civil courts to try a member of the armed forces of the Detaining Power in respect of the particular offence alleged to have been committed by the prisoner of war.

In no circumstances whatever shall a prisoner of war be tried by a court of any kind which does not offer the essential guarantees of independence and impartiality as generally recognized, and, in particular, the procedure of which does not afford the accused the rights and means of defence provided for in Article 105.

Article 85

Prisoners of war prosecuted under the laws of the Detaining Power for acts committed prior to capture shall retain, even if convicted, the benefits of the present Convention.

Article 86

No prisoner of war may be punished more than once for the same act, or on the same charge.

Article 87

Prisoners of war may not be sentenced by the military authorities and courts of the Detaining Power to any penalties except those provided for in respect of members of the armed forces of the said Power who have committed the same acts.

When fixing the penalty, the courts or authorities of the Detaining Power shall take into consideration, to the widest extent possible, the fact that the accused, not being a national of the Detaining Power, is not bound to it by any duty of allegiance, and that he is in its power as the result of circumstances independent of his own will. The said courts or authorities shall be at liberty to reduce the penalty provided for the violation of which the prisoner of war is accused, and shall therefore not be bound to apply the minimum penalty prescribed.

Collective punishment for individual acts, corporal punishments, imprisonment in premises without daylight and, in general, any form of torture or cruelty, are forbidden.

No prisoner of war may be deprived of his rank by the Detaining Power, or prevented from wearing his badges.

Article 88

Officers, non-commissioned officers and men who are prisoners of war undergoing a disciplinary or judicial punishment, shall not be subjected to more severe treatment than that applied in respect of the same punishment to members of the armed forces of the Detaining Power of equivalent rank.

A woman prisoner of war shall not be awarded or sentenced to a punishment more severe, or treated whilst undergoing punishment more severely, than a woman member of the armed forces of the Detaining Power dealt with for a similar offence.

In no case may a woman prisoner of war be awarded or sentenced to a punishment more severe, or treated whilst undergoing punishment more severely, than a male member of the armed forces of the Detaining Power dealt with for a similar offence.

Prisoners of war who have served disciplinary or judicial sentences may not be treated differently from other prisoners of war.

II. Disciplinary sanctions
Article 89

The disciplinary punishments applicable to prisoners of war are the following:

1. A fine which shall not exceed 50 per cent of the advances of pay and working pay which the prisoner of war would otherwise receive under the provisions of Articles 60 and 62 during a period of not more than thirty days.

2. Discontinuance of privileges granted over and above the treatment provided for by the present Convention.

3. Fatigue duties not exceeding two hours daily.

4. Confinement.

The punishment referred to under (3) shall not be applied to officers.

In no case shall disciplinary punishments be inhuman, brutal or dangerous to the health of prisoners of war.

Article 90

The duration of any single punishment shall in no case exceed thirty days. Any period of confinement awaiting the hearing of a disciplinary offence or the award of disciplinary punishment shall be deducted from an award pronounced against a prisoner of war.

The maximum of thirty days provided above may not be exceeded, even if the prisoner of war is answerable for several acts at the same time when he is awarded punishment, whether such acts are related or not.

The period between the pronouncing of an award of disciplinary punishment and its execution shall not exceed one month.

When a prisoner of war is awarded a further disciplinary punishment, a period of at least three days shall elapse between the execution of any two of the punishments, if the duration of one of these is ten days or more.

Article 91

The escape of a prisoner of war shall be deemed to have succeeded when:

1. He has joined the armed forces of the Power on which he depends, or those of an allied Power;

2. He has left the territory under the control of the Detaining Power, or of an ally of the said Power;

3. He has joined a ship flying the flag of the Power on which he depends, or of an allied Power, in the territorial waters of the Detaining Power, the said ship not being under the control of the last-named Power.

Prisoners of war who have made good their escape in the sense of this Article and who are recaptured, shall not be liable to any punishment in respect of their previous escape.

Article 92

A prisoner of war who attempts to escape and is recaptured before having made good his escape in the sense of Article 91 shall be liable only to a disciplinary punishment in respect of this act, even if it is a repeated offence.

A prisoner of war who is recaptured shall be handed over without delay to the competent military authority.

Article 88, fourth paragraph, notwithstanding, prisoners of war punished as a result of an unsuccessful escape may be subjected to special surveillance. Such surveillance must not affect the state of their health, must be undergone in a prisoner of war camp, and must not entail the suppression of any of the safeguards granted them by the present Convention.

Article 93

Escape or attempt to escape, even if it is a repeated offence, shall not be deemed an aggravating circumstance if the prisoner of war is subjected to trial by judicial proceedings in respect of an offence committed during his escape or attempt to escape.

In conformity with the principle stated in Article 83, offences committed by prisoners of war with the sole intention of facilitating their escape and which do not entail any violence against life or limb, such as offences against public property, theft without intention of self-enrichment, the drawing up or use of false papers, the wearing of civilian clothing, shall occasion disciplinary punishment only.

Prisoners of war who aid or abet an escape or an attempt to escape shall be liable on this count to disciplinary punishment only.

Article 94

If an escaped prisoner of war is recaptured, the Power on which he depends shall be notified thereof in the manner defined in Article 122, provided notification of his escape has been made.

Article 95

A prisoner of war accused of an offence against discipline shall not be kept in confinement pending the hearing unless a member of the armed forces of the Detaining Power would be so kept if he were accused of a similar offence, or if it is essential in the interests of camp order and discipline.

Any period spent by a prisoner of war in confinement awaiting the disposal of an offence against discipline shall be reduced to an absolute minimum and shall not exceed fourteen days.

The provisions of Articles 97 and 98 of this Chapter shall apply to prisoners of war who are in confinement awaiting the disposal of offences against discipline.

Article 96

Acts which constitute offences against discipline shall be investigated immediately.

Without prejudice to the competence of courts and superior military authorities, disciplinary punishment may be ordered only by an officer having disciplinary powers in his capacity as camp commander, or by a responsible officer who replaces him or to whom he has delegated his disciplinary powers.

In no case may such powers be delegated to a prisoner of war or be exercised by a prisoner of war.

Before any disciplinary award is pronounced, the accused shall be given precise information regarding the offences of which he is accused, and given an opportunity of explaining his conduct and of defending himself. He shall be permitted, in particular, to call witnesses and to have recourse, if necessary, to the services of a qualified interpreter. The decision shall be announced to the accused prisoner of war and to the prisoners' representative.

A record of disciplinary punishments shall be maintained by the camp commander and shall be open to inspection by representatives of the Protecting Power.

Article 97

Prisoners of war shall not in any case be transferred to penitentiary establishments (prisons, penitentiaries, convict prisons, etc.) to undergo disciplinary punishment therein.

All premises in which disciplinary punishments are undergone shall conform to the sanitary requirements set forth in Article 25. A prisoner of war undergoing punishment shall be enabled to keep himself in a state of cleanliness, in conformity with Article 29.

Officers and persons of equivalent status shall not be lodged in the same quarters as non-commissioned officers or men.

Women prisoners of war undergoing disciplinary punishment shall be confined in separate quarters from male prisoners of war and shall be under the immediate supervision of women.

Article 98

A prisoner of war undergoing confinement as a disciplinary punishment, shall continue to enjoy the benefits of the provisions of this Convention except in so far as these are necessarily rendered inapplicable by the mere fact that he is confined. In no case may he be deprived of the benefits of the provisions of Articles 78 and 126.

A prisoner of war awarded disciplinary punishment may not be deprived of the prerogatives attached to his rank.

Prisoners of war awarded disciplinary punishment shall be allowed to exercise and to stay in the open air at least two hours daily.

They shall be allowed, on their request, to be present at the daily medical inspections. They shall receive the attention which their state of health requires and, if necessary, shall be removed to the camp infirmary or to a hospital.

They shall have permission to read and write, likewise to send and receive letters. Parcels and remittances of money, however, may be withheld from them until the completion of the punishment; they shall meanwhile be entrusted to the prisoners' representative, who will hand over to the infirmary the perishable goods contained in such parcels.

III. Judicial proceedings
Article 99

No prisoner of war may be tried or sentenced for an act which is not forbidden by the law of the Detaining Power or by international law, in force at the time the said act was committed.

No moral or physical coercion may be exerted on a prisoner of war in order to induce him to admit himself guilty of the act of which he is accused.

No prisoner of war may be convicted without having had an opportunity to present his defence and the assistance of a qualified advocate or counsel.

Article 100

Prisoners of war and the Protecting Powers shall be informed as soon as possible of the offences which are punishable by the death sentence under the laws of the Detaining Power.

Other offences shall not thereafter be made punishable by the death penalty without the concurrence of the Power upon which the prisoners of war depend.

The death sentence cannot be pronounced on a prisoner of war unless the attention of the court has, in accordance with Article 87, second paragraph, been particularly called to the fact that since the accused is not a national of the Detaining Power, he is not bound to it by any duty of allegiance, and that he is in its power as the result of circumstances independent of his own will.

Article 101

If the death penalty is pronounced on a prisoner of war, the sentence shall not be executed before the expiration of a period of at least six months from the date when the Protecting Power receives, at an indicated address, the detailed communication provided for in Article 107.

Article 102

A prisoner of war can be validly sentenced only if the sentence has been pronounced by the same courts according to the same procedure as in the case of members of the armed forces of the Detaining Power, and if, furthermore, the provisions of the present Chapter have been observed.

Article 103

Judicial investigations relating to a prisoner of war shall be conducted as rapidly as circumstances permit and so that his trial shall take place as soon as possible. A prisoner of war shall not be confined while awaiting trial unless a member of the armed forces of the Detaining Power would be so confined if he were accused of a similar offence, or if it is essential to do so in the interests of national security. In no circumstances shall this confinement exceed three months.

Any period spent by a prisoner of war in confinement awaiting trial shall be deducted from any sentence of imprisonment passed upon him and taken into account in fixing any penalty.

The provisions of Articles 97 and 98 of this Chapter shall apply to a prisoner of war whilst in confinement awaiting trial.

Article 104

In any case in which the Detaining Power has decided to institute judicial proceedings against a prisoner of war, it shall notify the Protecting Power as soon as possible and at least three weeks before the opening of the trial. This period of three weeks shall run as from the day on which such notification reaches the Protecting Power at the address previously indicated by the latter to the Detaining Power.

The said notification shall contain the following information:

1. Surname and first names of the prisoner of war, his rank, his army, regimental, personal or serial number, his date of birth, and his profession or trade, if any;

2. Place of internment or confinement;

3. Specification of the charge or charges on which the prisoner of war is to be arraigned, giving the legal provisions applicable;

4 . Designation of the court which will try the case, likewise the date and place fixed for the opening of the trial.

The same communication shall be made by the Detaining Power to the prisoners' representative.

If no evidence is submitted, at the opening of a trial, that the notification referred to above was received by the Protecting Power, by the prisoner of war and by the prisoners' representative concerned, at least three weeks before the opening of the trial, then the latter cannot take place and must be adjourned.

Article 105

The prisoner of war shall be entitled to assistance by one of his prisoner comrades, to defence by a qualified advocate or counsel of his own choice, to the calling of witnesses and, if he deems necessary, to the services of a competent interpreter. He shall be advised of these rights by the Detaining Power in due time before the trial.

Failing a choice by the prisoner of war, the Protecting Power shall find him an advocate or counsel, and shall have at least one week at its disposal for the purpose. The Detaining Power shall deliver to the said Power, on request, a list of persons qualified to present the defence. Failing a choice of an advocate or counsel by the prisoner of war or the Protecting Power, the Detaining Power shall appoint a competent advocate or counsel to conduct the defence.

The advocate or counsel conducting the defence on behalf of the prisoner of war shall have at his disposal a period of two weeks at least before the opening of the trial, as well as the necessary facilities to prepare the defence of the accused. He may, in particular, freely visit the accused and interview him in private. He may also confer with any witnesses for the defence, including prisoners of war. He shall have the benefit of these facilities until the term of appeal or petition has expired.

Particulars of the charge or charges on which the prisoner of war is to be arraigned, as well as the documents which are generally communicated to the accused by virtue of the laws in force in the armed forces of the Detaining Power, shall be communicated to the accused prisoner of war in a language which he understands, and in good time before the opening of the trial. The same communication in the same circumstances shall be made to the advocate or counsel conducting the defence on behalf of the prisoner of war.

The representatives of the Protecting Power shall be entitled to attend the trial of the case, unless, exceptionally, this is held in camera in the interest of State security. In such a case the Detaining Power shall advise the Protecting Power accordingly.

Article 106

Every prisoner of war shall have, in the same manner as the members of the armed forces of the Detaining Power, the right of appeal or petition from any sentence pronounced upon him, with a view to the quashing or revising of the sentence or the reopening of the trial. He shall be fully informed of his right to appeal or petition and of the time limit within which he may do so.

Article 107

Any judgment and sentence pronounced upon a prisoner of war shall be immediately reported to the Protecting Power in the form of a summary communication, which shall also indicate whether he has the right of appeal with a view to the quashing of the sentence or the reopening of the trial. This communication shall likewise be sent to the prisoners' representative concerned. It shall also be sent to the accused prisoner of war in a language he understands, if the sentence was not pronounced in his presence. The Detaining Power shall also immediately communicate to the Protecting Power the decision of the prisoner of war to use or to waive his right of appeal.

Furthermore, if a prisoner of war is finally convicted or if a sentence pronounced on a prisoner of war in the first instance is a death sentence, the Detaining Power shall as soon as possible address to the Protecting Power a detailed communication containing:

1. The precise wording of the finding and sentence;
2. A summarized report of any preliminary investigation and of the trial, emphasizing in particular the elements of the prosecution and the defence;

3. Notification, where applicable, of the establishment where the sentence will be served.

The communications provided for in the foregoing subparagraphs shall be sent to the Protecting Power at the address previously made known to the Detaining Power.

Article 108

Sentences pronounced on prisoners of war after a conviction has become duly enforceable, shall be served in the same establishments and under the same conditions as in the case of members of the armed forces of the Detaining Power. These conditions shall in all cases conform to the requirements of health and humanity.

A woman prisoner of war on whom such a sentence has been pronounced shall be confined in separate quarters and shall be under the supervision of women.

In any case, prisoners of war sentenced to a penalty depriving them of their liberty shall retain the benefit of the provisions of Articles 78 and 126 of the present Convention. Furthermore, they shall be entitled to receive and despatch correspondence, to receive at least one relief parcel monthly, to take regular exercise in the open air, to have the medical care required by their state of health, and the spiritual assistance they may desire. Penalties to which they may be subjected shall be in accordance with the provisions of Article 87, third paragraph.

PART IV
TERMINATION OF CAPTIVITY
SECTION I
DIRECT REPATRIATION AND ACCOMMODATION IN NEUTRAL COUNTRIES

Article 109

Subject to the provisions of the third paragraph of this Article, Parties to the conflict are bound to send back to their own country, regardless of number or rank, seriously wounded and seriously sick prisoners of war, after having cared for them until they are fit to travel, in accordance with the first paragraph of the following Article.

Throughout the duration of hostilities, Parties to the conflict shall endeavour, with the cooperation of the neutral Powers concerned, to make arrangements for the accommodation in neutral countries of the sick and wounded prisoners of war referred to in the second paragraph of the following Article. They may, in addition, conclude agreements with a view to the direct repatriation or internment in a neutral country of able-bodied prisoners of war who have undergone a long period of captivity.

No sick or injured prisoner of war who is eligible for repatriation under the first paragraph of this Article, may be repatriated against his will during hostilities.

Article 110

The following shall be repatriated direct:

1. Incurably wounded and sick whose mental or physical fitness seems to have been gravely diminished.
2. Wounded and sick who, according to medical opinion, are not likely to recover within one year, whose condition requires treatment and whose mental or physical fitness seems to have been gravely diminished.
3. Wounded and sick who have recovered, but whose mental or physical fitness seems to have been gravely and permanently diminished.

The following may be accommodated in a neutral country:

1. Wounded and sick whose recovery may be expected within one year of the date of the wound or the beginning of the illness, if treatment in a neutral country might increase the prospects of a more certain and speedy recovery.
2. Prisoners of war whose mental or physical health, according to medical opinion, is seriously threatened by continued captivity, but whose accommodation in a neutral country might remove such a threat.

The conditions which prisoners of war accommodated in a neutral country must fulfil in order to permit their repatriation shall be fixed, as shall likewise their status, by agreement between the Powers concerned. In general, prisoners of war who have been accommodated in a neutral country, and who belong to the following categories, should be repatriated:

1. Those whose state of health has deteriorated so as to fulfil the conditions laid down for direct repatriation;

2. Those whose mental or physical powers remain, even after treatment, considerably impaired.

If no special agreements are concluded between the Parties to the conflict concerned, to determine the cases of disablement or sickness entailing direct repatriation or accommodation in a neutral country, such cases shall be settled in accordance with the principles laid down in the Model Agreement concerning direct repatriation and accommodation in neutral countries of wounded and sick prisoners of war and in the Regulations concerning Mixed Medical Commissions annexed to the present Convention.

Article 111

The Detaining Power, the Power on which the prisoners of war depend, and a neutral Power agreed upon by these two Powers, shall endeavour to conclude agreements which will enable prisoners of war to be interned in the territory of the said neutral Power until the close of hostilities.

Article 112

Upon the outbreak of hostilities, Mixed Medical Commissions shall be appointed to examine sick and wounded prisoners of war, and to make all appropriate decisions regarding them. The appointment, duties and functioning of these Commissions shall be in conformity with the provisions of the Regulations annexed to the present Convention.

However, prisoners of war who, in the opinion of the medical authorities of the Detaining Power, are manifestly seriously injured or seriously sick, may be repatriated without having to be examined by a Mixed Medical Commission.

Article 113

Besides those who are designated by the medical authorities of the Detaining Power, wounded or sick prisoners of war belonging to the categories listed below shall be entitled to present themselves for examination by the Mixed Medical Commissions provided for in the foregoing Article:

1. Wounded and sick proposed by a physician or surgeon who is of the same nationality, or a national of a Party to the conflict allied with the Power on which the said prisoners depend, and who exercises his functions in the camp.

2. Wounded and sick proposed by their prisoners' representative.

3. Wounded and sick proposed by the Power on which they depend, or by an organization duly recognized by the said Power and giving assistance to the prisoners.

Prisoners of war who do not belong to one of the three foregoing categories may nevertheless present themselves for examination by Mixed Medical Commissions, but shall be examined only after those belonging to the said categories.

The physician or surgeon of the same nationality as the prisoners who present themselves for examination by the Mixed Medical Commission, likewise the prisoners' representative of the said prisoners, shall have permission to be present at the examination.

Article 114

Prisoners of war who meet with accidents shall, unless the injury is self-inflicted, have the benefit of the provisions of this Convention as regards repatriation or accommodation in a neutral country.

Article 115

No prisoner of war on whom a disciplinary punishment has been imposed and who is eligible for repatriation or for accommodation in a neutral country, may be kept back on the plea that he has not undergone his punishment.

Prisoners of war detained in connection with a judicial prosecuti on or conviction and who are designated for repatriation or accommodation in a neutral country, may benefit by such measures before the end of the proceedings or the completion of the punishment, if the Detaining Power consents.

Parties to the conflict shall communicate to each other the names of those who will be detained until the end of the proceedings or the completion of the punishment.

Article 116

The costs of repatriating prisoners of war or of transporting them to a neutral country shall be borne, from the frontiers of the Detaining Power, by the Power on which the said prisoners depend.

Article 117

No repatriated person may be employed on active military service.

SECTION II

RELEASE AND REPATRIATION OF PRISONERS OF WAR AT THE CLOSE OF HOSTILITIES

Article 118

Prisoners of war shall be released and repatriated without delay after the cessation of active hostilities.

In the absence of stipulations to the above effect in any agreement concluded between the Parties to the conflict with a view to the cessation of hostilities, or failing any such agreement, each of the Detaining Powers shall itself establish and execute without delay a plan of repatriation in conformity with the principle laid down in the foregoing paragraph.

In either case, the measures adopted shall be brought to the knowledge of the prisoners of war.

The costs of repatriation of prisoners of war shall in all cases be equitably apportioned between the Detaining Power and the Power on which the prisoners depend. This apportionment shall be carried out on the following basis:

(a) If the two Powers are contiguous, the Power on which the prisoners of war depend shall bear the costs of repatriation from the frontiers of the Detaining Power.

(b) If the two Powers are not contiguous, the Detaining Power shall bear the costs of transport of prisoners of war over its own territory as far as its frontier or its port of embarkation nearest to the territory of the Power on which the prisoners of war depend. The Parties concerned shall agree between themselves as to the equitable apportionment of the remaining costs of the repatriation. The conclusion of this agreement shall in no circumstances justify any delay in the repatriation of the prisoners of war.

Article 119

Repatriation shall be effected in conditions similar to those laid down in Articles 46 to 48 inclusive of the present Convention for the transfer of prisoners of war, having regard to the provisions of Article 118 and to those of the following paragraphs.

On repatriation, any articles of value impounded from prisoners of war under Article 18, and any foreign currency which has not been converted into the currency of the Detaining Power, shall be restored to them. Articles of value and foreign currency which, for any reason whatever, are not restored to prisoners of war on repatriation, shall be despatched to the Information Bureau set up under Article 122.

Prisoners of war shall be allowed to take with them their personal effects, and any correspondence and parcels which have arrived for them. The weight of such baggage may be limited, if the conditions of repatriation so require, to what each prisoner can reasonably carry. Each prisoner shall in all cases be authorized to carry at least twenty-five kilograms.

The other personal effects of the repatriated prisoner shall be left in the charge of the Detaining Power which shall have them forwarded to him as soon as it has concluded an agreement to this effect, regulating the conditions of transport and the payment of the costs involved, with the Power on which the prisoner depends.

Prisoners of war against whom criminal proceedings for an indictable offence are pending may be detained until the end of such proceedings, and, if necessary, until the completion of the punishment. The same shall apply to prisoners of war already convicted for an indictable offence.

Parties to the conflict shall communicate to each other the names of any prisoners of war who are detained until the end of the proceedings or until punishment has been completed.

By agreement between the Parties to the conflict, commissions shall be established for the purpose of searching for dispersed prisoners of war and of assuring their repatriation with the least possible delay.

SECTION III
DEATH OF PRISONERS OF WAR
Article 120

Wills of prisoners of war shall be drawn up so as to satisfy the conditions of validity required by the legislation of their country of origin, which will take steps to inform the Detaining Power of its requirements in this respect. At the request of the prisoner of war and, in all cases, after death, the will shall be transmitted without delay to the Protecting Power; a certified copy shall be sent to the Central Agency.

Death certificates in the form annexed to the present Convention, or lists certified by a responsible officer, of all persons who die as prisoners of war shall be forwarded as rapidly as possible to the Prisoner of War Information Bureau established in accordance with Article 122. The death certificates or certified lists shall show particulars of identity as set out in the third paragraph of Article 17, and also the date and place of death, the cause of death, the date and place of burial and all particulars necessary to identify the graves.

The burial or cremation of a prisoner of war shall be preceded by a medical examination of the body with a view to confirming death and enabling a report to be made and, where necessary, establishing identity.

The detaining authorities shall ensure that prisoners of war who have died in captivity are honourably buried, if possible according to the rites of the religion to which they belonged, and that their graves are respected, suitably maintained and marked so as to be found at any time. Wherever possible, deceased prisoners of war who depended on the same Power shall be interred in the same place.

Deceased prisoners of war shall be buried in individual graves unless unavoidable circumstances require the use of collective graves. Bodies may be cremated only for imperative reasons of hygiene, on account of the religion of the deceased or in accordance with his express wish to this effect. In case of cremation, the fact shall be stated and the reasons given in the death certificate of the deceased.

In order that graves may always be found, all particulars of burials and graves shall be recorded with a Graves Registration Service established by the Detaining Power. Lists of graves and particulars of the prisoners of war interred in cemeteries and elsewhere shall be transmitted to the Power on which such prisoners of war depended. Responsibility for the care of these graves and for records of any subsequent moves of the bodies shall rest on the Power controlling the territory, if a Party to the present Convention. These provisions shall also apply to the ashes, which shall be kept by the Graves Registration Service until proper disposal thereof in accordance with the wishes of the home country.

Article 121

Every death or serious injury of a prisoner of war caused or suspected to have been caused by a sentry, another prisoner of war, or any other person, as well as any death the cause of which is unknown, shall be immediately followed by an official enquiry by the Detaining Power.

A communication on this subject shall be sent immediately to the Protecting Power. Statements shall be taken from witnesses, especially from those who are prisoners of war, and a report including such statements shall be forwarded to the Protecting Power.

If the enquiry indicates the guilt of one or more persons, the Detaining Power shall take all measures for the prosecution of the person or persons responsible.

PART V
INFORMATION BUREAUX AND RELIEF SOCIETIES FOR PRISONERS OF WAR

Article 122

Upon the outbreak of a conflict and in all cases of occupation, each of the Parties to the conflict shall institute an official Information Bureau for prisoners of war who are in its power. Neutral or non-belligerent Powers who may have received within their territory persons belonging to one of the categories referred to in Article 4, shall take the same action with respect to such persons. The Power concerned shall ensure that the Prisoners of War Information Bureau is provided with the necessary accommodation, equipment and staff to ensure its efficient working. It shall be at liberty to employ prisoners of war in such a Bureau under the conditions laid down in the Section of the present Convention dealing with work by prisoners of war.

Within the shortest possible period, each of the Parties to the conflict shall give its Bureau the information referred to in the fourth, fifth and sixth paragraphs of this Article regarding any enemy person belonging to one of the categories referred to in Article 4, who has fallen into its power. Neutral or non-belligerent Powers shall take the same action with regard to persons belonging to such categories whom they have received within their territory.

The Bureau shall immediately forward such information by the most rapid means to the Powers concerned, through the intermediary of the Protecting Powers and likewise of the Central Agency provided for in Article 123.

This information shall make it possible quickly to advise the next of kin concerned. Subject to the provisions of Article 17, the information shall include, in so far as available to the Information Bureau, in respect of each prisoner of war, his surname, first names, rank, army, regimental, personal or serial number, place and full date of birth, indication of the Power on which he depends, first name of the father and maiden name of the mother, name and address of the person to be informed and the address to which correspondence for the prisoner may be sent.

The Information Bureau shall receive from the various departments concerned information regarding transfers, releases, repatriations, escapes, admissions to hospital, and deaths, and shall transmit such information in the manner described in the third paragraph above.

Likewise, information regarding the state of health of prisoners of war who are seriously ill or seriously wounded shall be supplied regularly, every week if possible.

The Information Bureau shall also be responsible for replying to all enquiries sent to it concerning prisoners of war, including those who have died in captivity; it will make any enquiries necessary to obtain the information which is asked for if this is not in its possession.

All written communications made by the Bureau shall be authenticated by a signature or a seal.

The Information Bureau shall furthermore be charged with collecting all personal valuables, including sums in currencies other than that of the Detaining Power and documents of importance to the next of kin, left by prisoners of war who have been repatriated or released, or who have escaped or died, and shall forward the said valuables to the Powers concerned. Such articles shall be sent by the Bureau in sealed packets which shall be accompanied by statements giving clear and full particulars of the identity of the person to whom the articles belonged, and by a complete list of the contents of the parcel. Other personal effects of such prisoners of war shall be transmitted under arrangements agreed upon between the Parties to the conflict concerned.

Article 123

A Central Prisoners of War Information Agency shall be created in a neutral country. The International Committee of the Red Cross shall, if it deems necessary, propose to the Powers concerned the organization of such an Agency.

The function of the Agency shall be to collect all the information it may obtain through official or private channels respecting prisoners of war, and to transmit it as rapidly as possible to the country of origin of the prisoners of war or to the Power on which they depend. It shall receive from the Parties to the conflict all facilities for effecting such transmissions.

The High Contracting Parties, and in particular those whose nationals benefit by the services of the Central Agency, are requested to give the said Agency the financial aid it may require.

The foregoing provisions shall in no way be interpreted as restricting the humanitarian activities of the International Committee of the Red Cross, or of the relief Societies provided for in Article 125.

Article 124

The national Information Bureaux and the Central Information Agency shall enjoy free postage for mail, likewise all the exemptions provided for in Article 74, and further, so far as possible, exemption from telegraphic charges or, at least, greatly reduced rates.

Article 125

Subject to the measures which the Detaining Powers may consider essential to ensure their security or to meet any other reasonable need, the representatives of religious organizations, relief societies, or any other organization assisting prisoners of war, shall receive from the said Powers, for themselves and their duly accredited agents, all necessary facilities for visiting the prisoners, distributing relief supplies and material, from any source, intended for religious, educational or recreative purposes, and for assisting them in organizing their leisure time within the camps. Such societies or organizations may be constituted in the territory of the Detaining Power or in any other country, or they may have an international character.

The Detaining Power may limit the number of societies and organizations whose delegates are allowed to carry out their activities in its territory and under its supervision, on condition, however, that such limitation shall not hinder the effective operation of adequate relief to all prisoners of war.

The special position of the International Committee of the Red Cross in this field shall be recognized and respected at all times.

As soon as relief supplies or material intended for the above-mentioned purposes are handed over to prisoners of war, or very shortly afterwards, receipts for each consignment, signed by the prisoners' representative, shall be forwarded to the relief society or organization making the shipment. At the same time, receipts for these consignments shall be supplied by the administrative authorities responsible for guarding the prisoners.

PART VI
EXECUTION OF THE CONVENTION
SECTION I
GENERAL PROVISIONS
Article 126

Representatives or delegates of the Protecting Powers shall have permission to go to all places where prisoners of war may be, particularly to places of internment, imprisonment and labour, and shall have access to all premises occupied by prisoners of war; they shall also be allowed to go to the places of departure, passage and arrival of prisoners who are being transferred. They shall be able to interview the prisoners, and in particular the prisoners' representatives, without witnesses, either personally or through an interpreter.

Representatives and delegates of the Protecting Powers shall have full liberty to select the places they wish to visit. The duration and frequency of these visits shall not be restricted. Visits may not be prohibited except for reasons of imperative military necessity, and then only as an exceptional and temporary measure.

The Detaining Power and the Power on which the said prisoners of war depend may agree, if necessary, that compatriots of these prisoners of war be permitted to participate in the visits.

The delegates of the International Committee of the Red Cross shall enjoy the same prerogatives. The appointment of such delegates shall be submitted to the approval of the Power detaining the prisoners of war to be visited.

Article 127

The High Contracting Parties undertake, in time of peace as in time of war, to disseminate the text of the present Convention as widely as possible in their respective countries, and, in particular, to include the study thereof in their programmes of military and, if possible, civil instruction, so that the principles thereof may become known to all their armed forces and to the entire population.

Any military or other authorities, who in time of war assume responsibilities in respect of prisoners of war, must possess the text of the Convention and be specially instructed as to its provisions.

Article 128

The High Contracting Parties shall communicate to one another through the Swiss Federal Council and, during hostilities, through the

Protecting Powers, the official translations of the present Convention, as well as the laws and regulations which they may adopt to ensure the application thereof.

Article 129

The High Contracting Parties undertake to enact any legislation necessary to provide effective penal sanctions for persons committing, or ordering to be committed, any of the grave breaches of the present Convention defined in the following Article.

Each High Contracting Party shall be under the obligation to search for persons alleged to have committed, or to have ordered to be committed, such grave breaches, and shall bring such persons, regardless of their nationality, before its own courts. It may also, if it prefers, and in accordance with the provisions of its own legislation, hand such persons over for trial to another High Contracting Party concerned, provided such High Contracting Party has made out a prima facie case.

Each High Contracting Party shall take measures necessary for the suppression of all acts contrary to the provisions of the present Convention other than the grave breaches defined in the following Article.

In all circumstances, the accused persons shall benefit by safeguards of proper trial and defence, which shall not be less favourable than those provided by Article 105 and those following of the present Convention.

Article 130

Grave breaches to which the preceding Article relates shall be those involving any of the following acts, if committed against persons or property protected by the Convention: wilful killing, torture or inhuman treatment, including biological experiments, wilfully causing great suffering or serious injury to body or health, compelling a prisoner of war to serve in the forces of the hostile Power, or wilfully depriving a prisoner of war of the rights of fair and regular trial prescribed in this Convention.

Article 131

No High Contracting Party shall be allowed to absolve itself or any other High Contracting Party of any liability incurred by itself or by another High Contracting Party in respect of breaches referred to in the preceding Article.

Article 132

At the request of a Party to the conflict, an enquiry shall be instituted, in a manner to be decided between the interested Parties, concerning any alleged violation of the Convention.

If agreement has not been reached concerning the procedure for the enquiry, the Parties should agree on the choice of an umpire who will decide upon the procedure to be followed.

Once the violation has been established, the Parties to the conflict shall put an end to it and shall repress it with the least possible delay.

SECTION 11
FINAL PROVISIONS

Article 133

The present Convention is established in English and in French. Both texts are equally authentic. The Swiss Federal Council shall arrange for official translations of the Convention to be made in the Russian and Spanish languages.

Article 134

The present Convention replaces the Convention of 27 July 1929, in relations between the High Contracting Parties.

Article 135

In the relations between the Powers which are bound by The Hague Convention respecting the Laws and Customs of War on Land, whether that of July 29, 1899, or that of October 18, 1907, and which are parties to the present Convention, this last Convention shall be complementary to Chapter II of the Regulations annexed to the above-mentioned Conventions of The Hague.

Article 136

The present Convention, which bears the date of this day, is open to signature until February 12, 1950, in the name of the Powers represented at the Conference which opened at Geneva on April 21, 1949; furthermore, by Powers not represented at that Conference, but which are parties to the Convention of July 27, 1929.

Article 137

The present Convention shall be ratified as soon as possible and the ratifications shall be deposited at Berne.

A record shall be drawn up of the deposit of each instrument of ratification and certified copies of this record shall be transmitted by the Swiss Federal Council to all the Powers in whose name the Convention has been signed, or whose accession has been notified.

Article 138

The present Convention shall come into force six months after not less than two instruments of ratification have been deposited.

Thereafter, it shall come into force for each High Contracting Party six months after the deposit of the instrument of ratification.

Article 139

From the date of its coming into force, it shall be open to any Power in whose name the present Convention has not been signed, to accede to this Convention.

Article 140

Accessions shall be notified in writing to the Swiss Federal Council, and shall take effect six months after the date on which they are received.

The Swiss Federal Council shall communicate the accessions to all the Powers in whose name the Convention has been signed, or whose accession has been notified.

Article 141

The situations provided for in Articles 2 and 3 shall give immediate effect to ratifications deposited and accessions notified by the Parties to the conflict before or after the beginning of hostilities or occupation. The Swiss Federal Council shall communicate by the quickest method any ratifications or accessions received from Parties to the conflict.

Article 142

Each of the High Contracting Parties shall be at liberty to denounce the present Convention.

The denunciation shall be notified in writing to the Swiss Federal Council, which shall transmit it to the Governments of all the High Contracting Parties.

The denunciation shall take effect one year after the notification thereof has been made to the Swiss Federal Council. However, a denunciation of which notification has been made at a time when the denouncing Power is involved in a conflict shall not take effect until peace has been concluded, and until after operations connected with the release and repatriation of the persons protected by the present Convention have been terminated.

The denunciation shall have effect only in respect of the denouncing Power. It shall in no way impair the obligations which the Parties to the conflict shall remain bound to fulfil by virtue of the principles of the law of nations, as they result from the usages established among civilized peoples, from the laws of humanity and the dictates of the public conscience.

Article 143

The Swiss Federal Council shall register the present Convention with the Secretariat of the United Nations. The Swiss Federal Council shall also inform the Secretariat of the United Nations of all ratifications, accessions and denunciations received by it with respect to the present Convention.

IN WITNESS WHEREOF the undersigned, having deposited their respective full powers, have signed the present Convention.

DONE at Geneva this twelfth day of August 1949, in the English and French languages. The original shall be deposited in the Archives of the Swiss Confederation. The Swiss Federal Council shall transmit certified copies thereof to each of the signatory and acceding States.

ANNEX I

Model agreement concerning direct repatriation and accommodation in neutral countries of wounded and sick prisoners of war

(see Article 110)

I.-PRINCIPLES FOR DIRECT REPATRIATION

AND ACCOMMODATION IN NEUTRAL COUNTRIES

A. DIRECT REPATRIATION

The following shall be repatriated direct:

1.All prisoners of war suffering from the following disabilities as the result of trauma: loss of limb, paralysis, articular or other disabilities, when this disability is at least the loss of a hand or a foot, or the equivalent of the loss of a hand or a foot.

Without prejudice to a more generous interpretation, the following shall be considered as equivalent to the loss of a hand or a foot:

(a) Loss of a hand or of all the fingers, or of the thumb and forefinger of one hand; loss of a foot, or of all the toes and metatarsals of one foot.

(b) Ankylosis, loss of osseous tissue, cicatricial contracture preventing the functioning of one of the large articulations or of all the digital joints of one hand.

(c) Pseudarthrosis of the long bones.

(d) Deformities due to fracture or other injury which seriously interfere with function and weight-bearing power.

2. All wounded prisoners of war whose condition has become chronic, to the extent that prognosis appears to exclude recovery-in spite of treatment-within one year from the date of the injury, as. for example, in case of:

(a) Projectile in the heart. even if the Mixed Medical Commission should fail, at the time of their examination, to detect any serious disorders.

(b) Metallic splinter in the brain or the lungs, even if the Mixed Medical Commission cannot, at the time of examination, detect any local or general reaction.

(c)Osteomyelitis, when recovery cannot be foreseen in the course of the year following the injury, and which seems likely to result in ankylosis of a joint, or other impairments equivalent to the loss of a hand or a foot.

(d) Perforating and suppurating injury to the large joints.

(e) Injury to the skull, with loss or shifting of bony tissue.

(f) Injury or burning of the face with loss of tissue and functional lesions.

(g) Injury to the spinal cord.

(h) Lesion of the peripheral nerves, the sequelae of which are equivalent to the loss of ahand or foot, and the cure of which requires more than a year from the date of injury, for example: injury to the brachial or lumbosacral plexus, the median or sciatic nerves, likewise combined injury to the radial and cubital nerves or to the lateral popliteal nerve *(N. peroneus communes)* and medial popliteal nerve *(N. tibialis);* etc. The separate injury of the 'radial (musculo-spiral), cubital. lateral or medial popliteal nerves shall not, however, warrant repatriation except in case of contractures or of serious neurotrophic disturbance.

(i) Injury to the urinary system, with incapacitating results.

3. All sick prisoners of war whose condition has become chronic to the extent that prognosis seems to exclude recovery-in spite of treatment-within one year from the inception of the disease, as, for example, in case of:

(a) Progressive tuberculosis of any organ which, according to medical prognosis, cannot be cured, or at least considerably improved, by treatment in a neutral country.

(b) Exudate pleurisy.

(c) Serious diseases of the respiratory organs of non-tubercular etiology, presumed incurable. for example: serious pulmonary emphysema, with or without bronchitis, chronic asthma:* chronic bronchitis* lasting more than one year in captivity; bronchiectasis,* etc.

(d) Serious chronic affections of the circulatory system, for example: valvular lesions and myocarditis* which have shown signs of circulatory failure during captivity, even though the Mixed Medical Commission cannot detect any such signs at the time of examination; affections of the pericardium and the vessels (Buerger's disease, aneurism of the large vessels); etc.

(e) Serious chronic affections of the digestive organs, for example: gastric or duodenal ulcer-, sequelae of gastric operations performed in captivity; chronic gastritis, enteritis or colitis, having lasted more than one year and seriously affecting the general condition: cirrhosis of the liver, chronic cholecystopathy;* etc.

(f) Serious chronic affections of the genito-urinary organs, for example: chronic diseases of the kidney with consequent disorders; nephrectomy because of a tubercular kidney; chronic pyelitis or chronic cystitis: hydronephrosis or pyonephrosis; chronic grave gynaecological conditions-, normal pregnancy, and obstetrical disorder, where it is impossible to accommodate in a neutral country; etc.

(g) Serious chronic diseases of the central and peripheral nervous system, for example: all obvious psychoses and psychoneuroses, such as serious hysteria, serious captivity psychoneurosis, etc., duly verified by a specialist;* any epilepsy duly verified by the camp physicians.' cerebral arteriosclerosis-chronic neuritis lasting more than one year. etc.

(h) Serious chronic disease of the neuro-vegetative system, with considerable diminution of mental or physical fitness. noticeable loss of weight and general asthenia.

(i) Blindness of both eyes, or of one eve when the vision of the other is less than I in spite of the use of corrective glasses; diminution of visual acuity in cases where it is impossible to restore it by correction to an acuity of 1/2 in at least one eye;* other grave ocular affections, for example: glaucoma, iritis, choroiditis; trachoma, etc.

(k) Auditive disorders, such as total unilateral deafness, if the other car does not discern the ordinary spoken word at a distance of one metre;* etc.

(l) Serious affections of metabolism, for example: diabetes mellitus requiring insulin treatment; etc.

(m) Serious disorders of the endocrine glands, for example: thyrotoxicosis; hypothyrosis; Addison's disease; Simmonds' cachexia; tetany; etc.

(n) Grave and chronic disorders of the blood-forming organs.

(o) Serious cases of chronic intoxication, for example: lead poisoning, mercury poisoing, morphinism. cocainism, alcoholism; gas or radiation poisoning; etc.

(p) Chronic affections of locomotion, with obvious functional disorders, for example: arthritis deformans, primary and secondary progressive chronic polyarthritis; rheumatism with serious clinical symptoms; etc.

(q) Serious chronic skin diseases. not amenable to treatment.

(r) Any malignant growth.

(s) Serious chronic infectious diseases, persisting for one year after their inception, for example: malaria with decided organic impairment, amoebic or bacillary dysentery with grave disorders; tertiary visceral syphilis resistant to treatment; leprosy; etc.

(t) Serious avitaminosis or serious inanition.

---

*The decision of the Mixed Medical Commission shall be based to a great extent on the records kept by camp physicians and surgeons of the same nationality as the prisoners of war, or on an examination by medical specialists of the Detaining Power.

B. ACCOMMODATION IN NEUTRAL COUNTRIES

The following shall be eligible for accommodation in a neutral country:

1. All wounded prisoners of war who are not likely to recover in captivity, but who might be cured or whose condition might be considerably improved by accommodation in a neutral country.

2. Prisoners of war suffering from any form of tuberculosis, of whatever organ, and whose treatment in a neutral country would be likely to lead to recovery or at least to considerable improvement, with the exception of primary tuberculosis cured before captivity.

3. Prisoners of war suffering from affections requiring treatment of the respiratory, circulatory, digestive, nervous, sensory, genito-urinary, cutaneous. locomotive organs, etc., if such treatment would clearly have better results in a neutral country than in captivity.

4. Prisoners of war who have undergone a nephrectomy in captivity for a nontubercular renal affection; cases of osteomyelitis, on the way to recovery or latent; diabetes mellitus not requiring insulin treatment; etc.

5. Prisoners of war suffering from war or captivity neuroses.

Cases of captivity neurosis which are not cured after three months of accommodation in a neutral country, or which after that length of time are not clearly on the way to complete cure, shall be repatriated.

6. All prisoners of war suffering from chronic intoxication (gases, metals, alkaloids, etc.), for whom the prospects of cure in a neutral country are especially favourable.

7. All women prisoners of war who are pregnant or mothers with infants and small children.

The following cases shall not be eligible for accommodation in a neutral country:

1. All duly verified chronic psychoses.

2. All organic or functional nervous affections considered to be incurable.

3. All contagious diseases during the period in which they are transmissible, with the exception of tuberculosis.

II. GENERAL OBSERVATIONS

1. The conditions given shall, in a general way, be interpreted and applied in as broad a spirit as possible.

Neuropathic and psychopathic conditions caused by war or captivity, as well as cases of tuberculosis in all stages, shall above all benefit by such liberal interpretation. Prisoners of war Who have sustained several wounds, none of which, considered by itself, justifies repatriation, shall be examined in the same spirit, with due regard for the psychic traumatism due to the number of their wounds.

2. All unquestionable cases giving the right to direct repatriation (amputation, total blindness or deafness. open pulmonary tuberculosis, mental disorder. malignant growth, etc.)shall be examined and repatriated as soon as possible by the camp physicians or by military medical commissions appointed by the Detaining Power.

3. Injuries and diseases which existed before the war and which have not become worse. as well as war injuries which have not prevented subsequent military service, shall not entitle to direct repatriation.

4. The provisions of this Annex shall be interpreted and applied in a similar manner in all countries party to the conflict. The Powers and authorities concerned shall grant to Mixed Medical Commissions all the facilities necessary for the accomplishment of their task.

5. The examples quoted under (1) above represent only typical cases. Cases which do not correspond exactly to these provisions shall be judged in the spirit of the provisions of Article I 10 of the present Convention, and of the principles embodied in the present Agreement.

ANNEX II

Regulations concerning Mixed Medical Commissions

(see Article 112)

Article 1

The Mixed Medical Commissions provided for in Article 112 of the Convention shall be composed of three members, two of whom shall belong to a neutral country. the third being appointed by the Detaining Power. One of the neutral members shall take the chair.

Article 2

The two neutral members shall be appointed by the International Committee of the Red Cross, acting in agreement with the Protecting Power, at the request of the Detaining Power. They may be domiciled either in their country of origin, in any other neutral country, or in the territory of the Detaining Power.

Article 3

The neutral members shall be approved by the Parties to the conflict concerned, who notify their approval to the International Committee of the Red Cross and to the Protecting Power. Upon such notification, the neutral members shall be considered as effectively appointed.

Article 4

Deputy members shall also be appointed in sufficient number to replace the regular members in case of need. They shall be appointed at the same time as the regular members or, at least, as soon as possible.

Article 5

If for any reason the International Committee of the Red Cross cannot arrange for the appointment of the neutral members, this shall be done by the Power protecting the interests of the prisoners of war to be examined.

Article 6

So far as possible, one of the two neutral members shall be a surgeon and the other a physician.

Article 7

The neutral members shall be entirely independent of the Parties to the conflict, which shall grant them all facilities in the accomplishment of their duties.

Article 8

By agreement with the Detaining Power, the International Committee of the Red Cross, when making the appointments provided for in Articles 2 and 4 of the present Regulations, shall settle the terms of service of the nominees.

Article 9

The Mixed Medical Commissions shall begin their work as soon as possible after the neutral members have been approved, and in any case within a period of three months from the date of such approval.

Article 10

The Mixed Medical Commissions shall examine all the prisoners designated in Article 113 of the Convention. They shall propose repatriation, rejection, or reference to a later examination. Their decisions shall be made by a majority vote.

Article 11

The decisions made by the Mixed Medical Commissions in each specific case shall be communicated, during the month following their visit, to the Detaining Power, the Protecting Power and the International Committee of the Red Cross. The Mixed Medical Commissions shall also inform each prisoner of war examined of the decision made, and shall issue to those whose repatriation has been proposed, certificates similar to the model appended to the present Convention.

Article 12

The Detaining Power shall be required to carry out the decisions of the Mixed Medical Commissions within three months of the time when it receives due notification of such decisions.

Article 13

If there is no neutral physician in a country where the services of a Mixed Medical Commission seem to be required, and if it is for any reason impossible to appoint neutral doctors who are resident in another country, the Detaining Power, acting in agreement with the Protecting Power, shall set up a Medical Commission which shall undertake the same duties as a Mixed Medical Commission, subject to the provisions of Articles 1, 2, 3, 4, 5 and 8 of the Present Regulations.

Article 14

Mixed Medical Commissions shall function permanently and shall visit each camp at intervals of not more than six months.

ANNEX III

Regulations concerning collective relief

(see Article 73)

Article 1

Prisoners' representatives shall be allowed to distribute collective relief shipments for which they are sible, to all prisoners of war administered by their camp, including those who am in hospitals or in prisons or other penal establishments.

Article 2

The distribution of collective relief shipments shall be effected in accordance with the instructions of the donors and with a plan drawn up by the prisoners' representatives. 'Me issue of medical stores shall. however, be made for preference in agreement with the senior medical officers, and the latter may. in hospitals and infirmaries, waive the said instructions, if the needs of their patients so demand. Within the limits thus defined, the distribution shall always be carried out equitably.

Article 3

The said prisoners' representatives or their assistants shall be allowed to go to the points of arrival of relief supplies near their camps. so as to enable the prisoners' representatives or their assistants to verify the quality as well as the quantity of the goods received, and to make out detailed reports thereon for the donors.

Article 4

Prisoners' representatives shall be given the facilities necessary for verifying whether the distribution of collective relief in all sub-divisions and annexes of their camps has been carried out in accordance with their instructions.

Article 5

Prisoners' representatives shall be allowed to fill up, and cause to be filled up by the prisoners' representatives of labour detachments or by the senior medical officers of infirmaries and hospitals, forms or questionnaires intended for the donors, relating to collective relief supplies (distribution. requirements, quantities, etc.). Such forms and questionnaires, duly completed, shall be forwarded to the donors without delay.

Article 6

In order to secure the regular issue of collective relief to the prisoners of war in their camp. and to meet any needs that may arise from the arrival of new contingents of prisoners, prisoners' representatives shall be allowed to build up and maintain adequate reserve stocks of collective relief. For this purpose, they shall have suitable warehouses at their disposal; each warehouse shall be provided with two locks, the prisoners' representative holding the keys of one lock and the camp commander the keys of the other.

Article 7

When collective consignments of clothing am available each prisoner of war shall retain in his possession at least one complete set of clothes. If a prisoner has more than one set of clothes, the prisoners' representative shall be permitted to withdraw excess clothing from those with the largest number of sets, or particular articles in excess of one, if this is necessary in order to supply prisoners who are less well provided. He shall not, however, withdraw second sets of underclothing, socks or footwear, unless this is the only means of providing for prisoners of war with none.

Article 8

The High Contracting Parties, and the Detaining Powers in particular, shall authorize, as far as possible and subject to the regulations governing the supply of the population, all purchases of goods made in their territories for the distribution of collective relief to prisoners of war. They shall similarly facilitate the transfer of funds and other financial measures of a technical or administrative nature taken for the purpose of making such purchases.

Article 9

The foregoing provisions shall not constitute an obstacle to the right of prisoners of war to receive collective relief before their arrival in a camp or in the course of transfer, nor to the possibility of representatives of the Protecting Power, the International Committee of the Red Cross, or any other body giving assistance to prisoners which may be responsible for the forwarding of such supplies, ensuring the distribution thereof to the addressees by any other means that they may deem useful.

ANNEX IV.

A. IDENTITYCARD

(see Article 4)

[...]

B. CAPTURE CARD

(see Article 70)

[...]

C. CORRESPONDENCE CARD AND LETTER

(see Article 71)

[...]

D. NOTIFICATION OF DEATH

(see Article 120)

[...]

E. REPATRIATION CERTIFICATE

(see Annex II, Article 11)

REPATRIATION CERTIFICATE

Date:
Camp:
Hospital:
Surname:
First names:
Date of birth:
Rank:
Army number:
P. W. number:
Injury-Disease:
Decision of the Commission:
Chairman of the
Mixed Medical Commission:
A= direct repatriation
B= accommodation in a neutral country
NC= re-examination by next Commission

ANNEX V

Model regulations concerning payments sent by prisoners to their own country

1. The notification referred to in the third paragraph of Article 63 will show:

(a) Number as specified in Article 17, rank, surname and first names of the prisoner of war who is the payer;

(b) The name and address of the payee in the country of origin;

(c) The amount to be so paid in the currency of the country in which he is detained.

2. The notification will be signed by the prisoner of war, or his witnessed mark made upon if it he cannot write, and shall be countersigned by the prisoners' representative.

3. The camp commander will add to this notification a certiciate that the prisoner of war concerned has a credit balance of not less than the amount registered as payable.

4. The notification may be made up in lists, each sheet of such lists witnessed by the prisoners' representative and certified by the camp commander.

Pentagon plans to sell advanced missiles to Kuwait

Tue Jun 4, 7:09 PM ET WASHINGTON - The Pentagon is planning to sell Kuwait advanced air-to-air missiles to help the country protect itself against what the Defense Department called "hostile neighbors."

The Defense Security Cooperation Agency said Tuesday it had notified Congress that it plans a dlrs 58 million deal that would include 80 Advanced Medium Range Air-to-Air Missiles (AMRAAM), launch equipment, training missiles, software updates and other related equipment and services. The system allows a fighter pilot to launch the weapon from beyond visual range of his target. It also provides a greater capability to attack low-altitude targets.

"Kuwait is threatened by hostile neighbors with credible air, land and sea forces," the DSCA said in a statement. "While the nation depends on external support, the Kuwaiti Air Force must have adequate ... capabilities to protect its vital resources during the early part of a possible invasion until allies can arrive with reinforcements."

Small, oil-rich Kuwait is a strong ally of Washington, which led the international coalition that fought the 1991 Gulf War to end the seven-month Iraqi invasion and occupation of Kuwait. Kuwait still depends on its Western allies, mainly the United States and Britain, for defense. U.S. and British war planes fly from Kuwait to patrol a no-fly zone over southern Iraq established after the war to protect the Shiite Iraqi opposition from Iraqi troops.

Gephardt Supports Toppling Saddam

Tue Jun 4, 6:24 PM ET
By DAVID ESPO, AP Special Correspondent

WASHINGTON (AP) - House Democratic leader Dick Gephardt volunteered his support Tuesday if the administration resorts to force to topple Iraqi President Saddam Hussein adding, "I share President Bush 's resolve to confront this menace head-on."

As Gephardt spoke, Bush told reporters that "one option, of course, is the military option" when it comes to the Iraqi leader. The president added he has no plans to attack, but "nevertheless these nations that I have named need to take America seriously."

"We should use diplomatic tools where we can, but military means where we must to eliminate the threat he poses to the region and our own security," Gephardt, a likely 2004 presidential contender, said in remarks to a foreign policy organization.

Gephardt alternately praised, prodded and poked the administration in a speech that ranged over the diplomatic and military implications of the war on terrorism.

"President Bush was right Saturday to say we are fighting a new war and will have to be ready to strike when necessary, not just deter," Gephardt said in the speech to the Council on Foreign Relations. "But on the home front, we are moving too slowly to develop a homeland defense plan that is tough enough for this new war."

Gephardt said Homeland Security Director Tom Ridge should be made a member of the Cabinet and given authority over a security budget. Such suggestions would bring Ridge under formal congressional oversight, and Bush has thus far refused to go along with them.

Gephardt commended Bush for helping develop a stronger relationship between NATO and Russia. But he coupled those words with a call for additional funding to safeguard the remaining nuclear weapons from the former Soviet Union.

While he said the administration "deserves credit" for the military victory in Afghanistan Gephardt said it would be shortsighted "if we stop now and withhold support for expanding the international security presence beyond Kabul, as Chairman (Hamid) Karzai has urgently requested."

On defense issues, he said he would support adding troops to the armed forces, proposed an overhaul of a logistics and supply system that he described as sluggish, and offered to support a bipartisan commission to build support for military modernization.

On foreign policy, he urged the Bush administration to build on a tradition of worldwide engagement, not turn away from it.

He said the United States should abandon the use of the term "foreign aid," with its Cold War implications, and use its money to try and foster economic development, democracy and universal education abroad. Gephardt voted against the use of force in the run-up to the 1991 Persian Gulf War but in his prepared remarks, said he was ready to work with the administration "to build an effective policy to terminate the threat posed by" the Iraqi regime.

"New foreign policy initiatives can help remove one of the legs of Saddam's survival by reducing the desperation of many in the Arab world who see him as a defiant ray of hope," he said.

"At the same time, we should be prepared to remove the other leg with the use of force." Bush branded Iraq as a member of the "axis of evil" in a speech last winter, and administration officials have not discouraged speculation that the war on terrorism might involve an effort to oust Saddam.

Gephardt also urged the Bush administration to demonstrate leadership in the effort to resolve the conflict between Israel and the Palestinians.

"We cannot expect that the parties to this conflict will resolve it without the active support of the United States," he said.

"We must be steadfast in our support of Israel," he added. "There is no moral equivalence between suicide bombings and defending against them."

Within hours of the speech, the House Republican campaign committee said Gephardt's goal was to lay the groundwork for a presidential campaign and "change public perception about the Democratic party and national security." The group said Gephardt had voted in recent years to cut defense and intelligence spending from levels proposed by the GOP.

U.S. and British defense chiefs say military threat from Iraq is growing again

Wed Jun 5, 2:05 PM ET
By ROBERT BURNS, AP Military Writer

LONDON - Iraq poses an increasing threat that must be met, the defense chiefs of the United States and Britain said Wednesday, showing growing impatience with President Saddam Hussein.

"We know that Saddam Hussein's regime in Iraq has had a sizable appetite for weapons of mass destruction" and is finding ways to acquire the ingredients, Defense Secretary Donald H. Rumsfeld said. "We know the borders into that country are quite porous," he added, allowing Iraq to import technologies with applications in both civilian and military industries as well as illicit materials. "There is not a doubt in the world that with every month that goes by their programs mature," he said. Iraq denies it has or is developing any weapons of mass destruction, but it has refused to allow the international inspections that it agreed to accept as a condition of ending the 1991 Gulf War .

Rumsfeld would not discuss the possibility of U.S. military action to topple Saddam's government, saying that was a matter for President George W. Bush to decide. He spoke at a joint news conference with British Defense Secretary Geoff Hoon after meetings to discuss Iraq and other issues. Rumsfeld and Hoon both expressed their governments' hope for a lowering of tensions between nuclear rivals India and Pakistan. Rumsfeld's stop in London was the first on a 10-day journey that is to take him to the Indian and Pakistani capitals next week. For months the Bush administration has been publicly making the case for taking strong action—possibly military—against Iraq, but allied nations have been slow to offer support. In Washington on Wednesday, Senate Majority Leader Tom Dasch0 said his fellow Democrats support a push to unseat Saddam. "The question is when and how and under what circumstances," Daschle said. A day earlier, House Democratic leader Dick Gephardt volunteered his support if the administration resorted to force. "I share President Bush's resolve to confront this menace head-on," he said. Also on Tuesday, Bush said that "one option, of course, is the military option." The president added, however, he had no plans to attack. Hoon described the Iraqi military threat as increasing in recent weeks. Asked in a later interview to elaborate, Hoon said Iraq's air defenses are more aggressively trying to shoot down the U.S. and British pilots who regularly fly combat air patrols over northern and southern Iraq. Pilots have reported attacks in recent week by Iraqi anti-aircraft artillery and surface-to-air missiles. The allied planes have responded by bombing various elements of Iraq's air defense system. The recent aggressiveness would suggest a new, more worrisome Iraqi attitude, Hoon said. "Clearly they are feeling a little more confident than they have in the recent past," he said. Hoon said the United States and Britain "can only be deeply suspicious" of how far Saddam has progressed in developing weapons of mass destruction as long as United Nations inspectors are not allowed to freely monitor Iraq's military facilities. He said the best answer to the problem is to return U.N. inspectors, with Iraqi consent to freely monitor military facilities suspected of developing nuclear, chemical or biological weapon. Rumsfeld has cast doubt on that approach, asserting that previous efforts at U.N. monitoring accomplished little because of Iraqi denial and deception.

Traders, analysts say U.N. pricing dampening desire for Iraqi oil, but that Iraq tries to manipulate prices

Wed Jun 5, 11:07 AM ET
By TAREK AL-ISSAWI, Associated Press Writer
DUBAI, United Arab Emirates - Baghdad blames the United Nations or a pricing policy that is discouraging traders from buying Iraqi oil, but industry observers say Iraq is also responsible because of its attempts to manipulate prices. "The U.N. does not determine the price. The Iraqis do," Rasih Erbas, deputy head of a Turkish fuel dealers group, told The Associated Press Tuesday. A U.N. Security Council committee monitoring the sanctions—imposed to punish Iraq for its 1990 invasion of Kuwait—approves prices for Iraqi oil retroactively at the end of each month. The United States and Britain have pushed the policy to prevent Iraq from taking advantage of market fluctuations to impose an illegal surcharge on its oil customers. "Naturally, the Iraqis take a cut from the sales, up to 30 U.S. cents per

barrel," an oil dealer based in the United Arab Emirates told The Associated Press Wednesday on condition of anonymity. The U.N. retroactive pricing system "is an attempt to pressure Iraq to give up that policy." The dealer said traders were shying away from Iraqi oil. The retroactive pricing policy has been in place for months, but observers say Britain and the United States have been applying it more rigorously recently. Iraq has, in turn, stepped up criticism, saying its U.N.-monitored oil sales, which ran at about 1.5 million barrels per day in the second half of May, could drop sharply in June due to the retroactive policy. "Not all buyers can buy and resell oil without knowing its price," Iraqi Oil Minister Amer Mohammed Rashid told Iraqi television over the weekend. Iraqi Oil Ministry officials contacted by The Associated Press this week did not give figures to illustrate how Iraq's exports may have been affected by the pricing policy. There were reports this week that Iraqi exports had come to a halt, either because buyers had disappeared or because Iraq was trying to pressure the buyers. But Wednesday, a tanker named the Olympic Breeze arrived at Turkey's Ceyhan terminal Wednesday and was waiting offshore to load 2 million barrels of Iraqi crude, traders said. "The Iraqi claims are not true," said Erbas, deputy head of the Turkish Union of Employers of Fuel Oil Dealers and Petroleum and Gasoline Companies. James Reeve, an Economist Intelligence Unit analyst in London, said the decline in customers was being felt at Ceyhan, from where Iraqi exports head to Europe. He did not have figures. "Exports from the Gulf port of Mina al-Baker, which mainly head to the U.S. and the Far East, have been largely unaffected. This is because by the time a cargo reaches the U.S. (around 20 days), the U.N.-approved pricing formula will be known," Reeves said in an interview Wednesday. Reeves said oil shipping sources expect Iraq to back down and abandon its surcharge. Still, "the U.N. can hardly claim its strategy is succeeding if customers for Ceyhan crude are drying up completely, since the oil-for-food program and hence the humanitarian situation of most Iraqis depends on Iraq being able to sell its oil," Reeves said. The oil-for-food program was created in 1996 to ease Iraqi suffering under the strict U.N. economic sanctions. Under oil-for-food, Iraq can sell unlimited amounts of oil to buy food, medicine and other humanitarian supplies, and to pay war reparations. Benon Sevan, in charge of U.N. humanitarian programs in Iraq, told the U.N.

Security Council last month that the retroactive pricing policy has reduced Iraqi oil exports by about 25 percent and cost the oil-for-food program an estimated dlrs 1.2 billion since December. He said the pricing practice threatened efforts to improve the delivery of humanitarian goods to Iraqis. Wednesday, the United Nations announced that Iraqi oil exports surged to 15.3 million barrels in the last week of May, up from the previous week's low of 9 million barrels. Iraq had stopped exports from April 8 until May 8 in a gesture meant to show solidarity with the Palestinian uprising. It took some time for exports to resume previous levels, accounting for low figures in the first part of May. The U.N. Office of the Iraq Program said in a press release Wednesday that last week's shipments generated an estimated dlrs 333 million. Despite the surge, the statement said the humanitarian program is short on funds and cannot process contracts valued at dlrs 1.86 billion. ti,buros/db.

Rumsfeld: Iraq Poses Growing Threat

Thu Jun 6, 2:27 AM ET
By ROBERT BURNS, AP Military Writer

BRUSSELS, Belgium (AP) - The United States and Britain, partners for more than a decade in containing Iraq's military might, say the regime of Saddam Hussein poses an increasing threat. "We know that Saddam Hussein's regime in Iraq has had a sizable appetite for weapons of mass destruction," and it is finding ways to acquire their ingredients, Defense Secretary Donald H. Rumsfeld said Wednesday. "We know the borders into that country are quite porous," he added, allowing Iraq to import technologies useful for both civilian and military industries "as well as illicit materials that are helpful in their programs for weapons of mass destruction." "There is not a doubt in the world that with every month that goes by, their programs mature," he said in London before flying to Brussels for meetings Thursday and Friday with NATO allies. Iraq denies it possesses or is developing weapons of mass destruction, but it has refused to allow the international inspections that it accepted as a condition of ending the 1991 Gulf War. Rumsfeld would not discuss the possibility of U.S. military action to topple Saddam, saying that was a matter for President Bush to decide. He spoke at a joint news conference with

British Defense Minister Geoff Hoon after meetings to discuss Iraq and other issues. The two defense chiefs flew together to Brussels, where Iraq is expected to be a topic of discussion in NATO meetings Thursday, including the first-ever session of the NATO-Russia Council. Rumsfeld also was holding a one-on-one session with his Russian counterpart, Sergei Ivanov. Rumsfeld and Hoon both expressed their governments' hope for a lowering of tensions between nuclear rivals India and Pakistan. Rumsfeld's stop in London was the first on a 10-day journey that is scheduled to take him to the Indian and Pakistani capitals next week. For months the Bush administration has been publicly making the case for strong action—possibly by military means—against Iraq, but allied nations have been slow to offer support. In Washington on Wednesday, Senate Majority Leader Tom Daschle of South Dakota said his fellow Democrats expressed support for a push to topple Saddam. "The question is when and how and under what circumstances," Daschle told reporters. Hoon said the Iraqi military threat has increased in recent weeks. Asked in a later interview to elaborate, Hoon said Iraq's air defenses are more aggressively trying to shoot down the U.S. and British pilots who regularly fly combat air patrols over northern and southern Iraq. He was alluding to the fact that U.S. and British pilots have reported a series of attacks in recent week by Iraqi anti-aircraft artillery and surface-to-air missiles. The allied planes have responded by bombing various elements of Iraq's integrated air defense system. Since the start of U.S. and British enforcement of the "no fly" zones more than a decade ago, Iraq has considered them a violation of its sovereignty and has vowed to shoot down pilots. Hoon said that immediately after the Sept. 11 attacks in the United States, there was a marked decline in Iraqi targeting of allied pilots enforcing the "no fly" zones south and north of Baghdad. "We judged that the regime in Iraq seemed to have got the message that military action would follow if they were not very careful," Hoon said in an interview with reporters accompanying him and Rumsfeld aboard an Air Force jet en route from London to Brussels. The recent Iraqi aggressiveness would suggest a new, more worrisome Iraqi attitude, Hoon said. "Clearly they are feeling a little more confident than they have in the recent past," he said. from the June 14, 2002 edition

Common Virus Hit British Soldiers in Afghanistan

Thu Jun 6, 2:04 PM ET
By Paul Simao

ATLANTA (Reuters) - More than two dozen British soldiers and hospital staff who came down with what appeared to be a mystery illness in Afghanistan were exposed to a type of gastrointestinal virus common in military settings, U.S. health experts said on Thursday.

Military doctors were initially baffled last month when the soldiers developed severe vomiting, diarrhea and fever at Bagram Air Base, north of the Afghan capital Kabul.

But an investigation by the U.S. Centers for Disease Control and Prevention found that Norwalk-like viruses (NLV), usually spread through fecal-contaminated food and water and personal contact, were responsible for the outbreak which it said affected 29 British soldiers and staff at the base's field hospital.

The viruses, which often fail to be diagnosed or are misdiagnosed, cause an estimated 23 million people to become sick and lead to 50,000 hospitalizations and 300 deaths, usually due to dehydration, each year in the United States.

They were the most frequent cause of disability among soldiers serving in the 1991 Gulf War. There are no drugs to treat the viruses, though most people recover with fluid intake and prompt medical care.

Initial tests on the British soldiers at the hospital in Bagram were negative, prompting fears that they had been exposed to a "mystery infection" and causing British officials to airlift 11 of them to England and Germany.

Two medical staff involved in the airlift and a third person who had close contact with one of the patients in England subsequently developed gastroenteritis linked to NLV. All have since recovered.

"Our belief is that these people became severely dehydrated because the vomiting and diarrhea with NLV is pretty severe," said Dr. Reina Turcios, an epidemiologist in the CDC's National Center for Infectious Diseases in Atlanta.

Turcios added that some of the soldiers may have had a genetic predisposition for contracting NLV. At least one previous study found that people with blood type O might be more prone to developing the viruses.

The spread of NLV can usually be prevented by using a bleach solution to clean up areas contaminated with vomit or feces and through close monitoring of those who come into contact with infected patients.

The viruses can be shed in feces for up to two weeks after infection. The field hospital in Bagram has reopened under improved infection-control guidelines, according to British health officials.

Study Disputes Oil Well Smoke, Gulf War Illness Link

Fri Jun 7, 5:41 PM ET

NEW YORK (Reuters Health) - Available scientific evidence does not support a link between the long-term health problems experienced by some Gulf War veterans and exposure to smoke from Kuwaiti oil fires, US military scientists report.

"Since returning from the Gulf War in August 1991, some of the nearly 700,000 US military personnel who served in the Gulf have reported a wide range of symptoms that have been difficult to classify," according to Tyler C. Smith of the Naval Health Research Center in San Diego, California and colleagues.

While many studies have shown that veterans of this conflict are more likely than other military personnel to report a wide range of symptoms including rashes, fatigue or gastrointestinal disorders, "numerous research teams and expert panels have been unsuccessful in clearly implicating any specific Gulf War exposure as a cause of post-war symptoms," they note.

Potential causes of the "Gulf War illness" that are being investigated include exposure to biological and chemical warfare agents. In the current study, Smith's team investigated whether exposure to smoke from oil well fires could have played a role. Their report is published in the June issue of the American Journal of Epidemiology.

Iraqi troops set hundreds of oil wells ablaze as they withdrew from Kuwait. The fires, later extinguished one-by-one, burned for about 9 months and produced vast plumes of black, noxious smoke.

The team of researchers evaluated atmospheric data that included estimated emissions concentrations of the oil well-fire smoke and exposure data for more than 405,000 active-duty military personnel who were deployed in the Gulf region for one or more days during the oil fires.

The investigators also assessed all military hospital admissions between October 1988 and July 1999.

They divided the vets into seven groups, based on the length of time they were exposed to the smoke and the amount they were exposed to. No "dose-response" relationship was seen among the groups, the researchers report, meaning that hospitalization did not become more likely as exposure grew.

Although they concede that their study has limitations, Smith and his team conclude that "these data do not support the hypothesis that Gulf War veterans have an increased risk of post-war (illness) from exposure to the Kuwaiti oil well-fire smoke."

Persian Gulf Veterans Coordinating Board

The Persian Gulf Veterans Coordinating Board was established in January 1994 to work to resolve the health concerns of Persian Gulf veterans, including active duty personnel and reservists with Gulf service. The board, headed by the Secretaries of the Departments of Defense (DoD), Veterans Affairs (VA), and Health and Human Services (HHS), is coordinating government efforts related to research, clinical issues and disability compensation.

Background: Persian Gulf Veterans' Health Problems

Some 697,000 active duty service members and activated National Guard and Reserve unit members served in the Persian Gulf theater of operations during Operations Desert Storm and Desert Shield. The majority of troops were deployed to the Gulf theater of operations before the air war began on January 16, 1991, and more than half of the deployed troops were withdrawn from the area by the first week of May 1991. However, an additional 250,000 individuals have been deployed over the ensuing five years, with several thousand U.S. military members currently serving ashore and afloat in the Gulf region. Responding to concerns about the health problems of Persian Gulf War veterans, in 1992 VA created the Persian Gulf Registry Program for all veterans who served in the Persian Gulf, inviting them to come to VA for a free medical examination. In addition, DoD has established the comprehensive clinical evaluation program (CCEP), to provide care and systematically evaluate Persian Gulf veterans and their family members. Veterans have commonly reported that they suffer from a diverse group of symptoms, including fatigue, skin rash, headache, muscle and joint pain, memory problems, shortness of breath, sleep disturbances, gastrointestinal symptoms, and chest pain. DoD, VA and HHS are investigating possible causes of Persian Gulf veterans' health problems, including various chemical exposure combinations, leishmaniasis, health effects of oil well fires, petrochemical exposure, chemical/biological warfare agents, effects of vaccines and medications, and exposure to depleted uranium. The three departments are engaged in more than 80 federally supported Persian Gulf-related research and evaluation projects, including studies of general health and environmental effects. This includes grants to more than a dozen non-federal researchers, federal agencies and academic institutions examining a variety of health issues in Gulf veterans or studies of specific risk factors or illnesses. In May 1995, President Clinton formed an independent advisory committee to review the research agenda as well as other government activities related to the health of Persian Gulf veterans. Its final report is imminent.

VA Health Care - Persian Gulf Registry

VA's Persian Gulf Registry Program offers a free, complete physical examination with basic laboratory studies to every Persian Gulf veteran. A centralized registry of participants who have had these examinations is maintained to enable VA to keep them informed through periodic newsletters. This clinical database of more than 63,000 Persian Gulf veterans who have taken advantage of the physical examination program also provides a mechanism to catalog prominent symptoms, reported exposures and diagnoses. VA has named a physician at every VA medical center to coordinate the special examination program. In June 1994, VA expanded the basic examination protocol, which elicits information about symptoms and exposures, and directs baseline laboratory studies, including blood count, urinalysis, and a set of blood chemistries. In addition to this core laboratory work, for every veteran taking the Persian Gulf program examination, physicians may order additional tests and specialty consults as symptoms dictate. If a veteran's symptoms remain unexplained, VA provides an expanded assessment protocol, standardized in collaboration with DoD, for use in evaluation of unexplained illnesses. In addition to the Registry program, VA provides medical care to Persian Gulf veterans for illnesses possibly related to exposure to toxic substances or environmental hazards. Any Persian Gulf veteran who VA determines might possibly have an illness resulting from exposure to a toxic substance or environmental hazard in the Persian Gulf theater of operations has special eligibility for hospital and outpatient care. They have a higher eligibility for treatment than other nonservice-connected veterans. For Gulf veterans with unexplained symptoms, the local VA physicians also may refer veterans to a local tertiary care facility, or to one of VA's four Persian Gulf Referral Centers for additional specialty consultations. They are located at VA medical centers in Washington, D.C.; Birmingham, Ala.; Houston; and Los Angeles. Also, VA is inviting spouses and children of Persian Gulf War veterans to take advantage of special health examinations being scheduled through VA's national Persian Gulf Helpline. The free exams, administered by contractors of 33 VA medical centers, are available only to spouses and children of veterans who served in the Persian Gulf War and who have received a Persian Gulf Registry examination. VA estimates that the $2 million authorized by Congress for this program will provide physical examinations for approximately 4,500 individuals. The program does not provide follow-up, treatment or compensation for the veteran's spouses or children. VA offers a toll-free information line at 800-PGW-VETS (800-749-8387) where operators are trained to help veterans with questions about care and benefits and schedule the spouse and child examinations described above. Information also is being disseminated 24 hours a day through a national electronic bulletin board at 800-US1-VETS (800-871-8387) or (FTP/Telnet to VAONLINE.VA.GOV by Internet) as well as through a Persian Gulf Veterans' Illnesses page on VA's World Wide Web site at http://www.va.gov/health/environ/persgulf.htm. Realizing that research will take time to find answers to Persian Gulf veterans' health questions, the Clinton Administration supported legislation, enacted in

1994, to give VA authority to award compensation benefits to chronically disabled Persian Gulf War veterans with undiagnosed illnesses. Under a final regulation published Feb. 3, 1995, VA has begun paying compensation to Persian Gulf veterans suffering from chronic disabilities resulting from undiagnosed illnesses that became manifest during service in the Southwest Asia theater or within two years thereafter. Some 26,738 veterans with Persian Gulf service currently are receiving VA compensation or pension benefits for chronic disabilities, injuries or diagnosed illnesses of all kinds.

DoD's Comprehensive Clinical Evaluation Program

DoD, in collaboration with VA, developed the "Comprehensive Clinical Evaluation Program" in June 1994 to provide an in-depth medical evaluation to all eligible beneficiaries who have health concerns following service in the Gulf. All service members eligible for health care at DoD medical facilities, active, ready reserves or retired, who participated in Operation Desert Shield and Desert Storm, and their family members, are eligible for the program. To register, individuals should call the DoD hotline (800-796-9699) for Gulf War veterans. In April 1996, DoD issued its fourth report on 18,598 participants. DoD physicians find the majority of CCEP participants have clear diagnoses which include a variety of common conditions for which they are receiving treatment. The report concluded that based upon the CCEP experience to date, there is no clinical evidence for a single or unique syndrome among Gulf War veterans. However, a mild illness or a syndrome affecting a proportion of veterans at risk might not be detectable in such a case series. The results of the CCEP are consistent with the conclusions of a National Institutes of Health Technology Assessment Workshop Panel that no single disease or syndrome is apparent, but rather multiple illnesses with overlapping symptoms and causes. A specialized care center established at Walter Reed Army Medical Center in Washington, D.C., provides therapeutic care for some CCEP participants. The center uses multidisciplinary teams to provide intensive programs to improve the health of patients experiencing disabling symptoms. An additional specialized care center is located at Wilford Hall Medical Center in San Antonio, Texas. This center provides treatment for Gulf War returnees with chronic pain and other health concerns. In late 1996, DoD requested the National Academy of Sciences Institute of Medicine to reevaluate the relevancy of the CCEP examination process in light of the March 1991 demolitions at Khamisiyah, Iraq. This report is expected in early 1997. As of January 1997, 38,000 have requested participation in the CCEP. This number includes 9,300 individuals who have requested registration without examination.

Expanded Department of Defense Investigative Efforts

Since November 1996 DoD has been expanding its Gulf Illnesses Investigative Team from 12 to 110 people. This expanded organization is designed to add additional resources to help better understand what could be causing Gulf War illnesses. This greatly expanded team is building upon the very valuable work accomplished thus far by many organizations throughout DoD. The team is composed of representative elements of critical DoD components to ensure that research and analytical efforts and outreach programs are effective, coordinated and meaningful. In March 1995 DoD established a declassification effort encompassing research, medical, operational and intelligence records that could increase understanding of the causes of Gulf War Illnesses. By October 1996 the DoD declassification project had reviewed over 5.4 million pages of operational and intelligence information. Seven-hundred thousand pages were provided to the Analysis and Investigation Team for further review. About 23,000 pages of information were posted on the GulfLINK World Wide Web home page. In June of 1996, DoD learned U.S. troops destroyed large quantities of ammunition at Khamisiyah, a sprawling ammunition storage site in southern Iraq shortly after the Gulf War ended. Evidence that chemical weapons may have been among the munitions destroyed on 4 and 10 March has triggered an intensified effort on the part of DoD to reconstruct the events at that time. The Army Inspector General is conducting an in-depth inquiry into all the events and activities surrounding Khamisiyah. The Assistant Secretary of Defense for Intelligence Oversight is looking into the handling of intelligence information about Khamisiyah. In October 1996, the DoD announced a series of actions to seek the help of 20,000 Gulf War veterans who may have been near Khamisiyah, Iraq during the period March 4 - 15, 1991. The expanded outreach actually began in August 1996 when DoD began contacting 1,168 U.S. service members assigned to units involved in the March 4, 1991 demolition at the Khamisiyah bunker. Veterans are being asked to call the DoD Gulf Veterans hotline numbers to report any medical problems they may be experiencing and provide any information they believe is pertinent to this event. The incident reporting hotline number is 1-800-472-6719. The National Academy of Sciences has agreed to advise DoD on its overall approach to Gulf War Illnesses and to recommend any needed changes to that approach.

Research Activities

The federal government has steadily expanded research into the illnesses reported by Gulf War veterans, including the latest portfolio of 15 studies that include both non-federal researchers, federal agencies and academic institutions. The compendium of new projects brings to more than 80 the total of federally supported research projects detailed in the November 1996 update to *A Working Plan for Research on Persian Gulf Veterans' Illnesses*. The new initiative results from a nationwide request for protocols that brought a broad response of 111 scientific proposals. The proposed investigations were reviewed by independent panels of experts and graded for scientific merit and for program relevance to key questions surrounding health issues of Gulf veterans. The Persian Gulf Veterans Coordinating Board, through its Research Working Group, has intensified efforts related to possible effects of low-level exposures to chemical warfare agents. Based on the Coordinating Board's recommendation, three new peer-reviewed, basic science research projects in this area have been funded, and an additional $2 million has been identified for future studies. During 1996, DoD allotted $12 million for general research. In 1997, DoD has committed $12 million for general research and $5 million for studying the effects of low-level chemical exposure, oil well fires, depleted uranium, cancer incidence, birth outcomes and health risk assessments. The *Working Plan for Research on Persian Gulf Veterans' Illnesses* identifies major research questions and gaps in current knowledge, and required research that will close the gaps between what is known and what is needed. Among the 21 key research questions listed in the plan, the one identified as most important is the determination of whether Persian Gulf veterans are experiencing a greater prevalence of illnesses in comparison with an appropriate control population. Thirteen controlled scientific studies are being funded to address that question. Additional research goals include identifying possible risk factors for any excess illness or death, as well as finding appropriate diagnostic tools, treatment methods, and prevention strategies for any conditions found. The research plan helps coordinate federally sponsored research to ensure all the relevant research issues are targeted and unnecessary duplication is avoided. Persian Gulf veterans have expressed concern about birth defects in their children. While there are no current data supporting an increased rate of birth defects in the children of Persian Gulf War veterans, this is an important research question and deserves extremely careful review. A study conducted by the Mississippi State Department of Health in conjunction with the Centers for Disease Control and Prevention (CDC) showed no increase in birth defects or illnesses among children born to Persian Gulf veterans in two National Guard units. In addition, preliminary results of DoD epidemiologic research demonstrate no increase in the overall rate of birth defects among children born after active duty servicemembers returned from the Gulf compared to children of a control group of active duty service members who did not serve in the Gulf. Ongoing DoD, VA and CDC studies are examining the issue of birth defects, reproductive health, and family health status. Because of the broader importance of reproductive health to veterans, VA established a fourth environmental hazards research center at the Louisville, Ky., VA Medical Center in collaboration with the University of Louisville focusing on reproductive and developmental outcomes.

Research Studies and Evaluations

- A panel of nongovernment experts brought together at a *National Institutes* of Health-sponsored workshop in April 1994 examined data and heard from both veterans and scientists. The panel concluded that no single cause or biological explanation for the reported symptoms could be identified and indicated that it was impossible at that time to establish a single case definition for the health problems of Gulf veterans.

- VA and DoD have contracted with the *National Academy of Sciences* to review existing scientific and other information on the health consequences of Gulf operations. An interim report was issued Jan. 4, 1995, and a final report is expected in late 1996.
- The *Naval Medical Research Center* in San Diego, in collaboration with VA investigators, has begun epidemiological studies comparing Gulf veterans and control-group veterans (who served elsewhere) to detect differences in illnesses, hospitalizations, and birth outcomes in large cohorts of active duty service members.
- In its *National Health Survey of Persian Gulf Veterans,* the VA is conducting a mail survey of a random sample of 15,000 Persian Gulf veterans and active duty members with Gulf service to compare their health status with an equal-sized group not deployed to the Gulf. Results of initial responses now are being analyzed. Information on the health status of family members also is included, including birth outcomes and illnesses in the children born to veterans in the survey. A health examination will be offered to a representative sample to help evaluate participants' symptoms.
- CDC, in collaboration with the Iowa Department of Public Health and the University of Iowa, has conducted a telephone survey of approximately 4,000 active and retired *military personnel from Iowa* to compare the health status of veterans who served in the Gulf with that of veterans who served during the Gulf War but were deployed elsewhere. Publication of results is expected soon.
- CDC also is studying a group of *Air National Guard Persian Gulf War* **veterans** in the state of Pennsylvania for any pattern of unusual illnesses. In the June 16, 1995, *Morbidity and Mortality Weekly Report,* the CDC said preliminary findings indicate that some chronic symptoms were reported more commonly by Persian Gulf War veterans than by nondeployed Persian Gulf War-era service personnel. However, standardized physical examinations and reviews of laboratory test results did

not reveal consistent abnormalities. Final results of the study will be published within a few months.

- VA has analyzed cause-of-death data gathered from death certificates for its *Mortality Followup Study of Persian Gulf Veterans,* comparing Gulf-deployed veteran non-combat deaths with a control group of troops never deployed to the Gulf. As has been observed after other wars, veterans of the Persian Gulf War have experienced a higher incidence of death due to accidents. When this contributing factor is excluded, Persian Gulf veterans have not experienced a higher mortality rate due to disease-related causes. Both the Persian Gulf and non-deployed control group veterans had a lower death rate than Americans their age in general. A report was published Nov. 14, 1996, in the New England Journal of Medicine.

- In October 1994, VA established three *environmental hazards research* centers with an initial focus on the possible health effects of environmental exposures of Persian Gulf veterans. The centers are located at VA hospitals in Boston; East Orange, N.J.; and Portland, Ore. The centers are being funded for five years with a total annual budget of approximately $1.5 million and an additional $300,000 for equipment costs in the first year of operation. A total of 14 individual protocols are scheduled on a variety of interdisciplinary projects. A fourth environmental hazards research center focused on reproductive outcomes was announced in November 1996 to be located in Louisville, Ky.

- The Baltimore VA Medical Center is following the health status of individuals who retained embedded fragments of *depleted uranium* from injuries sustained during the Persian Gulf War.

- The Birmingham VA Medical Center is conducting a pilot clinical program that includes an extensive battery of neurological tests aimed at detecting the kind of dysfunction that would be expected after *exposure to nerve agents*.

- DoD will study the effects of chemical/environmental exposures.

- DoD is continuing its work as a world leader in developing a less invasive test for *viscerotropic leishmaniasis* that may provide for broader diagnostic screening in the future.
- DoD has developed a *geographic information system* (GIS), or troop location registry, that contains location information on more than 4,000 units from all Services. The GIS allows military unit locations during Operation Desert Storm to be compared with air quality measurements, reported SCUD attacks, chemical/biological weapon detection reports, weather reports and other factors. This data was used to identify units in the Khamisiyah area.
- Both VA and DoD are continuing to examine the role of stress from deployment and *post-traumatic stress disorder*, with a goal of developing intervention strategies.

Qatari delegation arrives in Baghdad for trade talks with Iraq
Fri Jun 7, 2:07 PM ET
BAGHDAD, Iraq - A Qatari delegation, headed by the Gulf state's trade and economy minister, arrived in Baghdad Friday on a three-day visit to boost trade ties with Iraq.

Qatari Trade and Economy Minister Sheik Hamad bin Faisal Al Thani told reporters that the delegation, comprising more than 50 businessmen and officials, would meet with Iraqi counterparts "to find opportunities of economic cooperation."

Sheik Hamad is also scheduled to take part in Iraqi-Qatari cooperation committee session.

Iraqi-Qatari trade ties have been improving since the U.N.-approved oil-for-food program began in late 1996.

Trade and political ties between both countries were cut after Iraq invaded Kuwait in August 1990, a move that sparked the 1991 Gulf War But Qatar was the first Arab state to send its foreign minister to Iraq after the war ended.

Iraqi Deputy Prime Minister Hikmat Ibrahim and Trade Minister Mohammed Mehdi Saleh greeted the Qatari delegation at Saddam International Airport.

Qatar has one of the world's largest reserves of natural gas and its per capita income of dlrs 17,000 is one of the world's highest.

Iraq has one of the world's largest oil supplies. But Baghdad says U.N.-imposed sanctions, which can only be lifted once Iraq verifies it has dismantled its weapons of mass destruction, have hurt the nation's economy.

Saddam Hussein
Iraqi President/Dead Man Walking

Saddam Hussein & the invasion of Kuwait

In 1979 the president, Ahmad Hassan al-Bakr, was replaced by Saddam Hussein, and once more the political situation flared into hostilities with Iran. The Iran-Iraq War, which began in 1980, lasted for eight years and had a crippling effect on the economy of both countries. Before Iraq had a chance to recover economically, it was once more plunged into war, this time with its invasion of Kuwait in 1990.

The invasion was the result of a long-standing territorial dispute, and Iraqi troops overran the country on 2nd August 1990. The UN security council condemned the Iraqi occupation of Kuwait, and demanded a complete withdrawal by 15th January 1991.

When Iraq failed to comply with this demand, the Persian Gulf War ensued, with allied troops led by the US launching an aerial bombardment on Baghdad. The war, which proved disastrous for Iraq, lasted only six weeks, and a cease-fire was announced by the US on 28th February 1991. UN terms for a permanent cease-fire were agreed by Iraq in April of that year, and strict conditions were imposed, demanding the disclosure and destruction of all stockpiles of weapons.

By early 1992, it became apparent that Iraq still possessed weapons of mass destruction, and intense international pressure to eliminate these was brought to bear, in the shape of UN economic sanctions. In 1993 the Security Council voted to maintain these sanctions, despite attempts by Iraq to have them lifted.

U.S. defense chief meet Nordic, Baltic counterparts; weighs progress in India-Pakistan feud.
Sat Jun 8, 8:10 AM ET
By ROBERT BURNS, AP Military Writer

TALLINN, Estonia - U.S. Defense Secretary Donald H. Rumsfeld discussed the expected expansion of NATO on Saturday with his counterparts from seven Baltic and Nordic nations and said he would consult with a top U.S. official who had just visited India and Pakistan.

In his meeting with the defense ministers, Rumsfeld discussed a range of issues, including the likelihood that the three Baltic countries—Estonia, Latvia and Lithuania—will be invited to join NATO when allied leaders meet in Prague, the Czech capital, in November.

Rumsfeld told reporters that "most of us favor a relatively robust" expansion of NATO, which now has 19 member countries.

He declined to be more specific but said U.S. President George W. Bush favors adding "a good number" of candidate countries, which include Albania, Bulgaria, Romania, Slovenia, Slovakia and Macedonia, in addition to the Baltic nations.

Macedonia and Albania are thought to be the least likely to gain membership invitations this year.

Rumsfeld said he planned to consult Saturday with the U.S. State Department's No. 2 official before deciding when to travel to India and Pakistan to continue efforts at averting war.

Until he meets with Richard Armitage, Rumsfeld said he had nothing he wanted to say about the situation. Armitage, the deputy secretary of state, met with Pakistani President Pervez Musharraf on Thursday and Indian Prime Minister Atal Bihari Vajpayee on Friday.

Rumsfeld spoke at a news conference after meeting with Baltic and Nordic defense ministers from Sweden, Norway, Denmark, Finland, Latvia, Estonia and Lithuania. That session focused on the global fight against terrorism and prospects for expanding NATO.

The U.S. defense secretary was scheduled to travel Sunday from Estonia to the Persian Gulf to meet with government officials in Kuwait, Qatar and Bahrain, before heading to Pakistan and India. Aides said Saturday that it was possible Rumsfeld would switch plans and go to South Asia before the Gulf.

Rumsfeld said Saturday before meeting with Armitage that he had not decided where he would travel next. Armitage was trying to persuade the nuclear-armed rivals to ease tensions along their frontier in the disputed province of Kashmir Both sides have massed 1 million troops along the Line of Control—the cease-fire line dividing Kashmir between India and Pakistan.

Iraq says it has not made weapons of mass destruction since 1991

Sun Jun 9, 2:18 PM ET

By WAIEL FALEH, Associated Press Writer

BAGHDAD, Iraq - Iraq has not made or possessed weapons of mass destruction since 1991, despite U.S. claims to the contrary, a Foreign Ministry statement said on Sunday.

"Iraq has said on many occasions that it is not concerned with entering the mass destruction weapons club ... We left it in 1991," said the statement in an apparent reference to nations that make such weapons.

The statement came as U.S. Defense Minister Donald Rumsfeld addressed about 1,000 U.S. servicemen in neighboring Gulf state Kuwait, the country Iraq invaded in 1990 and occupied for seven months until U.S.-led coalition routed its forces in the 1991 Gulf War.

"You are the people who stand between freedom and fear, between our people and a dangerous adversary that cannot be appeased, cannot be ignored and cannot be allowed to win," Rumsfeld said in an apparent reference to Iraq.

Washington accuses Baghdad of developing weapons of mass destruction and maintaining ballistic missile facilities. It also says Iraq is preventing U.N. weapons inspectors from entering the country to verify the dismantling of the weapons, a must for U.N. sanctions imposed in 1990 to be lifted.

U.N. inspectors left Iraq ahead of U.S.-British strikes in 1998 and have been barred from retiring.

The Iraqi Foreign Ministry on Sunday said such views were part of a U.S. campaign "of accusations and claims ... that are no more than lies." America has "provided no evidence for these claims," the statement said.

The statement said Iraq has fulfilled "its commitments under (U.N.) Security Council resolutions, including those related to weapons."

Baghdad has received nuclear weapons inspectors and invited a British fact finding team to see if Iraq is producing weapons of mass destruction, the statement said.

U.N. officials expressed hope Thursday that upcoming talks in Vienna on July 4-5 with Iraq will lead to the return of weapons inspectors.

Secretary-General Kofi Annan and Iraqi Foreign Minister Naji Sabri have had two rounds of talks since March that focused on the goal of getting U.N. inspectors back into Iraq. Both meetings, however, have been inconclusive.

U.S. defense secretary tells U.S. troops in Kuwait they are on front lines of war against terror
Sun Jun 9, 11:56 AM ET
By ROBERT BURNS, AP Military Writer
CAMP DOHA, Kuwait - Venturing into a sizzling desert 35 miles (55 kilometers) from the Iraqi border, U.S. Defense Secretary Donald H. Rumsfeld on Sunday told U.S. troops they are on the front lines against a foe that seeks to use terrorism to alter the American way of life.

"You are the people who stand between freedom and fear, between our people and a dangerous adversary that cannot be appeased, cannot be ignored and cannot be allowed to win," Rumsfeld told about 1,000 U.S. soldiers, sailors, airmen and marines assembled in a gymnasium.

In his prepared remarks, Rumsfeld left little doubt that he was aiming his anti-terror rhetoric at Iraq, which he frequently says is among nations that support international terrorist groups. He alluded to Iraq in describing the ultimate goal of U.S. President George Bush's war on terror.

"It will not end until state sponsors of terror are made to understand that abetting terrorism is unacceptable and will have deadly consequences," he said.

This sprawling, dusty military base, which Kuwait turned over to U.S. forces after the 1991 Gulf War bustles with activity. It is home to about 2,000 U.S. troops with tanks, surface-to-surface missiles, attack helicopters and other weapons and equipment for desert combat.

In his address to the troops, Rumsfeld emphasized that they could one day join the battle against terrorism.

"The global war on terrorism began in Afghanistan to be sure, but it will not end there," he said.

He refused, in a question-and-answer session with soldiers, to offer a clue where the next fight would be. He told one soldier there was no doubt that the full might of the American military would be called upon again.

"I'm certainly not in a position to tell you when, why or where," he said.

Rumsfeld later met with several senior Kuwaiti government officials.

Kuwait is the forward headquarters for U.S. Army Central Command, the land warfare component of U.S. Central Command. Its commander, Army Lt. Gen. Paul T. Mikolashek, greeted Rumsfeld upon his arrival.

U.S. F-15E Strike Eagles and F-16 Fighting Falcons use a Kuwaiti air base to launch patrol missions over southern Iraq. Supported by British fighters, they enforce a "no fly" zone that has been maintained since shortly after the war to contain Iraq's small air force.

A U.S.-led international coalition of ground forces liberated tiny Kuwait from Iraqi army occupation in February 1991.

It was Rumsfeld's first visit to Kuwait as defense secretary. He was in the Gulf in October to visit Saudi Arabia and Oman.

Rumsfeld's 10-day overseas trip began Wednesday in London, where his British counterpart, Geoff Hoon, told reporters there are worrying signs recently of Iraq's aggressively challenging the "no fly" zones and suggested it might require an allied military response.

Iraq also was a topic of discussion during Rumsfeld's two days in Brussels, Belgium, where he attended NATO defense ministers meetings. He met with Baltic and Nordic leaders in Estonia before heading to the Gulf.

Rumsfeld was to visit Bahrain on Monday and Qatar on Tuesday. Later in the week, Rumsfeld is expected in India and Pakistan in a bid to persuade the nuclear-armed neighbors to ratchet down military tensions over Kashmir

Iraq, Qatar Sign Free-Trade Agreement
Sun Jun 9, 8:43 AM ET
BAGHDAD, Iraq (AP) - Iraq and Qatar signed a free-trade agreement Sunday to drop customs duties and ease the flow of goods between the two Arab countries, further mending relations damaged by the 1990-91 Gulf War.

Iraqi Deputy Prime Minister Hikmat Ibrahim, who signed the accord with Qatari Trade and Economy Minister Sheik Hamad bin Faisal Al Thani, described the agreement as important for improving bilateral economic ties.

Sheik Hamad said contracts worth $200 million also were concluded during his three-day visit. More than 50 businessmen and officials accompanied him to Baghdad.

Total trade between Iraq and Qatar was a mere $18 million from 1997-2001, according to Iraqi Trade Ministry figures published this year. The ministry did not say what the two oil producers were trading.

Iraqi-Qatari trade and political ties were cut after Iraq's 1990 invasion of Kuwait, a move that triggered the 1991 Gulf War. But Qatar was the first Arab state to send its foreign minister to Iraq after the war ended, and ties have been improving in recent years.

Iraq now has free-trade agreements with 10 Arab countries.

Baghdad caught in a Catch-22

It was scarcely two days after the UN Security Council issued Resolution 1409 before Baghdad agreed to its provisions. This was a rapid response by Iraqi standards - especially compared to the 18 months it took them to agree to "oil-for-food" Resolution 968.

The reason behind this ready agreement was not that the Iraqis feared an American strike, but rather because 1409 was a victory for Baghdad: It was a giant step toward a total lifting of sanctions and regaining control over oil revenues.

The consensus within the Security Council that made 1409 possible (and which was trumpeted by the US as a great victory) had a price:

l Resolution 1284, which the Security Council passed on Dec. 17, 1999, linked a softening of the American position over sanctions to a return of UN weapons inspectors to Iraq. Resolution 1409, by contrast, gave Iraq all the inducements contained in 1284, but without linking these to any mention of a return of the inspectors. The new resolution also renewed the oil-for-food programs for a further six months without asking Baghdad for any new commitments.

l When Resolution 1284 was passed, Washington justified the "concessions"
it made by saying that it wanted to deprive Baghdad of using the suffering of the Iraqi people as a card to gain sympathy. But the Americans made even more concessions through 1409, underlining Baghdad's success in using sanctions to gain regional and world sympathy, and will continue to do so as long as its oil revenues remain under UN control.

l Resolution 1284 stipulated that Iraq would be allowed to freely import humanitarian goods included on a list without reference to the UN sanctions committee. Resolution 1409, by contrast, permits Iraq to import not only humanitarian supplies, but all civilian goods. Only dual use items would be referred to the sanctions committee for approval. It has to be said, though, that many items on this list (such as diving suits) are not traditional Iraqi imports anyway.

l Resolution 1409 stipulates that all Iraqi import contracts be decided upon by the UN weapons monitoring body and the International Atomic Energy Agency within 10 days of receiving them. When these bodies suspect that some goods are dual use, they must then refer the contracts in question to the sanctions committee made up of the Security Council members. Even then, this does not mean that such contracts would be rejected automatically.

l This mechanism ensures that neither the US, nor Britain, nor any other Security Council member state can henceforth be held responsible for delaying or rejecting contracts for goods bound for Iraq. The onus has been shifted to a UN technical committees. There is no doubt that these committees are more sensitive to Iraqi criticism and blackmail than were London and Washington when they ran the show.

l According to 1409, only certain items will be rejected if they are suspected of having dual use potential; the actual contract that included such items would not. All other items listed in such contracts would be shipped to Iraq while the suspicious ones are considered.

l The original smart sanctions idea envisioned the cooperation of Iraq's neighbors with the UN in monitoring border crossings in order to deter smuggling. Resolution 1409, however, dispenses with this provision, leaving matters much as they are now.

Syria, for example, still considers Iraqi oil supplies it receives to be for "technical analysis" purposes only! To get the Russians to agree to 1409, contracts to the value of $700 million they had signed with the Iraqis were approved.

But will the Iraqi people feel a positive difference in their living standards with the implementation of 1409?

Highly unlikely. The Iraqi regime simply does not have enough income to cover the requirements of the most recent phase of the oil-for-food program that ends on May 30. Baghdad's rash decision to stop oil exports for 30 days "in solidarity with the Palestinian intifada" lost the country in the region of $1.2 billion in revenues, thus increasing the deficit in the oil-for-food program to about $4 billion.

Resolution 1409 was an American admission of the failure of sanctions in isolating - much less overthrowing - the Iraqi regime. In other words, the US policy of containing Saddam Hussein's regime has failed. In fact, US President George W. Bush went even further when he said that a containment policy against Iraq would never work so long as Baghdad was intent on acquiring weapons of mass destruction (WMDs).

But Resolution 1409 would nevertheless be of some use to Washington, if only to deflect the humanitarian concerns associated with economic sanctions. It also enhanced unity within the Security Council, making it easier for the UN body to speak with one voice on the issue of Iraqi disarmament. The price for Washington's soft line on 1409 will be a much harder position on the issue of weapons inspectors.

The State Department is in no position to make concessions on this issue, especially after Sept. 11 and particularly as there are other circles (such as Congress and the Pentagon) that do not happen to believe that the return of weapons inspectors would be enough to neutralize the Iraqi threat.

Moreover, the Bush administration has designated the threat of WMDs as one of its top foreign policy priorities in the "war on terror." In addition, the recent rapprochement between Washington and Moscow does not give the Russians much room for maneuver in its efforts to help Iraq.

That is why the next confrontation with Iraq will revolve around a new resolution dealing with WMDs and the return of the inspectors.

Baghdad will only agree to cooperate if it was reassured that by doing so the US would try to overthrow the regime, and that sanctions would be lifted totally once the inspectors certify that the country is free of WMDs. Washington, on the other hand, is unprepared to give the Iraqis such assurances.

This being the case, Baghdad will view the return of the inspectors as a reconnaissance mission to prepare for a US invasion. Indeed, in the May 17 issue of the New York Times, James Dao wrote that one of Washington's most worrying concerns - and one of the main reasons for delaying military action against Iraq - is the fear of Iraq using chemical weapons against US troops.

It is not strange, therefore, for Baghdad to view the UN's mission as being intended to dispel these doubts. The Iraqis believe that far from making an invasion less likely, Washington's certainty that they do not have WMDs will actually encourage the US to invade.

On the other hand, it is surely not in Baghdad's interests to reveal that it does possess WMDs, since these weapons are the regime's ultimate deterrent against an American invasion and/or a popular uprising.

Russia and France have been trying to convince the Iraqis that by letting the inspectors back in, they would avoid a US military strike. So far, however, the Iraqis are unconvinced.

They believe that the inspectors, once back in Iraq, can instigate a crisis at any time and thus give Washington the pretext it needs to invade.

Conversely, by refusing to allow the UN team back in, the Iraqis would also give the US a pretext to strike, especially since Washington has so far failed to find a link between Saddam Hussein's regime and al-Qaeda.

Baghdad, in short, is in a Catch-22 situation.

On front line against Iraq, Rumsfeld says terrorist states must be punished

Mon Jun 10, 3:21 AM ET

By ROBERT BURNS, AP Military Writer

KUWAIT CITY, Kuwait - U.S. Defense Secretary Donald H. Rumsfeld on Monday dismissed claims by the Iraqi government that it has no nuclear, chemical or biological weapons and is making no effort to acquire them.

"They are lying," he told a news conference at Kuwait's international airport before flying to Bahrain.

The Iraqi Foreign Ministry in Baghdad issued a statement Sunday asserting the government of Saddam Hussein has neither made nor possessed weapons of mass destruction in more than a decade.

"Iraq has said on many occasions that it is not concerned with entering the mass destruction weapons club. ... We left it in 1991," the official statement said.

Earlier at Kuwait's Camp Doha, a desert encampment 35 miles from the Iraqi border, Rumsfeld told American troops that state sponsors of terrorism must be punished.

Without mentioning Iraq by name, Rumsfeld said the soldiers are on the front lines against a dangerous foe.

"You are the people who stand between freedom and fear, between our people and a dangerous adversary that cannot be appeased, cannot be ignored and cannot be allowed to win," he told about 1,000 troops assembled in an air-conditioned gymnasium on a 110-degree Fahrenheit (43 Celsius) afternoon Sunday.

Rumsfeld left little doubt he was aiming his words at Iraq, which he often says is among nations that support international terrorist groups and could help them gain access to weapons of mass destruction.

These states, he said, "do need to be stopped so that they cannot threaten or hold free people hostage to blackmail or terror."

He again alluded to Iraq in describing the ultimate goal of U.S. President George W. Bush's war on terrorism.

"It will not end until state sponsors of terror are made to understand that abetting terrorism is unacceptable and will have deadly consequences for the regimes that do so," Rumsfeld said.

Camp Doha, where Rumsfeld addressed the troops, is a sprawling military base that Kuwait turned over to U.S. forces after they evicted Iraq's occupation army in the 1991 Persian Gulf War It is home to about 2,000 U.S. troops with M-1A1 Abrams tanks, M2-A2 Bradley infantry vehicles, surface-to-surface missiles, self-propelled cannons, Patriot anti-missile batteries and Apache attack helicopters.

Rumsfeld met later Sunday with several senior Kuwaiti government officials.

Kuwait is the forward headquarters for U.S. Army Central Command, the land warfare component of U.S. Central Command.

U.S. F-15E Strike Eagles and F-16 Fighting Falcons use a Kuwaiti air base to launch patrol missions over southern Iraq. Supported by British fighters, they enforce a "no fly" zone that has been maintained since shortly after the war to contain Iraq's small air force.

A U.S.-led international coalition of ground forces liberated tiny Kuwait from Iraqi army occupation in February 1991.

Later this week, Rumsfeld is scheduled to travel to India and Pakistan to continue Bush administration efforts to persuade the nuclear-armed neighbors to defuse military tensions over Kashmir

Rumsfeld Dismisses Iraqi Claims
Mon Jun 10, 3:53 AM ET
By ROBERT BURNS, AP Military Writer
KUWAIT CITY, Kuwait (AP) - Defense Secretary Donald H. Rumsfeld on Monday dismissed claims by the Iraqi government that it has no nuclear, chemical or biological weapons and is making no effort to acquire them.

"They are lying," he told a news conference at Kuwait's international airport before flying to Bahrain.

The Iraqi Foreign Ministry in Baghdad issued a statement Sunday asserting the government of Saddam Hussein has neither made nor possessed weapons of mass destruction in more than a decade.

"Iraq has said on many occasions that it is not concerned with entering the mass destruction weapons club. ... We left it in 1991," the official statement said.

Earlier at Kuwait's Camp Doha, a desert encampment 35 miles from the Iraqi border, Rumsfeld told American troops that state sponsors of terrorism must be punished.

Without mentioning Iraq by name, Rumsfeld said the soldiers are on the front lines against a dangerous foe.

"You are the people who stand between freedom and fear, between our people and a dangerous adversary that cannot be appeased, cannot be ignored and cannot be allowed to win," he told about 1,000 troops assembled in an air-conditioned gymnasium on a 110-degree afternoon Sunday.

Rumsfeld left little doubt he was aiming his words at Iraq, which he often says is among nations that support international terrorist groups and could help them gain access to weapons of mass destruction.

119

These states, he said, "do need to be stopped so that they cannot threaten or hold free people hostage to blackmail or terror."

He again alluded to Iraq in describing the ultimate goal of President Bush's war on terror.

"It will not end until state sponsors of terror are made to understand that abetting terrorism is unacceptable and will have deadly consequences for the regimes that do so," Rumsfeld said.

Camp Doha, where Rumsfeld addressed the troops, is a sprawling military base that Kuwait turned over to U.S. forces after they evicted Iraq's occupation army in the 1991 Persian Gulf War It is home to about 2,000 U.S. troops with M-1A1 Abrams tanks, M2-A2 Bradley infantry vehicles, surface-to-surface missiles, self-propelled cannons, Patriot anti-missile batteries and Apache attack helicopters.

In his address, Rumsfeld emphasized to the troops that they could one day join the battle against terrorism.

"The global war on terrorism began in Afghanistan to be sure, but it will not end there," he said.

He refused, in a question-and-answer session with soldiers, to offer a clue where the next fight would be. He told one soldier there was no doubt that the full might of the American military would be called upon again.

"I'm certainly not in a position to tell you when, why or where," he said.

Rumsfeld met later Sunday with several senior Kuwaiti government officials.

Kuwait is the forward headquarters for U.S. Army Central Command, the land warfare component of U.S. Central Command.

U.S. F-15E Strike Eagles and F-16 Fighting Falcons use a Kuwaiti air base to launch patrol missions over southern Iraq. Supported by British fighters, they enforce a "no fly" zone that has been maintained since shortly after the war to contain Iraq's small air force.

A U.S.-led international coalition of ground forces liberated tiny Kuwait from Iraqi army occupation in February 1991.

It was Rumsfeld's first visit to Kuwait as defense secretary. He was in the Gulf in October to visit Saudi Arabia and Oman, but did not get to the smaller countries in the northern Gulf.

Later this week, Rumsfeld is scheduled to travel to India and Pakistan to continue Bush administration efforts to persuade the nuclear-armed neighbors to defuse military tensions over Kashmir

Rumsfeld Hopes to See Saddam's Downfall Through
Mon Jun 10, 4:49 AM ET
By Ashraf Fouad
KUWAIT (Reuters) - Donald Rumsfeld expressed hope on Monday Iraqi President Saddam Hussein would be toppled during his time as U.S. defense secretary.

"Oh, I would certainly hope so," Rumsfeld said when asked if he would see Saddam's downfall while still in office. "The world would be a better place without that regime."

"The solution in Iraq would be regime change," said Rumsfeld when told by a Kuwaiti journalist that his countrymen were "fed up" with the Iraqi leadership and threats from Baghdad.

On his first visit to Kuwait since becoming defense secretary last year, Rumsfeld dismissed an Arab summit attempt in March to reconcile Kuwait with Iraq, Kuwait's occupier during seven months ended by the U.S.-led Gulf War in 1991.

Arab states, including Kuwait, have collectively opposed fresh military action against Iraq.

The United States has accused Iraq of developing weapons of mass destruction and sponsoring terrorism, prompting speculation it might mount some type of military action against Baghdad.

"They are lying," Rumsfeld responded quickly when asked about Iraqi denials of involvement in mass-destruction arms. "They have them and they continue to develop them and they have weaponized chemical weapons, we know that. They have an active program to develop nuclear weapons. It is also clear that they are actively developing biological weapons," he added.

FATE OF 12 KUWAITIS DISCUSSED

Rumsfeld told a news conference before leaving for Bahrain that the United States has replenished stocks of ammunitions and arms in the region after a draw-down for use in the war on terrorism which was launched in Afghanistan in October.

Defense sources had noted a recent increase in U.S. military cargo traffic in the region, further boosting speculation that a military operation against Iraq was nearing.

"We began the process of replenishing stocks in ways that would be appropriate, including here (Kuwait), and we are very much in that mode right now," Rumsfeld said.

Rumsfeld said he discussed in Kuwait the fate of some 12 Kuwaiti men among U.S.-held prisoners accused of being fighters and members of the group al Qaeda and the toppled Taliban movement which ruled Afghanistan.

"We have invited representatives of the Kuwaiti government to visit and meet with the individuals we captured in Afghanistan during the conflict," Rumsfeld said.

He said the purpose of the visit, to Guantanamo Bay naval base, would be to help in intelligence gathering.

The United States launched its campaign in Afghanistan to flush out Saudi-born militant Osama bin Laden and his al Qaeda network, which it blames for the September 11 attacks on the United States, and to oust their Taliban protectors.

Relatives of some of the Kuwaiti detainees have said the men were involved in Muslim charity work in Pakistan and Afghanistan and not "terrorism."

Rumsfeld Slams Terrorists in Iraq
Mon Jun 10, 3:12 AM ET
By ROBERT BURNS, AP Military Writer
KUWAIT CITY, Kuwait (AP) - Defense Secretary Donald H. Rumsfeld on Monday dismissed claims by the Iraqi government that it has no nuclear, chemical or biological weapons and is making no effort to acquire them.

"They are lying," he told a news conference at Kuwait's international airport before flying to Bahrain.

The Iraqi Foreign Ministry in Baghdad issued a statement Sunday asserting the government of Saddam Hussein has neither made nor possessed weapons of mass destruction in more than a decade.

"Iraq has said on many occasions that it is not concerned with entering the mass destruction weapons club. ... We left it in 1991," the official statement said.

Earlier at Kuwait's Camp Doha, a desert encampment 35 miles from the Iraqi border, Rumsfeld told American troops that state sponsors of terrorism must be punished.

Without mentioning Iraq by name, Rumsfeld said the soldiers are on the front lines against a dangerous foe.

"You are the people who stand between freedom and fear, between our people and a dangerous adversary that cannot be appeased, cannot be ignored and cannot be allowed to win," he told about 1,000 troops assembled in an air-conditioned gymnasium on a 110-degree afternoon Sunday.

Rumsfeld left little doubt he was aiming his words at Iraq, which he often says is among nations that support international terrorist groups and could help them gain access to weapons of mass destruction.

These states, he said, "do need to be stopped so that they cannot threaten or hold free people hostage to blackmail or terror."

He again alluded to Iraq in describing the ultimate goal of President Bush's war on terror.

"It will not end until state sponsors of terror are made to understand that abetting terrorism is unacceptable and will have deadly consequences for the regimes that do so," Rumsfeld said.

Camp Doha, where Rumsfeld addressed the troops, is a sprawling military base that Kuwait turned over to U.S. forces after they evicted Iraq's occupation army in the 1991 Persian Gulf War . It is home to about 2,000 U.S. troops with M-1A1 Abrams tanks, M2-A2 Bradley infantry vehicles, surface-to-surface missiles, self-propelled cannons, Patriot anti-missile batteries and Apache attack helicopters.

In his address, Rumsfeld emphasized to the troops that they could one day join the battle against terrorism.

"The global war on terrorism began in Afghanistan to be sure, but it will not end there," he said.

He refused, in a question-and-answer session with soldiers, to offer a clue where the next fight would be. He told one soldier there was no doubt that the full might of the American military would be called upon again.

"I'm certainly not in a position to tell you when, why or where," he said.

Rumsfeld met later Sunday with several senior Kuwaiti government officials.

Kuwait is the forward headquarters for U.S. Army Central Command, the land warfare component of U.S. Central Command.

U.S. F-15E Strike Eagles and F-16 Fighting Falcons use a Kuwaiti air base to launch patrol missions over southern Iraq. Supported by British fighters, they enforce a "no fly" zone that has been maintained since shortly after the war to contain Iraq's small air force.

A U.S.-led international coalition of ground forces liberated tiny Kuwait from Iraqi army occupation in February 1991.

It was Rumsfeld's first visit to Kuwait as defense secretary. He was in the Gulf in October to visit Saudi Arabia and Oman, but did not get to the smaller countries in the northern Gulf.

Later this week, Rumsfeld is scheduled to travel to India and Pakistan to continue Bush administration efforts to persuade the nuclear-armed neighbors to defuse military tensions over Kashmir

Rumsfeld calls Iraqi leader a 'world-class liar,' a danger to the world
Mon Jun 10, 4:06 PM ET
By ROBERT BURNS, AP Military Writer
MANAMA, Bahrain - Iraqi President Saddam Hussein is a "world-class liar" who is trying to fool the world into thinking he has no interest in weapons of mass destruction, Defense Secretary Donald H. Rumsfeld told U.S. troops Monday on this island nation in the Gulf.

Addressing several hundred sailors and Marines at U.S. Navy Central Command headquarters, Rumsfeld left no doubt he believes Iraq is pursuing stocks of nuclear, chemical and biological weapons in defiance of U.N. resolutions that ended the 1991 Gulf War

In emphatic tones, the defense secretary noted a public assertion by Saddam's government that it has no weapons of mass destruction and is making no effort to acquire them.

"He's lying. It's not complicated," Rumsfeld said.

The Iraqi Foreign Ministry in Baghdad issued a statement Sunday asserting the government has neither made nor possessed weapons of mass destruction in more than a decade.

"Iraq has said on many occasions that it is not concerned with entering the mass destruction weapons club. ... We left it in 1991," the official statement said. The reference was to the six-week-long Persian Gulf War.

"If you want to know a world-class liar, it's Saddam Hussein," Rumsfeld told the troops, who gathered in a courtyard, fans stirring the sticky night air.

Earlier Monday, at a news conference in Kuwait, Rumsfeld said the Iraqi claim cannot be trusted.

"It is false, not true, inaccurate and typical," he said.

"They have had an active program to develop nuclear weapons," Rumsfeld said. "It's also clear they are actively developing biological weapons" and used chemical weapons against their own Kurdish population in the 1980s.

Without saying it explicitly, Rumsfeld left a clear impression that he believes the United States may take pre-emptive military action against Iraq.

Vice President Dick Cheney also cited Iraq as a threat in making a case Monday for an active U.S. attitude toward countering terrorism. President George W. Bush who spoke of "pre-emptive action when necessary" in a graduation speech this month at the U.S. Military Academy, plans to formalize the "strike-first" policy this year when he presents his first national security strategy to Congress.

In Kuwait and Bahrain, Rumsfeld met with senior government officials, including Kuwaiti Defense Minister Sheik Jabir al-Mubarak and his Bahraini counterpart, Gen. Khalifa bin Ahmed al-Khalifa.

Rumsfeld said he invited Kuwaiti government representatives to meet with a dozen Kuwaitis who are among the more than 300

Taliban or al-Qaida fighters captured in Afghanistan and held prisoner at a U.S. Navy base in Cuba.

Rumsfeld told reporters the Kuwaitis' meeting at Guantanamo Bay, Cuba, would have two purposes: to glean additional intelligence from the prisoners and to determine "if there is any law enforcement interest" in them.

It marked the first time Rumsfeld has acknowledged publicly the nationality of Arabs held at Guantanamo Bay and specified how many of any specific nationality are imprisoned.

Rumsfeld Questions Iraq Weapons Stash
Mon Jun 10, 3:44 PM ET
By ROBERT BURNS, AP Military Writer

MANAMA, Bahrain (AP) - Iraqi President Saddam Hussein is a "world-class liar" who is trying to fool the world into thinking he has no interest in weapons of mass destruction, Defense Secretary Donald H. Rumsfeld told U.S. troops Monday on this island nation in the Persian Gulf.

Addressing several hundred sailors and Marines at U.S. Navy Central Command headquarters, Rumsfeld left no doubt he believes Iraq is pursuing stocks of nuclear, chemical and biological weapons in defiance of U.N. resolutions that ended the 1991 Gulf War.

In emphatic tones, the defense secretary noted a public assertion by Saddam's government that it has no weapons of mass destruction and is making no effort to acquire them.

"He's lying. It's not complicated," Rumsfeld said.

The Iraqi Foreign Ministry in Baghdad issued a statement Sunday asserting the government has neither made nor possessed weapons of mass destruction in more than a decade.

"Iraq has said on many occasions that it is not concerned with entering the mass destruction weapons club. ... We left it in 1991," the official statement said. The reference was to the six-week-long Persian Gulf War.

"If you want to know a world-class liar, it's Saddam Hussein," Rumsfeld told the troops, who gathered in a courtyard, fans stirring the sticky night air.

Earlier Monday, at a news conference in Kuwait City, Rumsfeld said the Iraqi claim cannot be trusted.

"It is false, not true, inaccurate and typical," he said.

"They have had an active program to develop nuclear weapons," Rumsfeld said. "It's also clear they are actively developing biological weapons" and used chemical weapons against their own Kurdish population in the 1980s.

Without saying it explicitly, Rumsfeld left a clear impression that he believes the United States may take pre-emptive military action against Iraq.

Vice President Dick Cheney also cited Iraq as a threat in making a case Monday for an active U.S. attitude toward countering terrorism. President Bush who spoke of "pre-emptive action when necessary" in a graduation speech this month at the U.S. Military Academy, plans to formalize the "strike-first" policy this year when he presents his first national security strategy to Congress.

Cheney said U.S. officials are especially worried by "any possible linkup" between Saddam's government and terrorist networks, given Saddam's propensity for using chemical weapons.

"We have a responsibility to answer this growing peril," Cheney said in a Washington speech to the International Democrat Union, a group of mostly conservative officials from several countries. "Deliverable weapons of mass destruction in the hands of terrorists would expose the civilized world to the worst of all possible horrors, and we will not allow it."

In Kuwait and Bahrain, Rumsfeld met with senior government officials, including Kuwaiti Defense Minister Sheik Jabir al-Mubarak and his Bahraini counterpart, Gen. Khalifa bin Ahmed al-Khalifa.

A reporter asked Rumsfeld what he thought of Iraq's recent pledge to respect Kuwait's sovereignty and to restore full relations with the Kuwaiti government. He said accepting Iraq's word of good intentions toward Kuwait "would be like the lion inviting the chicken to embrace."

"What good, in the past, have Iraqi representations of good will to its neighbors been? Precious little," he said. "Should hope spring eternal? Maybe, maybe not. It depends on the risks."

127

Rumsfeld said he invited Kuwaiti government representatives to meet with a dozen Kuwaitis who are among the more than 300 Taliban or al-Qaida fighters captured in Afghanistan and held prisoner at a U.S. Navy base in Cuba.

Rumsfeld told reporters the Kuwaitis' meeting at Guantanamo Bay, Cuba, would have two purposes: to glean additional intelligence from the prisoners and to determine "if there is any law enforcement interest" in them.

It marked the first time Rumsfeld has acknowledged publicly the nationality of Arabs held at Guantanamo Bay and specified how many of any specific nationality are imprisoned.

"You are the people who stand between freedom and fear, between our people and a dangerous adversary that cannot be appeased, cannot be ignored and cannot be allowed to win," he told about 1,000 troops assembled in an air-conditioned gymnasium on a 110-degree Kuwait afternoon Sunday.

Rumsfeld left little doubt he was aiming his words at Iraq, which he often says is among nations that support international terror groups and could help them gain access to weapons of mass destruction.

These states, he said, "do need to be stopped so that they cannot threaten or hold free people hostage to blackmail or terror."

From Bahrain, Rumsfeld was scheduled to visit Qatar on Tuesday, then travel to India and Pakistan to continue Bush administration efforts to persuade the nuclear-armed neighbors to defuse military tensions over Kashmir

Bush lays foundation for potential attack on Iraq

Fri Jun 14, 2:06 AM ET

By RON FOURNIER, AP White House Correspondent

WASHINGTON - President Bush is methodically laying the foundation to overthrow Iraq's Saddam Hussein perhaps with military action, and he may feel compelled to strike without warning.

In recent weeks, the administration has intensified its rhetoric against Saddam and unveiled a new policy that calls for pre-emptive action against enemies armed with weapons of mass destruction.

Aides say Bush's resolve has not been weakened by the Mideast crisis, tension in southeast Asia or qualms of U.S. allies.

Behind closed doors at the White House, the president reacted with dismay to reports that U.S. military leaders were lobbying against an Iraqi invasion anytime soon.

"I don't know what they're talking about," two senior U.S. officials quoted the president as saying. They interpreted the remark to mean Bush is seriously considering military action despite opposition.

Bush himself told supporters this week: "When we see evil—I know it may hurt some people's feelings, it may not be what they call diplomatically correct—but I'm calling evil for what it is. Evil is evil, and we will fight it with all our might."

Bush may choose diplomatic pressure or covert action to undermine Saddam. If he decides to go to war, there will be more choices—such as whether to follow his father's blueprint or launch an unconventional attack.

Most analysts assume Bush would slowly generate support inside and outside the country with a series of warnings to Saddam and a deliberate marshaling of U.S. troops. After all, the world saw the Persian Gulf War coming for six months before Bush's father ordered the attack.

But there may be little or no warning this time.

If the United States' estimation of Iraq's weapons of mass destruction program is correct, a long buildup to war could be catastrophic, analysts say.

Given notice, Saddam might strike the United States first or help a terrorist group do so. He could become cornered and desperate—and presumably armed with a greater arsenal of deadly weapons than he had during the Gulf War.

"We're now beginning to understand that we can't wait for these folks to deliver the weapons of mass destruction and see what they do with them before we act," said Philip D. Zelikow, a University of Virginia history professor who worked for the National Security Council under Bush's father.

"And we're beginning to understand that we might not want to give people like Saddam Hussein advance warning that we're going to strike," he said.

Some top military leaders favor delaying an Iraqi invasion until next year and perhaps not do it at all. They warn that at least 200,000 troops would be needed. They want the focus to be on covert intelligence operations.

But if Bush decides to strike without warning, there are alternatives to a conventional military buildup.

One strategy first proposed by retired Army Gen. Wayne A. Downing four years ago calls for attacking Iraq with a combination of airstrikes and special operations attacks in coordination with Iraqi fighters opposed to Saddam.

From Kuwait, carrier battle groups in the nearby waters or Kurdish-controlled northern Iraq the forces could launch surprise attacks against the nation's weapons facilities—or even target Saddam himself.

A sneak attack would create a huge uproar in the international community and expose Bush to criticism at home, particularly if troops get bogged down in a post-Saddam Iraq.

Leaving a White House meeting with Bush, Sen. Joseph Biden, D-Del., chairman of the Senate Foreign Relations Committee, said he told Bush: "There's a reason why your father stopped and didn't go to Baghdad."

Bush won't reveal his plans, but said again Thursday, "We'll use all tools at our disposal to deal with him."

Under his new policy, which has evolved since the Sept. 11 attacks, the U.S. military can take pre-emptive action, if necessary, against terrorist-harboring nations that have weapons of mass destruction.

Iraq may fit the bill:

_ Bush increasingly suspects that Saddam still supports terrorism, despite repeated warnings since Sept. 11.

_ Defense Secretary Donald H. Rumsfeld recently dismissed claims by the Iraqi government that it has no nuclear, chemical or biological weapons. "They are lying," Rumsfeld said.

The president's views toward Iraq have hardened since Sept. 11, when he condemned terrorist-harboring nations but did not mention weapons of mass destruction.

On Nov. 16, he warned for the first time that Osama bin Laden was seeking chemical, biological and nuclear weapons. He had been told that al-Qaida may have access to those weapons through Pakistan.

The chilling news is said to have crystalized Bush's thinking that terrorist groups and nuclear nations are a deadly combination.

That led to the State of the Union address and Bush's outing of an "axis of evil"—Iraq, Iran and North Korea

Standing before Congress, he offered the first hint of his "strike first" doctrine and, perhaps, his plans for Iraq.

"I will not wait on events while dangers gather," Bush said.

U.S. Warplanes Attack Iraqi Air Defense Targets
Fri Jun 14, 9:32 AM ET
WASHINGTON (Reuters) - U.S. warplanes on Friday attacked a military air defense radar facility in a "no-fly" zone in southern Iraq in response to threats against western aircraft patrolling the zone, the U.S. military said.

The U.S. Central Command, based in Tampa, Florida, said in a statement that the strike was in response to attempts to shoot down U.S. and British warplanes on Thursday.

Damage to the radar command and control target at Al Amarah about 165 miles southeast of Baghdad was still being determined, the command said.

The latest in a long series of tit-for-tat exchanges in policing by western warplanes of no-fly zones in northern and southern Iraq since the 1991 Gulf War came at 1:20 p.m. Iraq time (5:20 a.m. EDT), the command said.

Those exchanges have increased in recent months amid speculation that the United States might be preparing to invade Iraq to overthrow President Saddam Hussein accused by Washington of actively trying to develop chemical, biological and nuclear weapons.

British Defense Secretary Geoff Hoon said in Brussels last week that Iraq, which does not recognize the no-fly zones, had become more aggressive in threatening U.S. and British jets and that might require a response from the allied forces.

But he also stressed after talks with Defense Secretary Donald Rumsfeld that he was specifically referring to action related to the western-imposed no-fly zones and not to any broader military action.

U.S. attacks Iraqi radar site for fourth time in a month
Fri Jun 14, 8:39 AM ET
By PAULINE JELINEK, Associated Press Writer
WASHINGTON - U.S. aircraft bombed an Iraqi military facility Friday in the fourth such strike in a month, American defense officials reported.

The strike was in answer to an Iraqi attack the previous day on aircraft patrolling the southern "no-fly" zone that U.S. and British coalition forces have been maintaining since shortly after the 1991 Gulf War

"Coalition strikes in the no-fly zone are ... a self-defense measure in response to hostile Iraqi acts against coalition forces and their aircraft," said a statement from U.S. Central Command, which oversees the patrols.

Friday's strike was on a radar facility at Al-Amarah, about 165 miles (265 kilometers) southeast of the capital, Baghdad, said Pentagon spokesman Lt. Col. Dave Lapan.

"The facilities struck today had been targeted because they were used to direct yesterday's attack against the coalition aircraft monitoring the no-fly zone in southern Iraq," it said.

Top British and American defense officials have said it is a worrying sign that in the past month Iraq's air defenses have been more aggressively trying to shoot down the U.S. and British pilots on patrol.

Pilots have reported attacks by Iraqi anti-aircraft artillery and surface-to-air missiles. As they did Friday, the allied planes have responded by bombing various elements of Iraq's air defense system.

Lapan said Iraq has shot at coalition aircraft about a half dozen times since the beginning of May. And coalition forces have struck back four times since mid-May, he said.

Iraq blasts US claims on terrorism

Iraq blasted a report released by the US Department of State which included a repeated language of threats against some independent world countries.

An official spokesman for Iraqi Foreign Ministry condemned the report which enlisted Iraq as one of seven countries claimed to be states supporting terrorism.

He told INA that the US chose certain states and described them as supporting terrorism, but it did not offer any evidence for such accusation; this again means that the U.S uses the so called 'combating terrorism' theme as a pretext to implement its aggressive policy against states that refuse its hegemony.

The spokesman added "the US claims that Iraq had not uphold international drive to combat terrorism is not but distorting of facts, Iraq was and is still facing terrorism over 30 years and it rejected US use of force in contradiction with UN Charter against states." Iraq stressed the necessity of giving a clear UN definition to terrorism that treat its causes in compliance with international law and the UN charter.

The spokesman inquired "how the report accused Iraq with sponsoring terrorism as it supported Palestinian Intifada at time Palestinian people defend their land and confront the Zionist occupation, and at the same time the US administration exempts the Zionist entity from terrorist occupation and all war crimes and killing," he added.

"The US administration supported the Zionist occupation with money, weapons and international protection, which makes it full culprit in the terrorist operations against Palestinian people," he elaborated.

He pointed out that the US belittle international law and human rights principles in addition to international charters when it considered Palestinian people's struggle to restore their rights as terrorism that should be combated.

"However, the US named the Zionist Prime Minister with his horrible crimes against humanity as a "peace man", besides, they expressed understanding to the Zionist occupation and vowed support for their crimes in the occupied territories," the spokesman said.

133

International law is a united one like principles of combating terrorism while US double-standard policies would hurt motives of combating terrorism for they harbor some terrorists at the same time they attack some countries under the same pretext.

He affirmed "the Iraqi people had been the first victim of US terrorism for more than 30 years when many civilians and officials had been subjected to assassination across borders by many US trained and armed agents while the US had proclaimed it spent tens of millions of dollars for its agents to commit terrorist actions against the Iraqi people under a US so-called "Law of Liberating Iraq."

He added that the US had admitted that they harboured since 1991 a number of criminals who fled into a neighbouring state after they had perpetrated terrorist crimes against civilians

The US Department of State declared during a news conference on May 21 that it had released a report in which seven countries, including Iraq, accused of terrorism.

The spokesman said that Iraqi cities and economic and scientific installations are being exposed to daily raiding since 1991, pointing out that the imposition of the so-called 'no-fly zones' by the US and Britain against Iraq constitutes a violation of international law and the UN Charter.

He stressed that the only way to combat terrorism is that the US should give up domination, arrogance and intervention in peoples' affairs and should come back to the UN principles in international relations and dialogue.

Concerning 11 September attacks victims, the spokesman said "Iraq had paid condolences to the victims and families inflicted in the attacks, he stressed that the civilian victims of 11 September attacks is a painful matter, it is as painful as millions of victims died owing to US and Zionist aggressive acts and embargoes.

He elaborated that President Saddam Hussein, in view of UN principles and charters, had sent a letter to the US government and people and called on them to deal with the event wisely and with responsibility. The President called them to review their policy against the world peoples in order to reach international peace and stability, he concluded

Dear FRONTLINE,

I served on the frontlines as a cavalry scout during the Gulf War and you could say I experienced some stress! I found your report to be very well put together and fairly unbiased. I have experienced some of the "symptoms" that were reported. I also believe I suffered a mild case of PTSD after leaving the Gulf. I do not think people really understand the physiological changes caused by stress. Many vets think stress means that they are suffering some kind of mental illness and just couldn't "hack it". That is not the case. Stress causes many of your bodily functions to change. Your body and senses are alert and ready to go at a moment's notice. This is not without some cost to us my comrades in arms. I truly believe stress/PTSD to be the MAJOR problem we are facing. I also am not so naive as to believe there were not other health risks. I remember receiving a daily intel brief that some of our engineers had been exposed to a chemical agent (possibly mustard gas) while examining ammunition bunkers and prepping them for demolitions. They blew it up as far as I know but why hasn't anyone heard of this? I was briefed on the incident and precautions to take and I was only a PFC in a cavalry squadron! No one asked me and I wasn't keeping it secret. What IS going on? I hope we find where the problem lies and fix it.

Dan Ebker
Bloomington, IL

Dear FRONTLINE,

We have just seen "Last Battle of the Gulf War" on tape and judge it to be among the finest documentary efforts of recent decades. Today, when newspapers and television stations are financially rewarded for sensationalism, it is rare to see a piece that truly informs and educates. PBS escapes the bondage of circulation figures and Nielsen ratings, but seldom escapes the desire to look as "courageous" as its commercial cousins. This time you did. You informed and educated. You are to be congratulated.

Dear FRONTLINE,

Your program was interesting but, to us, lacking in a couple of important areas. Firstly, while the U.S. may have been the biggest 'person power' contributor there were many other nationals of other countries present and probably civilian contractors and observers as well. Is the incidence of GWS the same for these people and how do their troubles relate to their war time location in the Gulf?

Secondly, which makes the first question somewhat rhetorical, what happened to information on this subject that has been developed by the British? Within the last two years PBS aired a program, wholly or partly produced in Britain on this very subject. The gist of it as I remember was that they named some chemical compounds that they believed might be at fault. Also they said that British GWS researchers were receiving scant cooperation from the U.S. government and technical people. One might say that in addition to the U.S. government P.B.S. also has an Anglo blind eye.

David Banks
Hayes. Va

Dear FRONTLINE,
It should not matter at this point what the cause of Gulf War Syndrome, just take care of them!

It was frustrating to see these great panels, in the exquisite certainty of their technical expertise, override this simple fact: these soldier are sick, need medical help, and should have it without question or delay—as should any citizen in this Country.

That "universal health coverage" is so easily dismissed in our Country as if it does not even matter...is truly embarrassing and morally damning. As has always been the case, once again you have shown courage to cover controversy in your depiction of Gulf War Syndrome. With the conservative congress and lobbyists for corporations threatening your very existence, I must commend you for your attempt to yet educate the American public on issues they otherwise will not even really hear about. You were conscientiously careful to show "both sides" and it is clear that there are two sides in this issue. Clearly the soldiers are sick, sick for whatever reason—and as you revealed this has been the case in all previous wars as well. It is my belief that the panels (for better, for worse) really did try to find a single cause or symptom, and to the degree this represents a legitimate "other side," you were fair to give coverage to their conclusion: that their is no single cause but that these soldiers are mostly suffering from illnesses due to severe stress.

And this is my point. When all is said and done, and no single cause can be pin-pointed, the fact remains that these men and women are truly sick and need care—as do all Americans when they are clearly sick—and without question!

Sincerely,

Curtis P. Fallgren

Dear FRONTLINE,

As someone who studies the social impact of war upon veterans, I was unsurprised by your conclusions regarding Gulf War Syndrome. Like other American conflicts, the eventual costs of war—whether medical or political—are being paid by whom bore the burden of service.

What surprised me is that there was never any systematic economic analysis of those that claim disability due to GWS. America has always taken better care of our wounded veterans than our other disabled populations. Might not Gulf War Syndrome have an economic cause, rather than a medical one?

Timothy Haggerty, Ph.D.

Murfreesboro, TN

Dear FRONTLINE,

Bravissimo! Finally, a voice in the wilderness of popular media cries out for reason! You deflated the myth of GWS in part by letting the so-called "victims" tell their own stories, to telling effect. Frontline pulled a few punches (for instance, you sidestepped the mass hysteria factor) but any intelligent viewer must agree that the "syndrome" is in fact a popular media invention, and that the real tragedy lies in the anguish and false hope needlessly stirred up amongst those brave soldiers and their families by self-serving journalists, politicians, and medical charlatans.

Thank you, thank you, and thank you!

Sincerely,

Brian Adams
Reno, NV

Dear FRONTLINE,
Is it really surprising that medical science funded by Washington is just as corrupt as everything else funded by Washington? The hubris demonstrated by your Government "experts" is simply amazing. The total lack of humanity comes across on the TV screen and feeds what has become the oxymoron of "medical ethics," with which anyone acquainted with the Government's role in chronic fatigue syndrome is already only too familiar.
Jerry S. McKee
Sulphur Springs, TX

Dear FRONTLINE,
Congratulations, you've done it again. With your program on Gulf Syndrome, you have convincingly shown how media and congressional hype irresponsibly tried to overwhelm careful and extensive scientific inquiry. It is clear to anyone who understands the scientific process that there is no evidence that there was a "Gulf Syndrome" that caused damage to U.S. troops in the Gulf War.
Albert B. Reynolds
Charlottesville, Virginia

Dear FRONTLINE,
I am a Gulf War Veteran. I have had health problems since returning from Saudi Arabia. I am concerned that, if I don't take time every time I get sick to go to a doctor and have it documented, I will have problems in the future trying to get help from the VA. I do not think that the powers that be can blame stress for the afflictions that are plaguing veterans from Desert Shield and Storm. I was lucky to have a relatively easy assignment in Saudi Arabia and felt that there is more stress in my life now than there ever was then.
I started feeling sick before I left the service in 1992 and haven't felt fully healthy since. My shot records were removed

from my medical file after I returned from Saudi and before I ETS. I was also told that the problems I checked off on my ETS medical form (headaches, dizziness, fatigue, etc.) were all in my head. I want some answers from an impartial review. Why not get the Iraqi soldiers and other people who are suffering the same problems as the rest of us involved in this so we can get more facts and figure this dilemma out. They are suffering just as much as we are and, should have an explanation. Thank you for this opportunity to express my views.

W. Cramer
SPC USA (ETS)
19K (Tank Driver)
Tupper Lake, New York

Dear FRONTLINE,
Frontline: It is quite refreshing to see such a non-emotional approach taken on such an emotional issue. I am a veterans service officer for a state veterans agency and am office in a VA Regional Office. I see may veterans first hand who are attempting to have their disabilities recognized as service connected by the VA. I have felt for a long time that these Gulf War maladies were in some way stress related. It is important to remember that the vast majority of those personnel deployed to the Gulf region never even conceived of the possibility that they would be called upon to actually fight a war during their military service. It is readily understandable how reservists were even more greatly affected, after being uprooted from friends and family, and then having to cope with such hostile living conditions so far from home, friends, and family.

I also have had the misfortune to speak personally with Dr. Nicolson (the wife). Until recently we lived in the same community. She sent me volumes of their research and expounded endlessly on their theories. The less said about their "pseudo-science"... the better.

Being a Vietnam veteran myself, I fully understand and appreciate the frustration these veterans feel. However I sincerely urge them to take to heart the evidence presented by your program.

Dennis A. Lawrence

Dear FRONTLINE,
Excellent and well balanced reporting! As a Viet Nam veteran
I know the feelings these heroes are experiencing and there was a
time that I would have whole-heartedly supported their assertions.
But time is the test of truth. We age, we decline, we disease and we
look for reasons other than the nature of human frailty. It is so
much easier to lay blame with a government or a perceived cover-
up of negligence than to recognize that we have fallen into a range
of statistical probability. Sometimes accepting the fact that there is
no one to blame can be the most effective therapy.

Dear FRONTLINE,
"Dear" Frontline: As a person with CFIDS, I am terribly upset
by your distorted report. Many of us CFIDS sufferers, as well as
the GW vets, have had to put up with this "it's all in your head"
attitude for much too long. You have obviously, not investigated
all the facts thoroughly. I feel a new investigation is in order, with
an apology to our brave soldiers! Shame on you for your shabby
reporting! The cover-up continues...
    JNW
    MA FMS/CFS Support Group Co-Leader

Dear FRONTLINE,
Frontline has proven itself to be the best investigative
journalism to be found in any medium, from your excellent
coverage of breast implants, to now this, the controversy
surrounding Gulf War Syndrome.
    If there was any deficiency in your presentation—and this is
nit-picky because I realize you have time and production
constraints—is that you did not mention Mr. Michael Fumento,
who has been one of the only print journalists I am aware of that
has questioned the validity of Gulf War Syndrome (March 1997,
Reason magazine) as reported in other media.
    That the New York Times, self-righteously adhering to
disclosure of public and private information only when it suits
their own interests, would refuse an interview is not very

surprising. I think it is important to draw up a short but health list of journalists who really blew this story, starting with none other than Ed Bradley. People may have forgotten about Alar, but let's not forget what Bradley has done here.

In sum, you have done a great service not only to objective science-policy reporting, but a service to our veterans who deserve to know the truth.

Sincerely,
Eric "Ace" Croddy
San Francisco, CA

Dear FRONTLINE,
The story unfolds before me on the TV screen. I am appalled upon the manipulation of ideas and truth that has been seen by my eyes for 8 years now. There are specific things that have been left out. For example the notion of the use of bug juice as being a probable item in the problem. However there was no mention of the bugs that were constantly at our sites of operation. The flies and sand fleas. The other indigenous life there also had effects on us that can not be denied. With the massive amounts of information that was brought back from there, where could all the information be? There have been too many friends that have ended up in the hospital that served with me in the gulf to say that it is coincidence.

New Salisbury, IN

Dear FRONTLINE,
Your show on the Gulf War syndrome was very enlightening and well done. I thought it was interesting Captain Hyams had been able to find similar "syndromes" dating back to the Civil War. It appeared to me from the information presented Gulf War syndrome, Da Costa syndrome, Effort syndrome etc. were all by-products of the various wars. When you consider war overrides the basic instinct of self-preservation is it any wonder there is lasting damage? I found it sad and ironic that the wife of the gentleman with Lou Gehrig's disease attributed her symptoms to "stress" even though she'd been "diagnosed" with Gulf War syndrome!

It was refreshing to here about the facts without the media hype. I learned from your report 1. There is little difference between the National Enquirer and the New York Times and 2. Politicians are and always will be "politicians".
Muldrow, OK

Dear FRONTLINE,
I was appalled at the comment from Dr. Joseph's stab at those who offered theories (no matter how unfounded they were) stating that they were pseudo-scientists. What were many of the great men/women of science before his or her break through? That is what science is about, trying something different and testing it, not discrediting it because you were PAID OFF. I am not a vet, nor do I consider myself patriotic, I just hate wrongdoing.
Mitch Brown
Atlanta, GA

Dear FRONTLINE,
As an ailing Gulf War veteran, I thank you sincerely for your presentation tonight. I thought it was researched very well and presented in a well-balanced manner.

Two points I would like to touch on in regard to your show:

1. Dr. Joyce Lashoff (Chairperson of the President's Advisory Committee on Gulf War Illness) stated that her observations of the oil-well fires left her believing that the flumes blew upward and away from the troops on the ground. She is absolutely wrong in her conclusions. There were no less than three days when the smoke flumes "hugged" the ground and turned the sunlit, bright day into a dark of night. Myself and others traveled the "coastal highway" from Kuwait City down to Saudi Arabia on April 1st, 1991, and the petroleum-thickened air was so impregnated that we choked on oil while breathing through our doubled-up scarves and we were forced to stop and clear the raw petroleum off vehicle windshields and our goggles constantly. At some points on the highway the oil-thickened air was so thick our vehicle headlights could not penetrate the air further than 10-15 feet, and Marine escorts were needed to walk on foot ahead of the vehicles to keep us on the

highway. I was there, and I saw this. Dr. Lashoff hung her hat on erroneous information, as so many others in government have done.

2. Secondly, Dr. Stephen Joseph made the amusing remark on camera that we sick veterans "…wanted a label…" for our illnesses. The sad truth is that we didn't, and don't want for a label for our illness - the Veteran's Administration DOES. Veterans can not be treated, nor compensated for any illness that does not fall under a "labeled" category of disability or illness. We're just trying to satisfy the bureaucratic "wickets" established and enforced by Dr. Joseph and the others in Congress and the DoD.

Respectfully
David Fournier (Mustang)
Captain, US Marine Corps (retired)
Vietnam and Gulf War veteran

Dear FRONTLINE,
I think the program was right on target. It's time to move on and accept that there is no Gulf War Syndrome. Almost every pro Syndrome letter speaks about cover-ups, etc. Get a grip. This is the same government that couldn't even end the war! 7 years later Saddam is still winning. How in heavens name would this same government conduct a cover up that would have to include other soldiers, media, doctors, nurses, medical journals and thousands of minor bureaucrats? The same science you want to cure you is the same science that you say is covering it up. Which way do you want it? I wish someone else would pay my medical bills and provide me with a pension too but I didn't do anything to deserve it. And yes, I am a veteran.
Ft Myers, FL

Dear FRONTLINE,
I found your program on the Gulf War Syndrome to be very informative. I also appreciated the clarity of Dr. Lashof's and Dr. Joseph's answers and statements. When people get sick, they want to know the name of their illness, the expected length, severity, and cause. The unknown can be very scary. However, when stress is named as the cause, many people take offense. Somehow, we wish

143

to see ourselves as capable of dealing with all of life's stresses. After all, it appears as though everyone else does. Denial is a useful tool when reality is overwhelming, but sadly, it can also prevent people from receiving valuable help. Our health care system also reflects this lack of trust by contributing minimal funds towards mental health. Are there qualified psychologists available for those Veterans who are willing to try therapy?

Dear FRONTLINE,
As an Explosive Ordnance Disposal technician during Desert Storm it was my job to "blow-up" or burn any captured or unexploded ordnance found in order to protect lives and property. My one question over all this senseless arguing is; why aren't more troops that were with me on the 'front lines' in Kuwait and Iraq (tank crews, Special Forces, etc.) getting sick? We were right there in the middle of the oil fires, DU rounds all around, explosives cooking off, and yet I can still run 5-minute miles.

Also, older nerve agents such as GA and GB (that were in the Iraqi inventory) have cumulative effects. This means that after even a tiny exposure (hoping you survive the atropine and 2PAM-chloride injections) the evidence of exposure will be with you forever.

Overall, a good and balanced piece Frontline.
SSgt Michael Kohler
Arlington, TX

Dear FRONTLINE,
What motive do you have to make one of our nation's top scientist's look so foolish? Dr. Garth Nicolson's finding of HIV-1 env gene within the Mycoplasma is the story, not that he treated one incurable veteran. Why didn't you talk about his findings rather than his theories? You're no better than The New York Times that you also critiqued. Why are scientists finding antibodies to Squalene? Why did the DOD say that they didn't even know what Squalene was (highly experimental adjuvant) but now we know that they even produce it? And about the hospitalization study (The Postwar Hospitalization Experience of Persian Gulf Veterans)-Didn't Dr. Rostker work at the DMDC

when those records were gathered for the study? Isn't he now in charge of the investigation of the illnesses? Isn't he responsible for the Manpower and Reserve Affairs? (Isn't this a conflict of interest?) When you interviewed Joseph, you let him get away with comparing our CHRONIC ILLNESS with a large city's population which would have the same number of hospitalizations, but WE ARE STILL GOING TO THE HOSPITALS! WE ARE STILL SICK! (And dying) And didn't the hospitalization report find that prior to the war we were at less risk of hospitalization? NOT NOW! And didn't that study contradict itself about how many service member's records were used? VA's literature for September 1993 shows that the study's number of participants would have to be 120,000 less than reported. Who did those other 120,000 records belong to? Start asking the real questions!

Mark Langenkamp
Ozark, AL

Dear FRONTLINE,
I'm a former Marine who served time in the Gulf from start to finish. Over the past years my health has turned poor. I'm 28 years old and feel like I'm 80. I went to the VA for help but it was no good. I have bad heart and stomach. Were do we go for help? We served our country with pride but now they have turned their backs on us. If we were locked up at one of the many Federal Prisons the government would have to take care of us!

Mark Prater
Memphis, TN

Dear FRONTLINE,
I am a Gulf War Vet and am currently 60% disabled. I was in perfect health prior to going to the Gulf. I believe that we were exposed to something that is causing us to age rapidly. The current investigations only make conjectures that it was a combination of things we were exposed to. I do not believe this as I did not use pesticides, PB, etc. I did, however, receive the anthrax vaccine. This is the only difference I have found between those in my unit who are ill and those who are not.

Vera Roddy

Milwaukee, WI

Dear FRONTLINE,
As much as one must sympathize with the suffering of many gulf war vets, I strongly believe that there is no physiological basis for a "gulf war syndrome". I think frontline's very balanced report showed this clearly.

It is a fact of life that when bad things happen to people, one of the first responses is to try and place blame. How sad that so many have fueled the fire on this subject, only adding to the suffering already being experienced by those involved.

It should be clear to any OBJECTIVE observer that those have manufactured the "syndrome" seeking to advance their own interests. Shame on them! They are providing much more damage than comfort!
Washington, DC

Dear FRONTLINE,
After seeing the program this evening I feel even stronger now that this was a major cover up by the US government. All the special panels set up to review the situation were only created as smoke screens to take the public's focus away from the cover up. The government stands to loose public support for any future military action in the Gulf in the event that the UN weapons inspectors cannot properly verify Saddam's weapons capabilities. Here we are seven years later and we still cannot get this thorn (Saddam) out of our side. I have a very high distrust for our government. It's amazing the level of incompetence at the Pentagon, and our taxes are paying for this.
Bill Hoddy
Tempe, AZ

Dear FRONTLINE,
What a load of crap. And so well done. It's clear that real professionals wrote this propaganda and that this is a staged event for the benefit of the Pentagon.

I am disgusted that PBS has broadcast this sad excuse for journalism. Did anyone read the Shays committee report? Did anyone read Patrick Eddington's book? Has anyone investigated why more than 10 Gulf War vets have ALS, Lou Gehrig's disease, a rate that is more than 10 times the norm? Or why the fabled birth defect study only counted births through the end of 1993? And only children born to active duty soldiers? What about the Czech chemical weapons detections? Why was Dr. Jonathan Tucker summarily dismissed from the Presidential Advisory Commission after he indicates that he thought vets were exposed to chemical weapons?

The Pentagon and PBS as its mouthpiece are suffering from a serious case of terminal denial.

You can bet that PBS will never get a dollar of my money. And I can guess where the money for this load of crap came from.

Andrew Cederstrom
Massachusetts

Dear FRONTLINE,

I spent seven months in the Gulf where I served as the Chemical Officer for the 11th Air Defense Brigade (the SCUD Busters). If chemical agents were used I would have known since had units form my Brigade stationed all over the theater of war. Not a single soldier ever reported a single incident. How do you hide a chemical incident? This would be the Mother-of-all cover-up of which, by default, I would be a part. Let's stop the hype and distortion and find what is causing the health problems that Gulf vets are having.

Earl Henderson
Rome, New York

Dear FRONTLINE,

I am completely shocked that Frontline would stoop to a new low in tabloid journalism. Your entire hour of one-sided coverage on Gulf War Syndrome was nothing more than propaganda for the military-industrial complex. Where were the many, highly-respected medical researchers who have shown with numerous brain SPECT and PET scans, immunological testing, brain-mapping, balance-testing, and so forth, that the symptoms of the Gulf War vets could not have been caused simply by stress. You gave that "spin" doctor from the DOD about half an hour of airtime and the only opposing view was a few minutes from some flaky doctor.

I am really sick that PBS would have the gall to present this program as "journalism." I guess when your bills are paid by ADM; we have to be a lot more skeptical about your biases.

Laurel Ballou
Bothell, WA

Dear FRONTLINE,
The things that I noted in the show had more to do with what the "scientists" didn't do with regard to investigating the causes of this syndrome. Mainly, they didn't even make an expedition to those sites to gather data about the conditions, soil samples, etc.

I would say that what they were accomplishing was more of a debating society than proper scientific methodology. I'm curious as to whether or not these esteemed (sic) individuals have any notion of what proper scientific investigational techniques are. They seemed to place more credence in the literature of the past and their own theories than today's data and letting that create the theory. They might also be well advised to realize that Gulf War Syndrome might be a variety of sources rather than a single one. Anything can be a factor right down the powdered camel dung dust stirred up by the passage of armored vehicles. NO factor is too insignificant.

Rick Fallstrom
Bremerton, WA

Dear FRONTLINE,
Excellent program, very thorough examination of the issues and the protagonists. Disturbing to see the publicity-hungry politicians in action with no real interest in defining the problem. The President's Commission did us all proud the way that they conducted their thorough and logical examination of the facts. Their findings that the Gulf Veterans illnesses were not a unique syndrome, but were what could be expected in any population group of 750,000.

Does anyone else see the similarity to the medical studies that showed that the silicon breast implant population of 1,000,000 has the same percentage of the same medical problems as 1,000,000 women without implants...and that the implants are just as much in denial of the medical facts as the Gulf War Syndrome Vets!

Redondo Beach, CA

Dear FRONTLINE,

On the subject of the program you just aired on the Persian Gulf War and the effect on Gulf War Veterans - Gulf War Syndrome/Illness, I am very disturbed that you had someone like Dr. Joseph make the statements that he made at the end of the program.

This man has done nothing for the Gulf War Veterans, but call us nothing more then stressed out crazies, who are suffering from nothing more then their own sick mind games.

I, as a veteran am appalled by his remarks, and I am here to tell you that the government tried that with me, thanks to an Army shrink that knew nothing about me, and without even doing any testing, he hung on me the PTSD anchor. It took me almost three years, and five different shrinks to finally get them to admit that I didn't have PTSD, Combat Stress, or any other stress related effects of the war.

Why don't you do something more constructive then have a program that is orchestrated to the slant of the government who have been trying to hide the truth from the veterans and the public for the past seven years. I thought that your Network was for truth and based on facts, not on lies and deception.

We veterans are not like our father, grandfathers or great grandfathers, who took the words of the government as the truth, even though they knew that it wasn't, when it came to Vietnam, Korea, WWII, WWI. The government has always lied to its soldiers when it was for the good of the government. All they want to do is cover their own behinds to secure that they don't go to jail for putting their soldiers in harms way.

We are the soldiers of the new military, who are smarter, able to think on our feet faster fight better and with less effort then our forefathers did. We know how to use the deadliest weapons on

149

earth known to man today. We can analyze situation come to a conclusion and act on the conclusion, ten times faster than our forefathers ever could imagine.

Why don't you do something on the Gulf War Veterans, who are sick, but are fighting from every corner of this country from our homes, because we can't do the fighting anymore on our feet, because they don't work that well nowadays, due to degenerative joint diseases, chronic fatigue, memory loss and a multitude of other ailments that make us less then half as what we were before the war.

I am posting this also to the Veterans Web Net to let all veterans know who we are, and what we are. We will not, and have not taken a back seat to the governments inability of not telling us the truth, and we will get the truth told as to what has happened to all of us.

Respectfully,
Ken Rogers, Sr.
PGWVIRC
Leavenworth, Ks

Dear FRONTLINE,
Thank you Frontline for finally putting together a report that was factual on GWS! I have watched the sensationalist reporting from many other groups in the press, and vote-grabbing politicians with dismay for years. I am a Gulf War vet and can speak from first hand experience that there has been made "much to do about nothing". Yes, there are stress-related symptoms in many vets, and the expected number that have contracted real illness since the war but there is no "syndrome". Maybe we can let this fiasco die and help these vets get on with their lives. Believing a lie is the worst way to waste one's life.

Seattle. WA

Dear FRONTLINE,
There is absolutely no scientific evidence that stress caused the Gulf veterans' illnesses. Psychiatric diagnoses are diagnoses of exclusion. Chemicals may have caused the veterans' illnesses via a general mechanism known as "toxicant-induced loss of tolerance,"

150

a theory of disease we have published on in the NIH journal Environmental Health Perspectives. The theory, which is backed by numerous clinical observations, states that a subset of more susceptible persons who are exposed to various chemicals or chemical mixtures may lose their prior, natural tolerance for common low-level chemical exposures, foods, and drugs that never were a problem for those individuals before and that don't affect most people. Subsequently, symptoms are triggered by such exposures. Classical toxicology does not explain this problem.

I am a university researcher who serves as a consultant to the VA, is a member of the VA's national advisory committee on the Gulf War veterans' illnesses, and has done research on low level organophosphate (related to nerve agent) health effects. I also testified before Congressman Shay's committee and the Presidential Advisory Committee at their invitation. The latter made no mention of the research on toxicant-induced loss of tolerance (the TILT Theory of Disease, as it has been dubbed) in its final report. The TILT theory of diseases poses a testable hypothesis that has not been explored adequately by the federal agencies concerned with the Gulf veterans' illnesses.

Because TILT involves a general mechanism for disease (like the germ theory), there may be diverse symptoms reported by those affected, just as the symptoms of infectious disease run the gamut. Dr. Nicholas Ashford of M.I.T. and I just published the second edition of our book, Chemical Exposures: Low Levels and High Stakes (which has received professional acclaim by JAMA and other mainstream medical and scientific, peer-reviewed journals. The book details this theory and it potential to explain the Gulf veterans' health problems. Unfortunately, the research recommendations other scientists and we have made for testing this theory have not been pursued by either the VA or DOD. Congressman Sanders is aware of our work and its relationship to the Gulf veterans problems as well as to the problems reported by civilians with exposure to new carpet emissions and other low level mixtures. If you are interested in further information, please contact me.

It is important to bear in mind that until just recently most physicians believed that ulcers were caused by stress. The physician who first proposed that ulcers were due to the bacterium, Helicobacter pylori was ridiculed, until he proved its causative role by infecting himself with this agent. We must not be too hasty to invoke stress as a cause for illnesses we do not fully understand before we have exhaustively ruled out other plausible (and testable) etiologies.

Claudia S. Miller, MD
San Antonio, TX
millercs@uthscsa.edu

Dear FRONTLINE,
Good program. Raise new question. Why doesn't DOD list Stress as a "Line of duty" disability. Why doesn't acknowledge the Stress related medical illness as a Disability. Why doesn't the VA acknowledge the same? Until that happens Veteran will denied treatment and compensation for Stress and Stress-related illnesses. The DOD and VA have not put action behind the statements in this program. The senate arms committee and veterans affairs committee has not acted on this issue yet.

V.Hammack
Lynn, MA
ckdc05a@prodigy.com

Dear FRONTLINE,
It is painfully obvious that the producers began this project with the preconceived notion that the syndrome doesn't exist. There also seemed to be a bias against the veterans.

Speaking as a veteran of the Agent Orange (Dioxin) struggle, I am experiencing deja vu. We were not taken seriously, then abandoned, too. The Gulf War Vets are being treated with the same disdain that my unfortunate brothers in arm who served in Southeast Asia. (Dioxin use was not confined to just South Vietnam).

The Veterans of my era were asking for the same answers as the Gulf War Vets are seeking now. They want to know everything the DOD is hiding that will provide a definitive answer about what is causing their ailments (and it is NOT STRESS). Next, the veterans want the government to provide effective treatment for the aching muscles, fatigue, insomnia, etc. that seems to afflict most of them. Finally, those who are disabled by this syndrome want the VA to recognize that it is a 100% disability and compensate them accordingly without the obstacles that Vietnam Era veterans were forced to endure.

The issue is treating many seriously ill veterans. It is not about protecting some bureaucrats' or generals' retirement benefits.

Dear FRONTLINE,

I think your show missed the point. The point is that, this "all in your head," answer is the standard answer that I received from the VA. For me, I really did not have an opinion one way or another about this. Then after three years of the VA telling me there was nothing wrong with me I had back pain? A civilian doctor saw me and found out that instead of my head it was in my back. Bad enough that I had spinal fusion a year ago. My wife and I even tried to have a child, it ended in miscarriage. So what is my point? I actually had something wrong with me that was not in my head. And because of the miscarriage I am not all that sure about trying again. As for Doctor Joseph, his association with early aids researches? If I remember right, did they get that right at first?

I would have liked to see your program show the facts not someone tell me what the facts are. Like calling cape fear hospital in Fayetteville and ask them how many birth defect babies they had before the gulf war and then after? I think that is called research? See, a majority of families go to a civilian doctor using this thing called champus and that means the military families have the kids at civilian hospitals, not military hospitals. Which means if that data DOD uses is based on births at military hospitals? The data would at the very least be incomplete? Yes or no?

Bottom line I expected better from your show then what I saw.
Mike R
Sanford, NC
airthief@aol.com

Dear FRONTLINE,

It appears as if PBS/Frontline is the last remaining pocket of scientific objectivity left in the American media. Shame on Life Magazine, the NY Times, and all the other tabloids who are unwilling or unable to understand the statistical facts of (the imaginary) Gulf War Syndrome.

I wish Frontline did the daily news too. There would be no need to watch any other channel!

Tom Gilson
Salt Lake City

Dear FRONTLINE,

This was a perfect example of PBS putting their heads in the sand. The CDC (William Reeves, M.D.) said in September that GWS was CFS. Major General Blank said the same thing several years ago. If the right tests were done, each GWS patient would show abnormalities...i.e. SPECT scans, full lymphocyte panel, and a circulating blood volue test. It seems PBS is as determined to sweep this under the rug. Why such a non-scientific interview with Dr. Garth Nicolson? Why not even say what MI was? He has published in peer reviewed medical journals. Why was he driven from the MD Cancer Institute in Texas? Why not let outside experts that have asked test the serums of the inoculations given to GWS vets such as Dr. W. John Martin, formally of the NCI? Your show had less scientific knowledge but was certainly strong in the field of government psychobabble. Shame on you!

National CFIDS Foundation, Inc.
Needham, MA
Gailronda@aol

Dear FRONTLINE,

I watched in great interest your Frontline report on the Gulf War Syndrome. As a Gulf War veteran myself I am greatly concerned with the apparent governmental cover-up on this issue. I served as a Marine in a forward area on the border between Kuwait and Saudi Arabia and witnessed first-hand the many chemical detection alarms that sounded daily. It is my opinion that so many detection units sounding so many times, at the same time, was not a "glitch in the system", as much government reporting agencies would have you believe.

I was a first-hand witness to many unexploded and exposed chemical munitions that absolutely littered certain areas of the theater of operations. That a number, however small, of our troops became exposed at one time or another to chemicals cannot be refuted. Bureaucrats in Washington who have more than likely never even seen, much less set foot in, the areas in question cannot make a fair judgment on whether or not our troops were exposed to chemicals. Exposure by accident or by design is not the issue.

The issue is that some of our troops were exposed and is experiencing the aftermath of that exposure—no matter what all the documentation that tries to prove otherwise says. That many veterans cannot be suffering from mass delusions or hysteria.

I, myself, have suffered from extreme depression and memory loss. Due to the fact that depression seems to run in my family I have not tried to seek any reparations from the government. However, due to my memory problems I have given up my job as an Intelligence Analyst in the Marine Corps and have had to settle with the menial job of delivering appliances for a living. The depression that I have suffered through has, in my opinion, been the cause of my divorce and a recent suicide attempt. The Veteran's Administration, however, has been taking steps to recognize that there is a serious problem with us Gulf War veterans. I have had the opportunity to take part in counseling sessions that related directly to depression caused by the "Syndrome" and have made great progress. A lot of other Veterans of the Gulf War are not being taken as seriously and is seemingly being brushed aside by our own government. This is a genuine travesty and shouldn't be tolerated.

Thank you again for your candor and open mindedness in the reporting of this issue. I hope that it opens some eyes and brings to light the genuine problems that our great nation has in dealing with concerns of this nature and scope.

Gary A. Adelhardt, Jr.
ex-LCpl. USMC
Albuquerque, NM

Chapter VII

Dealing with the stress

On April 26, 2000, I found out that SGT David Kagels was in a nursing home in the Buffalo New York from his wife via email.

She told me that he was in for a broken leg but he also was in with MS that was diagnosed 2 years ago.

He was rated at 30% from the Veterans Administration in New York, at which time I started calling and sending email to my Senators and Congressman and finally to President Clinton but no response except an electronic message saying that they received and someone would look into the issue.

And at that time I decided to fly to New York when his wife can change her work schedule with Wal-Mart and spend the weekend to at least show that I care since I am going through some of the same problems that David is at this time.

Chapter VIII
The Return Home

Returning home back in Europe after the Gulf War while supporting the 1st Infantry Division since they were assigned to VII Corps from Stuttgart Germany. It was like something that you only see in films and imagine from time to time. Instead of going to the United States we had to return back to our home base which was Ludwigsburg Germany right outside of Stuttgart. We arrived to the Stuttgart Flughaven and went through processing and were loaded on busses and it was like a rush that is really hard to explain to anyone.

On August 5, 1999 My son Mark Anthony Krob enlisted in the US Army he wanted to go Infantry Airborne, Ranger but what he got was Signal Airborne and Fort Bragg, North Carolina. He is going to the XVIII Airborne Corps... Just talked to a friend of mine SGM Luis Lopez and asked him to look after my kid eventhough he does not need that. I am proud of him and I have no doubt 4 years after I got out that he will be all he can be... August 6, 1999, I decided to go to the Dallas Cowboys Training Camp in Wichita Falls in north Texas and would like to talk to another gulf war veteran number 95 of the Cowboys Chad Hennings... I would like to get his view on this and would like to interview him if he has the time. One of the few benefits left for retirees is staying on a military installation for $8.50 a night... It was Worth the drive here to see them since that is one thing I wanted to do before I die and with what is going on it could be tomorrow. Right now I am taking 33 pills a day and trying to function normally if there is such a thing. Well, I tried to speak with Cowboys Defensive Lineman but was not able to get closer than 30 feet, but if you look at it like it should be viewed they like their personal time as much as we want ours in civilian life. This morning it was pleasant outside and not too muggy. I was hotter than hell today at the training camp in Wichita Falls Texas it seemed like it was 105 degrees outside.

Chapter IX
After Effects

Fibromyalgia

Coping with the pain

Originally published in Mayo Clinic Health Letter, October 1997

You hurt all over. Your muscles are so stiff in the morning it's hard to get moving. You feel constantly fatigued but have trouble sleeping. Yet, your doctor can't seem to find anything specifically wrong with you.

This is a familiar scenario for people with fibromyalgia. Recently, the diagnosis of fibromyalgia has increased. Some estimates suggest that as many as 2 percent of all Americans are affected.

But there's still much that remains unknown about fibromyalgia. For that reason, it's controversial and a focus of medical debate. Here's what we know and don't know about the condition, and what you can do to try to relieve symptoms.

Widespread pain

Fibromyalgia is a disorder involving chronic pain in your muscles, ligaments and tendons. It's often called fibromyalgia syndrome, meaning that it's not a specific illness but a condition that involves several symptoms that occur together.

Before the American College of Rheumatology endorsed the term fibromyalgia in 1990, the condition was referred to by names such as fibrositis, chronic muscle pain syndrome, psychogenic rheumatism and tension myalgias.

The main symptom of fibromyalgia is chronic pain—an "aching all over." The pain may be a deep ache or a burning sensation. It's often accompanied by stiffness and discomfort in your muscles, tendons and ligaments.

Although the condition may feel like a joint disease, it isn't a form of arthritis and it doesn't cause deformity in your joints.

Fibromyalgia may be associated with difficulty sleeping, fatigue, anxiety, stress, depression, numbness, headaches, tingling in your hands and feet, digestive problems and sensitivity to weather and temperature changes.

Symptoms may come and go but typically never disappear completely. They're often most severe during the first year you have the condition. Although it tends to be chronic, fibromyalgia isn't progressive, crippling or life-threatening.

Theories as to a cause

Doctors have yet to learn what causes fibromyalgia. There are many theories, but none has been proven. One theory is that certain factors—such as stress, poor sleep, physical or emotional trauma or being out-of-shape—may trigger the condition in people who are more sensitive to pain.

Some scientists believe the syndrome may be linked to an injury or trauma that affects your central nervous system. Researchers are also exploring possible associations with chemical or hormonal differences, infections or psychological or psychiatric factors.

The condition is diagnosed much more often in women than men. Some doctors theorize that fibromyalgia may be more common in men than figures indicate, but that men are less likely to see a doctor for general aches and pains.

Not a simple diagnosis

Fibromyalgia is difficult to diagnose. There isn't a test that can confirm or rule out the condition. In addition, many of its symptoms mimic other diseases, such as low thyroid hormone production, Lyme disease and rheumatoid arthritis.

Often, people with fibromyalgia will go through several medical tests, only to have the results come back normal—yet their pain is very real. It's usually when other conditions have been dismissed that a diagnosis of fibromyalgia is made.

The American College of Rheumatology has established some general diagnostic guidelines for fibromyalgia to help in the assessment and study of the condition. They include having widespread aching for at least 3 months and at a minimum of 11 locations on your body that are abnormally tender under relatively mild pressure. These areas are called tender points.

However, not all doctors agree with the guidelines. Some believe that the criteria are too rigid and that you can have fibromyalgia even if you don't meet the required number of tender points. Others question how reliable and valid tender points are as a diagnostic tool.

There's also some controversy among physicians whether fibromyalgia is really a distinct condition or part of a larger group of disorders.

What you can do

There's no known cure for fibromyalgia. But a combination of these steps may help reduce symptoms:

Stress reduction—Develop a plan to avoid or limit overexertion and emotional stress. Allow yourself time each day to relax. That may mean learning how to say "no" without guilt. But, don't change your routine totally. People who quit work or drop all activity tend to do worse than those who remain active.

Regular exercise—At first, exercise may increase your pain. But doing it regularly often improves symptoms. Appropriate exercises include walking, swimming, biking and water aerobics. Aim for at least 20 to 30 minutes of exercise four or more times a week. Stretching and good posture are also helpful. Keep your activity on an even level. If you do too much on your "good" days, you may have more "bad" days.

Adequate sleep—Fatigue makes symptoms worse. Try to develop regular sleep hours and get adequate rest each night.

Education—Learning more about fibromyalgia and its symptoms is often helpful. You may also find comfort from support groups.

Medications—Modest doses of over-the-counter pain relievers may eliminate some of your pain and stiffness. Your doctor may also prescribe small doses of certain antidepressant medications that help promote deep sleep. Side effects of the antidepressants can include dry eyes and mouth, constipation and increased appetite.

Other techniques—Some people get relief from massages, hot baths and relaxation techniques.

Fortunately, doctors have found that these lifestyle changes, sometimes coupled with medications, can relieve symptoms or even make them disappear.

For more information Fibromyalgia - Coping with very real pain

The Iraqi Assets claim

There is quite a bit of controversy of this issue, and so the material on this page is purely subjective.

In September 1990 George Bush signed a executive order freezing Iraqi Assets held in the states.

The big bank in question is the "Banca Nazionale del Lavoro", and nearly $4 billion in funds used for Iraqi weapons purchases. The bank was in Atlanta Georgia and faced criminal proceedings, including legislative action. The CIA, Department of Agriculture, Department of Energy, State Department, and several others had varying ties to this.

The Department of Justice sluggishly moved on it, and Congress as well as the DOJ would be squeezed into forgetting the deal. The rulings by the Supreme Court left so many loop holes, and even stated for the record that the Government has with held vital data concerning this.

The BNL scandal was happening while we fought for America in Iraq. The $1.5 billion held in the vaults would end up matching the money lost in the BNL scandal, thus leading to the Iraqi Central Bank that both British and American officials believed were above international law (immunity from prosecution).

George had been dealing with Saddam Hussein throughout the Reagon administration, and helped in countless arms deals with Iraq. He had at one time divulged intelligence data to Iraq (during a meeting with them) on key locations to strike in Iran during the Iran/Iraq war.

He also supplied weapons grade biological samples to Iraq to help with their bioweapons program in the 1980's.

I believe as long as George Bush is in the political circles he will make sure that the money is forgotten, thus not drawing Iraq, and others to move the world courts to file against the US for criminal actions. The insuing trial would no doubt show Bush's ties from 1984 to present over the Iraqi War machine.

A while back Congress moved to free the assets, and this quickly fell apart. The big problem was that the Tobacco Industry was first in line for a piece of the pie, that however has been changed.

The whole thing still dissolved in the usual Congressional manner.

What does this mean to me the veteran:

Why you file a claim against Iraq for damages done to your person. Health, financial, and lively hood. You might see .10 cents on the dollar for your claim when they finally release these assets someday.

Something is better than nothing.

How to file

Mail the 1-96 Form CERTIFIED receipt to the address listed here:

Foreign Claims Settlement Commission
Attn: Iraq Claims Registrant
Washington, DC 20579
OMB control No. 1105 - 0067

Misinformation from the Special Assistant for Gulf War Illnesses: On January 23rd, 2002 they finally announced the members for the Gulf War Advisory Panel to the VA. Only 3 years after it was supposed to be constituted. In keep with VA tradition of helping the vets too late. It has some good names on the list like Steve Robinson, James Tuitte, and Lea Steele—but Dr. Vinh Camm wasn't brought on board. No doubt because of the efforts of Roger Kaplan and Kelly Brix. On January 24th, 2002 - the House Committee on Veteran Affairs and the House Committee on Government reform had hearings on Gulf War Illness. It was a all star line up of the good, the bad, and the ugly. Former Senator Donald Reigle spoke at the VA subcommittee - and he rocked the house. Ross Perot spoke at the Reform Committee, speaking out against OSAGWI's stress team PR campaign to hurt vets. Warren Rudman defended DOD policy and decision, which is no surprise to the Gulf War veterans he has insulted to impose his twisted ideas of what he believes is right. Both committees believe GW veterans deserve better, they did not defend Bioport or DOD in any way. On the DOD / VA death squad defended their programs, and that is why most of us was want the following removed from office:

Dr. Mark Brown
Dr. John Feussner

Dr. Susan Mathers
Dr. Mike Kilpatrick
Dr, Francis Murphy
Kelly Brix
Roger Kaplan
Sue Bailey

These people are not only out of touch with the veterans; they have insulted veterans rather than help them myself included. Then we have the VA's recent **Gulf War Birth Defect survey** only confirming earlier GAO reports that Gulf War veterans had reproductive disorders. Too late to benefit the families, and the poor children of these families. Yet, **Walter Reed Army Hospital** and the **Naval Research Group** struggle to make the **Millennium Cohort Study** produce bogus results showing a happy and healthy Army. They already tried to make Hep C sound nonexistent, though VA figures show otherwise. In the **CHIPPM MWMR** report the fact that 33% of Illness suffered while serving the Military overseas are *UNDEFINED*. In Military terms, if it was something we dot want the public to know about - we use the term undefined and push the soldier's aside. This has gone on for 10 years with Gulf War vets.

The **Gulf War Presumption Bill** is now Public Law **107-103** as the House Committee forgets to update the language to reflect 5 years instead of ten year extension window. We win a bonus by accident. While the new **Clinical Practice Guidelines** leave active duty Gulf War soldiers in IATROGENIC SOMATIZATION hell - we wait to see if programs like the **Military Health Veterans Coordinating Board** will even have their charter renewed to continue some sort of cross communication between agencies to regulate any Gulf War programs. It has come to our attention that altering the **Feres Doctrine** maybe our only hope of getting anything meaningful out of the Pentagon. Since the Commanding staff lacks the integrity to own up to its mistakes, it is necessary for changes to the doctrine to allow these soldiers the same rights other American citizens have. The Pentagon doesn't believe its soldiers have rights, and yet these people were first on the scene to defend this country overseas. So by altering the Feres Doctrine we can hopefully speed up legal channels, and improve the quality of life for those veterans suffering at the hands of

163

a dishonest Pentagon.. Not to worry, by joining our list you will see that OSAGWI will also see your message as well - they (and many other government agencies) monitor us daily for news and updates.

Sincerely

Kirt P. Love

Disabled Gulf War Veteran and Webmaster

The Army Security Review Protocols

When the Army was first tasked to review its own classified records, this would spark the beginning of the real cover-up. In these Army records, they basically admit that the records database was massive, and damaging to National Security. There would be more than 21,000,000 Army records alone.

These records groups would be deliberately milked, tampered with in mass, and even many records deliberately destroyed.

OSAGWI stated they had reviewed materials since 1996 based on medical relevance. These protocols were the buzzwords used to screen those military record groups.

Hundreds of thousands of damaging files never made it to daylight. "Excluded" from Gulf War Records Group and "Exemption 1" were continually used to death.

Anyways, here is the Security Review Protocols for the United States Army. They were also used by the Marines, Navy, Air Force, and other declassification teams as the template. See for yourself.

Chapter X
Hassles with the Government

I called Senator Phil Gramms office and was told by him that we had to wait on the outcome from the VA medical board and he would let me know of their findings. Attached mail to President Clinton and Vice President Gore and the responses that you get via electronic Email... Then someone from the Veterans Administration calls you back wanting to know what the

problems are, but have been helpful on one occasion and helped my claim only took one week after 1 and ½ years in the Waco Veterans Administration. Below is a actual letter that was sent to and not even a response, this is how our money is going to work for us lonely people that serve our country.

Honorable Sam Gejdenson, Ranking Democrat House Committee of International Relations 2304 Rayburn House Office Building Washington, DC 20515

Dear Sir,

This is in reference to H.R. 618, "The Gulf War Veterans' Iraqi Claims Protection Act." I believe that when this bill comes in front of The House Committee on International Relations someone up on the HILL should finally stand up for the Veterans like myself that are really falling apart and should stand up for our rights as AMERICANS. If it was not for normal people like myself that give their life to our nation and lost an excellent career due to health problems and that continue to worsen on a daily basis.

To give you a little insight I have lost jobs since arriving to the Civilian Sector and trying to maintain a normal life of some sort. Just about to loose everything that I have worked for in my 39 years of life and 15 years of Excellent Military Service until having to take the early retirement as an Sergeant First Class in the United States Army in May 1995. At which time I am getting behind on medical bills and on the verge of loosing another job at which I make 56K a year. I have a Graduate Degree in Computer Systems Engineering. The last person that I wrote to was Senator Phil Gramm and still no response.

If a bill comes to anyone in the Congress or Senate there should be no Questions asked except what can we do for our Veterans? But Since arriving back from the Gulf War it seems that not only my personal life but physical being has constantly been hurt in one way or another. So the final questions is what have you done for a Veteran lately?

Finally, could you please respond back to this letter so that I know you did receive it from me and what you and your associates are willing to do?

PLEASE Below is a list of all of the medications that I take on a daily basis.

Acetaminophen 500 mg 6 tablets a day
Buspirone 10mg 3 tablets a day.
Ambien 10 mg at bedtime
carisprodol 350 mg 3 tablets a day
allopurinol 300 mg 1 tablet a day
prednisone 20mg tablet a day
nortriptyline 10 mg a day
Cimetidine 400mg 2 tablets a day
Fluoxetine hcl 20mg 2 tablets a day
Atenolol 25mg 1 tablet a day
Isomthptn 2 tablets a day

Some of the problems that I am having are as follows: And am rated at 70% disability from the Veterans Administration. But still not able to say that this is Gulf War problems. I have lost 2 jobs since leaving the military due to medical problems. I have been to 6 different hospitals in and out of the Army and to this day eventhough I have been through multiple testing environments and weeks of testing no one still seems to know what the problem is of even how to deal with this for the rest of our lives. At the last count about 250,000 service members were sick and that is totally unacceptable by anyones standards.

Fibromalgya - Headaches, joint and muscle pain, memory loss, sleeping problems
Sarcoidosis
Hypertension
Gastritis
GAUT

PTSD (Post Traumatic Stress Disorder)
The main doctors that I am seeing are:

Dr. James Woessner, MD, PhD, FCERA
214-353-4950
2 times a week for pain

Dr. John H. Harney, M.D.
Dallas Neurological Associates
375 Municipal Drive Suite 222
Richardson, Texas 75080
972-783-8900

Dr. Michael Brophy, MD Dallas VA
214-857-0912
Every 6 months or when needed, Medication monitor

Dr. Emmitt, MD Dallas VA
214-857-0916
Working on the PTSD Evaluation for the Gulf War since there are none at the present time.

All of your help is appreciated.

Randy Stamm
Sergeant First Class (ret)
United States Army
General Frederick Franks (Commander, VII Corps)
Q: How big a force was this that you were commanding, how destructive?
Franks: You can go back to the battle in the Ardennes and General Patton's Third Army… Third Army essentially making a 90-degree turn and going to the relief of the forces in Bastogne, I believe that whole unit that went to the relief there was about the size of maybe one and a fraction of another one of our divisions, so we were .. VII Corps was a World War II army, probably about the size of George Patton's Third Army in World War II terms .. considerable combat power and the capability of the equipment, Apache

167

helicopters, M1/A1 tanks, 120 millimeter tanks the British .. certainly a British equivalent tank, and infantry fighting vehicles, so considerable combat power to fight day and night, fight day and night, fight in bad weather, capability to reach out and hit the Iraqi forces before they even knew we were coming. As a matter of fact some of their prisoners said to us afterwards, one of them said, hey, the tank to the right of me blew up, the tank to the left of me blew up, I couldn't even see what was firing at us, and that was because we were able to hit them in some cases at extended ranges, so a considerable amount of combat power, but the combat power is only realised by superbly trained and motivated soldiers and that's really what made the corps, British and American soldiers, superbly trained, motivated, tough, took the fight to the enemy, well led.

Q: Can you tell the story of that first briefing with General Schwarzkopf...

Franks: We met with General Schwarzkopf, I believe it was Tuesday, we had gone to Saudi Arabia on a leaders reconnaissance, we got notified Thursday, late Thursday evening, we flew down there on Sunday and we met Tuesday. The setting was a dining facility, essentially a mess hall, with flat tables, a small room, and we were all in there, all the senior commanders from all the services were in there, in our case, in 7 Corps, these were all fellow soldiers and members of .. the other services that I knew, we were all combat veterans of Vietnam, of another generation of US soldiers, we had all been products of our own military schooling system, so we all knew each other, so there was a very calm professional atmosphere in the room. On the walls were maps, it turned out they were aerial photographs with covers over the top, and in the front of the room was essentially a podium and General Schwarzkopf came in and delivered the whole briefing himself as the Commander, laid out the whole enemy situation, friendly situation and the four phases of the scheme of manoeuvre, and there was no particular excitement among those of us there in the room, people were calmly taking notes, looking around at each other, a couple of small chit-chats passed back and forth as General Schwarzkopf gave the briefing. He was very clear, very precise in the description we didn't know at the time if we would execute this or not but certainly if you're going to get called on to execute an offensive operation, you need to start to prepare for it well in advance, so that's what the purpose of the briefing was and it was very clear and at the end of it he asked if there were any questions, as I recall there weren't any, and then he invited us.. all to get up and take a look at the maps which showed the Iraqi positions and then showed roughly the sector of operations that we would get to operate in. So I recall, we got up, those of us that would comprise 7 Corps, the US commanders, and walked up to the map - at that point I didn't know that we would have the 1st British Armored Division as part of the US 7 Corps, went up and looked at the map, quickly internalised what I had heard General Schwarzkopf say, I'd never been to Saudi Arabia before and so this was all relatively new to all the commanders, the geography, the names, the Iraqi positions and so forth, so this was rapid internalisation of what had just been said and I was looking at the map and rapidly making up in my own mind schemes of manoeuvre for the Corps, I'd been in command of the Corps well over a year at that point so we had had some operations, and General Schwarzkopf walked up and he said what do you think, Fred, and I .. looking at the map, I said, this'll work, we can do it, and that was it.

Q: You took these guys seriously, they were the fourth largest army in the world ...

Franks: Oh, we were very serious professional soldiers there taking a look at the conditions of the mission, the enemy forces, the terrain, the troops we had available to us and the amount of time that we had to get to the theatre, to essentially make a Cold War Central European Corps into a contingency Corps tailored for that particular mission, which was a considerable undertaking, so all of those things were going through my mind at the time and, no, we did not underestimate the enemy - I don't think we overestimated the enemy either, I believe we were .. we had reasonable information about what their capabilities were, how they fought against the Iranians, so we were .. very sober-minded about Iraqi capabilities.

Q: How did it come about that the Big Red One were the guys who made the breach?

Franks: I went to see General Tom ... who commanded the 1st Infantry Division, the Big Red One, and I really wanted the Big Red One to do the breach so I knew that they had done a lot of work at our national training centre at Fort Owen in California, practising a breach, and I said to Tom, look, I need the division to conduct a breach

169

operation, you've done a lot of that, he said, we'll do it, we know how to do that, we'll do it and we'll do it right and we'd like the mission, and I said, okay Tom, you got it, that was early December.

Q: It was a tough mission.

Franks: It was a tough mission, it was a tough mission on two counts, one the actual breach operation, clearing 24 lanes for the passage then—it turns out the first British armored division to pass through them—and secondly the logistics of the Corps to pass through, and then third it turns out the 1st Cavalry Division to pass through the breach as well, so yes, it was a tough, complex mission, required a lot of rehearsal, required some new techniques developed there in the desert and developed a lot of co-ordination with the 1st British armoured division, so a tough mission but Tom and the Big Red One did it superbly, the soldiers and leaders, they thoroughly rehearsed it and I was very proud of them.

Q: And they were the obvious division, they've got a history.

Franks: Well, they've got great tradition in breach operations, the division was awarded an Arrowhead device for the heroic actions at Omaha Beach, D-Day in Normandy, June 6th 1944, and so it was in that tradition that they carried off this breach superbly and I was proud of them, soldiers and leaders of the Big Red One.

Q: At that stage, you were aware that the life expectancy of the first guys through that breach was not necessarily great and you were going to do everything you could to increase it.

Franks: I knew that I was giving the Big Red One a very tough mission, I knew that the soldiers, especially in the lead vehicles, were going into—they were out on the tip of the spear so to speak, particularly the Arrowhead as it turned out, and that it was a tough mission, and so what I wanted to do was to do everything that I could to provide them the kind of support to minimise our own casualties in the accomplishment of that mission and to be very aggressive in the accomplishment of that breach, and so we did that.

Q: Could you sum up for me, as you prepared for the war, what was your plan?

Franks: As I looked at the disposition of the Iraqi forces, the mission we were given, the troops I had available to me and the time that we had, we had three fights, we had to fight against the front line Iraqi infantry, in essence the Iraqi 7th Corps, as it turns out, then it was a fight against the tactical reverse which was positioned right behind the front line infantry divisions, then it was a fight against the Republican Guards. So those three fights had to be sequenced in a way that would allow us to have our point of main effort initially at the breach and when the success of the breach was assured then to shift that point of main effort to mass against the Republican Guard, so essentially we had three fights, those three.

Q: And you wanted to mass?

Franks: I wanted to mass, I knew that again in the breach mass of fires and rapidly push through the breach, and then secondly to ensure that when we hit the Republican Guards we would go in at full speed, full speed, and that we were massed into a fist - I didn't want to poke at the Republican Guards with some extended fingers or hit them piecemeal, I wanted to hit the Republican Guards with a left hook, with a fist, with a three division fist, and when we hit 'em we'd hit them hard and be through them in a minimum amount of time.

Q: What happens to people who attack in fingers rather than fists?

Franks: What you get is, you get piecemeal commitment, you get lack of coherence in the attack or lack of synchronisation of fires with manoeuvre forces, with ground and air co-ordination, and what you get is you get a chance, a probability of increased casualties, you get the probability of an attack that starts and stops and starts and stops, loses momentum, and you get all those things that you really don't want - what you want to do is you want to hit .. you want to hit at max. speed, you want to hit massed and you want to hit the enemy from an unexpected direction and at a speed that they just can't handle, and that's what we were after.

Q: What sort of forces did you have, I mean I don't know if there's a Second World War analogy or something, but what is a corps, what did you have in Corps?

Franks: We had in 7 Corps, we had 146,000 American and British soldiers, we had 5 divisions, essentially 5 armoured divisions, although one was a mechanised infantry division and one was a cavalry division, essentially 5 armoured divisions. We had close to 1600 tanks, American and British, a sizeable force, a lot of moving parts, we consumed well over 2 million gallons of fuel a day, we had a support command, vital logistics support command of over 26,000 soldiers, we had 15 hospitals, we had over 800 helicopters, a sizeable force, a lot of moving parts.

Q: Is there a sort of Second World War analogy—how big a force was this you were commanding, how destructive?

Franks: Well you can go back to the battle in the Ardennes and General Patton's Third Army, essentially making a 90-degree turn and going to the relief of the forces in Bastogne, I believe that whole unit that went to the relief there was about the size of maybe one and a fraction of another one of our divisions, so we were .. 7th Corps was a World War II army, was about .. probably about the size of George Patton's Third Army in World War Two terms .. considerable combat power and the capability of the equipment, Apache helicopters, M1 .. M1/A1 tanks, 120 millimetre tanks the British .. certainly a British equivalent tank, and infantry fighting vehicles, so considerable combat power to fight day and night, fight day and night, fight in bad weather, capability to reach out and hit the Iraqi forces before they even knew we were coming - as a matter of fact some of their prisoners said to us afterwards, one of them said, hey, the tank to the right of me blew up, the tank to the left of me blew up, I couldn't even see what was firing at us, and that was because we were able to hit them at .. in some cases at extended ranges, so a considerable amount of combat power, but the combat power is only realised by superbly trained and motivated soldiers and that's really what made the corps, British and American soldiers, superbly trained, motivated, tough, took the fight to the enemy, well led.

Q: How serious a force was yours?

Franks: This was a force designed, trained and equipped to defeat the best the Soviets had in Central Europe. It was a powerful maneuvre force, mounted maneuvre force, five armored divisions, 146,000 American and British soldiers, superbly trained, motivated, tough, well led, and a force that could take the fight to the Iraqis day and night, in sandstorms and in the rain, 24 hour capability on the ground and in the air, a considerable combat capability.

Q: You did all that superbly well, but if you hadn't done it ..

Franks: Actually if we hadn't done it, if we'd have committed ourselves piecemeal, if we'd have gotten lack of coherence, you're talking 20,000 plus vehicles in the Corps, if we had done it in a way that would have caused units to attack the Iraqis piecemeal, certainly the probability of casualties would have gone up.

Q: What was the nightmare scenario, why didn't it happen?

Franks: The thing we were most concerned about was getting stalled in the breach and then getting hit by enemy artillery fire that could have included chemicals if the Iraqis had chosen to use a chemical, and to take casualties from artillery, from chemical and also from getting stalled in the breach and getting hung up on mines, so we didn't let that happen, we prepared an exact replica of the Iraqi defensive position and the Big Red One rehearsed it time and time and time again, so that every soldier knew their particular duty, knew their assignment and knew their mission. We also rehearsed the first British armored division passing through the US 1st Infantry Division, so it was thoroughness, it was preparation, it was synchronisation of all of the capabilities available to the Corps air, attack helicopters, artillery, and seeing to it that we did not put ourselves at that kind of disadvantage and so we worked hard at it, we worked hard at it, that's why I wanted to tell General Tom R... early on that, okay Tom, you've got the mission, that would allow him the time to talk it over and to rehearse it and to go over it and make very thorough battle plans. We said in the intent of the Corps that the breach operation would be very detailed planning and very detailed in its preparation and a very closely synchronised, co-ordinated operation, and once that was completed then the rest of the operation would be much more free-falling and much more adept and be force oriented, but the breach had to be very carefully rehearsed and orchestrated in order to accomplish the mission at least cost to the attacking force.

Q: Could you describe the February 8th briefing with Dick Cheney, what was the message you wanted to get across to them?

Franks: The message that I wanted to get across at the 8th of February briefing to both Secretary of Defence, Dick Cheney, and General Powell, Chairman of the Joint Chiefs of Staff, that VII Corps was prepared to fight, VII Corps would accomplish its mission with the plan that I was about to brief. I also wanted to be candid and say this was the 8th of February, all our forces had still not completely closed into the theatre, I wanted to be candid and up front and say there were a few concerns that we still had, but that they were all soluble within the theatre and that the Corps was committed to fight. I also wanted to communicate the message that the support and continuing support of the American people back home, which we felt there in the theatre of operations, that was coming through in cards and letters and the news that we did get, that that was very important, that that was combat power, that that mattered to our soldiers on the battlefield, so those were the messages I wanted to get across, the bottom line being the Corps was ready to fight and the Corps would accomplish its mission.

Q: Cal Waller afterwards grabbed you in the corridor, can you tell me that story?

Franks: We took a break afterwards and Cal thought I had used more than the time that had been allotted to me, I guess I did run over time a little bit but I was talking about a five-division operation here, I was talking about the main attack, and I felt as if this needed to be communicated very clearly, that we would accomplish the mission at least cost, how we envisioned the plan unfolding, and so I felt that those points needed to be made.

Q: Schwarzkopf believed that VII Corps kept treating the Iraqis like they were Soviet army, what do you say to that?

Franks: We treated the Iraqi forces as the Iraqi forces. There was no particular comparison with potential opposing forces in Central Europe with the Soviet forces, we knew they were well equipped, we knew they had recently fought and we also knew that they were essentially two different forces, their front line infantry and their mounted forces, so I don't believe for a minute that we overestimated the capabilities of the Iraqi forces - we didn't want to underestimate them either and certainly numbers do count, there were 11 plus divisions squared up in our zone of attack. To begin our attack, 4 attacking 11, and so our goal was to make sure that the fewer who were massed at places where our speed and our combat power and our training of our soldiers would be to best advantage against those numbers.

Q: But the idea you could have a mad cavalry charge going up to Baghdad, that just wasn't on...

Franks: No. First of all in the VII Corps sector we were in a very tight restricted piece of real estate for a five division Corps and so it required some intense co- ordination and synchronisation and co-ordination of the forces, you're talking about tank cannons that fire a projectile at a mile a second at ranges in excess of 2500 metres, 3,000 metres, and whatever they hit at that range they're going to destroy in a flat piece of terrain, so you're talking about maneuvering five divisions in a relatively confined piece of real estate that isn't rolling but is flat and where the possibilities of units running into each other, of fratricide, is very probable if you don't maintain a coherent direction of attack, so we knew thatin our enveloping force I had two Army divisions on a 40-kilometre front. One of the divisions was on a 15-kilometre front, he was in a column of brigades, if you stretch a US armor division in a column of brigades on a 15-kilometre front, it'll stretch for about 120 kilometres, there is a lot of vehicles, a lot of moving parts. So based on the mission we had and the numbers of Iraqi units in our sector, we felt as if our attack needed to be massed and in coherent combat formations rather than in pursuit or exploitation, which we certainly were not in, at least for the first two days of the war.

Q: When you got this news there was going to be a ground war... the head of this great force, what did you as a person feel?

Franks: It came over the telephone, I think I was in my .. I had a trailer built up on a back of a truck is really what I was living in there at the time, at the Corps main C.T., and I remember talking on the phone and I got the word that, yes, the attack would .. G-Day would be the 24th of February, now originally we were going to attack at G plus one, that's essentially on the 25th, and I thought to myself, this is it now, all questions are removed, we're going to get .. we're going to attack on the 24th and I said to myself then, we've got to use the time we've got remaining to ensure we've done everything we need to do to give our soldiers the best possible advantage to accomplish the mission at least cost to them. I said to myself .. first I wanted to get the word out to my subordinate commanders and so I did, then what I wanted to do since there weren't many more preparations I could do as the Corps commander, what I wanted to do was go out and visit some of the units and I particularly wanted to visit the units who were going to conduct the breach, so I went to visit General Bert Maggert, then Colonel Bert Maggert, 1st Brigade of the Big Red One, to talk to him, his soldiers, talk to his subordinate commanders, and I came away from there sensing an air of confidence, not over confidence, certainly a sense of awareness of the toughness of the mission they were about to go on, but a sense of confidence in their own capabilities, in the plan, in their knowledge of the plan, that they had rehearsed it, so they were confident, they were ready to go, and I came away from that feeling as if the Corps was ready to attack, and what I had told the Secretary of Defence certainly was confirmed for me by those soldiers that afternoon in that visit.

Q: You knew all about combat, what did you feel as you were talking to Bert Maggert's guys there, looking around all those young faces?

Franks: Well I had seen battle, of course, in Vietnam, many of us had, I had been wounded in Vietnam twice, so what I wanted to do was to make sure we had done everything in terms of preparation, in terms of seeing to it that the soldiers understood the mission, they were well trained, to give them the best possible chance to accomplish the mission at least cost, get them at the right place at the right time in the right combination and they'd do the rest, I was confident in that, they were confident in themselves, but as I looked around .. and I had visited hospitals before the ground attack started, we had had some casualties in the 1st Cavalry Division in their great actions in the R... pocket, so I was well aware that it was the young soldiers in the front line vehicles, the Bradleys and the tanks and the Challengers and the Warriors in the case of the British who would be at the tip of the spear and so I wanted to go out and talk to them, see how they felt, they felt confident, I visited the 1st Armored Division, one of the platoons called themselves the Raiders, they wanted to get a picture taken, this was the day before the attack, I still have it .. I told them good luck, I knew what they were about to go through, I maybe knew better than some of them. I told 'em good luck, shook their hands, you know, pat on the back, just wanted to talk to them soldier to soldier, see how they felt. I happened to run into that platoon on the way home, I'd wished 'em good luck, the 1st Battalion of the 7th Infantry, they were originally part of the 3rd Infantry Division but fighting with the 1st Armoured Division - I saw them on the way home, the day before they went home and went back, I said how did you do, they said, hey sir, we did great, we accomplished our mission and there was not a single soldier killed or wounded in our platoon.

Q: The air war had been going on for over a month, did it give you what you wanted?

Franks: Yes, what the air war did for our scheme of maneuvre, it essentially froze the Iraqis in the configuration they were in at the start of the air war, now they could move around and make some minor adjustments but in terms of extending the barrier further to the west, in terms of repositioning large units, they couldn't do that, so essentially they were fixed in position so the scheme of manoeuvre . that I had issued to the Corps in early January at a war game we had in King Khalid military city, essentially was a scheme of manoeuvre that would work, because the Iraqis were essentially fixed in position. Now we had some disagreements in the air as to the air that was made available in the VII Corps sector, what targets they would attack. Now we had some intense discussions over those targets, which ones would be attacked in what priority and that's just in the nature of air/ground operations, sometimes I got what I wanted, sometimes I didn't.

Q: The strategic guys who played an important part in this, they were into bombing residential palaces and buildings in Baghdad. Meanwhile you're worried about artillery pieces that are going to land chemical weapons on a lot of young soldiers, did the Air Force understand that?

Franks: My goal was to see to it that the air that was flown in the VII Corps assigned sector was flown against targets whose priority would contribute to the success of our scheme of manoeuvre to accomplish our mission, in other words I was given a mission by the theatre commander to destroy the Republican Guards forces command forces in our sector - we knew how to do that. Air was in support of that, so whatever numbers of air would be flown in our sector, I wanted to be the commander who would determine the priority of what they would attack. Now whether it was two sorties or attacks or a hundred, that wasn't my decision, that's the theatre commander's decision, but if the two flew then I wanted them to fly against the target priorities that would contribute to the success of the ground manoeuvre, so my priorities were first artillery within range of the breach, back to the success of the breach operation, and because the Iraqis had chemically .. chemical capable artillery systems. Secondly I wanted to go after their .. essentially their command control of the Iraqi VII Corps which was in front of us, so they couldn't notify the Republican Guards the speed and direction of the main attack, this fist that was coming after them. And third, I wanted to go after the tactical reserve, I didn't want the 1st British Armored Division to get stuck in the breach by an Iraqi tactical reserve that was right up against where they were breaking out of the breach, so there was a brigade sitting right there of tactical reserves so I remember pounding the map, saying make this brigade go away, some of the staff picked up on it as the 'go away brigade', but essentially that was to emphasise that that brigade was prioritised .. a priority of attack, so those were our priorities. Now sometimes we got that and sometimes we didn't.

Q: What did you want the Air Force to hit and did they hit it?

Franks: I wanted the priority of air to go after artillery in range of the breach, second to go after the command control of the Iraqi VII Corps which was directly in front of us, to prevent them from telling the Republican Guards the direction and the speed of our attack, and then third I wanted the air to go after the tactical reserve positioned close to the exit to the breach so they would not interfere initially with the 1st British Armoured Division. I had some amount of difficulty getting those priorities struck because of other theatre priorities in terms of number of air available to the Corps and then even which wasn't my decision, but even that air that was made available in the Corps sector, to get it to attack in accordance with those priorities, sometimes other priorities would override those particular priorities. In the end we got it all done, now we got a lot of it done through the use of our own MLRS rocket system and the use of unmanned aerial vehicle to locate the targets and then fire MLRS, the bomblets, after Iraqi artillery.

Q: So you never managed to get air to hit artillery in the way you wanted?

Franks: No, we went after Iraqi artillery mainly with artillery raids by the Corps.

Q: That must have been pretty frustrating.

Franks: Well, there was some intense discussions about priorities of air and the targetry and correlation between targets requested to be hit and those that were actually hit, so that's in the nature of things in a theatre of operation.

Q: You've got a whole bunch of troops who are going to die if they have chemical weapons landed on them and there's long range artillery sitting nearby and you're telling me you can't get the Air Force to hit them...

Franks: Of all the things that got me heated up prior to the attack or the ground campaign, as a matter of fact I went down to Riyadh in person to talk about it, was my lack of success in getting the air that was forming in the VII Corps sector to attack artillery within range of the breach, because we were concerned about artillery as artillery and also chemical capable artillery firing into the Big Red One as they conducted the breach .. so I appealed to the Third Army commander, the G-3, General Steve ..., who carried, you know, that argument in the targeting council that went on and then finally appealed to General Cal Waller who finally General Schwarzkopf put General Waller in charge of essentially target prioritisation and when Cal got into it then the correlation between the priorities of targets that I had requested in VII Corps and what actually got much better.

Q: What were you saying to Cal Waller?

Franks: What I said to Cal Waller was, Cal, how much air flies and attacks targets in the VII Corps zone is not my decision, that's a theatre decision, but what does fly in there needs to attack targets in the priority that I as the ground commander set in order to support the ground scheme of maneuvre to accomplish a mission that I've been given by the C-in-C.

Q: What were you saying to Cal Waller about artillery?

Franks: I was saying to Cal Waller, Cal, the air has got to go after artillery, especially artillery in range of the breach, this will assure success of the breach and if the Iraqis choose to use chemicals it'll also prevent the Iraqis from firing chemicals on to our troops in the breach, Cal understood that and so did John Yeosock and so between the two of them and especially after Cal Waller was given the mission to see to it that the correlation between the ground commander targets request and what was flown was better, it got better.

Q: So after Cal Waller intervened, all the artillery was bombed by the Air Force?

Franks: No, that's not true either, no, because there were other priorities for air in the theatre, they were going after Scuds and other strategic targets and that was not my decision so that was certainly none of my concern, but what I wanted to do was destroy the artillery in range of the breach, that was our top priority, so because of disagreements over priorities of air and then the lack of air to go after those targets, we began a series of artillery raids using all the artillery

179

in the Corps in combination with our own targeting apparatus in the corps, unmanned aerial vehicles and also other platforms that could detect these targets, to go after these artillery in range of the breach, and so I wanted to .. first of all I wanted every unit in the Corps to have some combat action prior to the attack and so we used artillery raids to go after the artillery, the Iraqi artillery.

Q: You did it yourself in the end.

Franks: Yes, it was a team effort, it was a team effort, but what I couldn't get the air to go after we went after with our own capabilities.

Q: The day the war started, you spoke about going to see the troops .. you were asked if you could go earlier and you flew up to see Tom R…, what did you say to him?

Franks: I got a call about 9.30 in the morning of the first day, the 24th of February, from General John Yeosock saying could we attack early and I didn't know the reasons why, all I knew was could we attack early and John told me that the answer he got from 18th Corps was with two hours notice they could go. I said that sounds okay with me, let me go check with my subordinate commanders but that's .. it's a go with VII Corps, so then I left the corps tactical C.P. which is a small collection of vehicles and flew on up to visit General Tom Rhame. and talked to Tom and he said yes, he was ready to go right at that moment, he and the 2nd Cavalry, but it required some considerable adjustment, we had a two hour artillery preparation plan for the breach, we reduced that to half an hour, it required considerable adjustment on the part of General Rupert Smith and the 1st British Armored Division, who had to move from there 80 kilometres or so, they were south of the breach, they had to move early, so considerable adjustment on their part, and then to get the word out to all the troops. But Tom told me he was ready to go, as a matter of fact he probably would have requested to go early even if we had not gotten the call, since he had done some initial probes in the Iraqi security zone and was encouraged by the initial success that he was having and so he was going to ask to push forward at least through the security zone on that first day, as had Colonel Don Holder who was commanding the 2nd Cavalry.

Q: There's a picture of the two of you looking at some maps, Tom R… and yourself, just before the breach—what was the last thing you said to him as you headed off?

Franks: Well, what I said to Tom was, good luck, you've got a tough mission but you're up to it, the division's well trained, you've rehearsed it, good luck, but also you're not done when you're finished with the breach, be prepared for future missions because I'm not going to leave you behind, because I knew I needed three divisions in this fist and I didn't know where I was going to get the third division from. At that point I didn't know whether I would be given command of the 1st Cavalry Division, who at that time were CENTCOM reserve, so I told Tom, good luck, you know what to do, go for it and to .. well, I'm not going to leave you behind, be prepared for a follow-on mission, because I wanted him thinking ahead, you always try to think 24, 48, 72 hours ahead.

Q: Where were you when the breaching operation took place?

Franks: I went out to visit Tom late that afternoon, heard the operation going on, firing going on, went out and met with him and General Rupert Smith, the 1st British Armored Division commander, right out there in the middle of the breach.

Q: Describe what was going on around you, what was the scene?

Franks: Well, the scene was of a lot of vehicles moving, of completing the lanes so to speak, you could hear artillery, you'd got aircraft flying, you could hear the sharp crack of tank cannons and the pop of 25- millimetre Bradley cannons, so a lot of fighting still going on but there was also the prisoners who had been captured by the Big Red One, and a sense of early success .. a feeling of success and confidence on the part of the Big Red One.

Q: When did you first realise that it was beginning to work?

Franks: The first indication I had was when the artillery was able to take what was going to be a two hour preparation and position themselves to fire a 30-minute prep. and for that to go off like clockwork and to have then followed up by the co-ordinated attack of two brigades of the Big Red One who attacked at 1500 on Sunday afternoon as opposed to first light the following morning. I said to myself, if the Corps is able to adjust that quickly, then we're going to build on success here and then I got some of the radio reports that the breach was going well.

Q: Do you remember any particular conversation or report from Bert Maggert or Tom R... that made you think we're okay - once the fighting had started?

Franks: No, I had gotten radio reports, I was monitoring that at the corps tactical C.P., then I got in a helicopter and went on out to the breach and talked to Tom and I could see it in his face and I could see the sense of confidence in the Big Red One that what they had done to this point had been very successful, they were very confident, they were very pleased that the plan had gone very well, so I could sense it, I could feel it, I could see it, I could see it in their conversations and I also could talking to the 2nd Cavalry and also the 1st and 3rd Armored Divisions, they were moving well, so the whole thing was beginning on a .. on a note of great success and the Corps was gaining confidence rapidly and quickly.

Q: All the time you've been talking about speed, why didn't you pause the guys in the breach that night? Franks: We had a decision to make, because we attacked early, what we were going to do the first night. I was thinking 48 hours ahead, I wanted to be in a posture that when we hit the Republican Guards, that we would hit 'em with a fist massed from an unexpected direction at full speed, and so what I needed to do was get the Corps in a posture that would allow that to happen over the next 48 hours. In addition to that I wanted to talk to both commanders involved, General Tom R... commanding the Big Red One and Colonel Don Holder who was commanding the 2nd Cavalry out in front of the two armored divisions. I asked both of them, Colonel Holder was concerned about getting too far out in front of the two armoured divisions and attacking the Republican Guards piecemeal, as was I. And General R... was concerned about being able to complete the breach during the hours of darkness with the thoroughness required to allow rapid passage of the 1st UK Armored Division and also to allow passage of the logistics vehicles that we needed to position on the other side of the breach in order to support the enveloping two armoured divisions, 1st and 3rd Armoured Divisions, so I determined from the sensing of the commanders, from the need to synchronise the British passing through and attacking and destroying the tactical reserve, which could have gotten into the logistics tail of the attacking armoured divisions, and the need to be at full speed when we hit the Republican Guards - taking all those things into consideration, I told the units to conduct local reconnaissance, continue the artillery fights, continue to pressure up and to resume full scale operations at first light the next morning.

Q: Because otherwise there was going to be a horrible night-time traffic jam with the possibility of friendly fire incidents...

Franks: Correct. It seemed to me the it was more of a gamble to continue the breach that evening. Now I briefed my immediate commander in Third Army, I told him what we were doing, and he said okay and I presume he had told General Schwarzkopf and that everybody at Central Command knew what we were doing.

Q: If they'd continued that night, what could have happened?

Franks: Well, . there was a lot of possibilities of things, you could have had difficulties in navigation which could have led you to some fratricide incidents, you could have had Iraqi stay behind units that could have gotten in behind .. it's easy enough to by-pass dug-in infantry during the day, it's of course much easier at night when you can't see them, they can come up and shoulder fired anti-tank weapons can get .. interfere with following logistics vehicles and we figured we needed all 24 lanes cleared, so if for example you had two or three or four or five lanes that would have damaged vehicles in them, burning vehicles, our own, in those, that would in a sense lengthen the time it would take the 1st British armored division to pass through.

Q: More haste, less speed.

Franks: So speed was necessary to get them through to attack the tactical reserve, so the tactical reserve of the Iraqis could not interfere with the enveloping force, so it was all tied together, it was all tied together, so it seemed to us .. there's an old German saying that says, 'go slow now and go fast later' and so the scheme of maneuver based on my own assessment and my discussions with the tactical commanders, I informed my headquarters that it would be actually faster, we would conduct the mission faster if we did not continue during hours of darkness but we continued it at first light, in fact the 1st British Amoured Division began passing through...

Q: And Schwarzkopf, as you have heard, was absolutely furious about the slowness of the Corps advance...

Franks: I had heard later, about the next day, through my chief of staff, that was there was some concern about the pace of the Corps operation and I had talked this over then with General Yeosock and he understood, I talked to him on almost on a continuing basis about the pace of the Corps, what we were doing, the manever of the Corps, and assumed that all of that was well known. So it was hard for me to understand why there was a lack of understanding about what the Corps was up to, especially correlating it to the intelligence we had about what the Republican Guards were doing at that point in time.

Q: But Schwarzkopf throwing the tantrum, is that the way he should do business?

Franks: Well, I think every commander does things their own way, I felt as the commander of the main attack, if there was some problem with either direction or the pace of the attack, then someone would tell me that and I got no such communication during the four days of the ground war. As a matter of fact, I talked to General Schwarzkopf on Tuesday, the 26th, and told him that we had made our right turn, that was a call we made in the Corps, and that we were about to conduct .. it turns out a four-division night attack against the Republican Guards. He seemed pleased with that, he told us to press the attack, he gave me a piece of intelligence about the H... division had been seen loading on to hit vehicles so he said he wanted us to continue to press the attack and I told him that we would. I also told him I was not happy with a mission I had gotten to attack, the 1st British Armored Division south and clear essentially Wadi al Batin, which we had gone around to avoid, and eventually we did not do that.

Q: But Schwarzkopf was going around saying that you and the VII Corps, these 146,000 men you had, were stuck into European mode, it was NATO, they didn't have any fire, any dash. What do you say to that? ..

Franks: The pace of the attack depends on first of all the scale of the map you're looking at, as to time and distance. The movement of actually four divisions at that point in time, since the 1st Cavalry Division did not .. was not part of the Corps, we were moving and attacking continually, from the time we got the word on 1500 on Sunday afternoon, either ground or air, until cessation of offensive operations at 8 o'clock on Thursday morning. Now .. I did halt the large unit movement the evening of the 24th and we've discussed that ..

Q: I'll come on to that later.

Franks: Correct, we've discussed it. But the pace of the Corps attack and synchronising and co-ordinating large unit movement on flat terrain in very confined maneuver space and turning a Corps, two Armoured Divisions, 90 degrees and attacking 90 degrees to the east while on the move, with no pause, and doing essentially a four-division night attack, I was enormously proud of the soldiers and the leaders of VII Corps then and I'm even more proud of them now, I think it was an enormously powerful achievement by the soldiers and leaders of the VII Corps British and American soldiers.

Q: If you could have been transported that morning to that room and sat next to General Schwarzkopf, what would you have said to him?

Franks: What I was trying to do was to describe what I was seeing, the battle as I was seeing it, on the ground, up front, with my own commanders, seeing with my own eyes, ...having been in battle before in Vietnam, sensing the battle, sensing the pressure, seeing what the soldiers and the leaders were doing, going around visiting commanders, I would have .. and I tried on a continuing basis with General Yeosock, who was back in Riyadh, to describe the situation as I was seeing it and the pace of operations, and I felt the pace was swift, that the soldiers were moving, the soldiers units were changing, in major formations going from a column of brigades to brigades, making a night passage of lines, a division through a cavalry regiment, under fire, very difficult operations - all of this was done with enemy resistance, we had 11 plus divisions in the Corps sector of operations, there were some gaps in where enemy forces were but most of our units were in contact almost on a continuing basis, there were a lot of prisoners, contacts, units that were by-passed, there was a considerable amount of Iraqi forces, so I felt .. I was proud of the pace of the Corps and of the soldiers and their willingness and drive and toughness to take the fight to the enemy, day and night, sandstorms and in the rain, and I think that'll be forever etched in the desert sands of Iraq and Kuwait.

Q: It's one thing to sit in a war room in Riyadh, it's another to be in a tank.

Franks: You get different perspectives, looking at different scale maps, you get perhaps an incomplete view of the battlefield, you get different perspectives, I had a perspective and I was conducting the pace and the synchronisation of the combat power of VII Corps in accordance with the mission that I was given. T accomplish that mission at least cost to the soldiers, and if that pace needed to be increased and I felt as if one of my commanders would call me and tell me that and none of them did.

Q: What was the significance of 73 Easting?

Franks: 73 Easting was really the first large scale fight that we got in, ...the breach of course was a separate operation, the 1st British Armored Division, as soon as they broke out of the breach, began a series of tough fights against the Iraqi reserve. The 73 Eastingwas the first indication we had of the Republican Guard's positioning and the role that they would fight, and so it was significant in setting up the battle that followed.

Q: Were you out there at the time of 73 Easting- did you see the battle?

Franks: I heard it, it went on late. No, I did not, the particular battle, I'm not sure they named it 73 ... until later, but that particular battle that discovered .. the initial success against the Republican Guards, where their main battle positions were and the fact that we had caught them by surprise, I knew then that our armored divisions would be successful as the British 1st Armored Division was being very successful against the Iraqi tactical reserve.

Q: So the Iraqis by now, the J-STARS were showing that they were beginning to peel off, they're beginning to retreat, they'd left a defensive screen, what was your perception of how the battle was at that stage, as we go into Tuesday night/Wednesday morning?

Franks: My instructions to the Corps were we had to keep up the intensity of attack for the next 24 or 36 hours, a straight message to the Corps. My perception was we would have .. the 3rd Armoured Division, General Butch ..., 3rd Armored Division, hit the Tawakalna right in the centre, the 1st Armoured Division to the north and the Big Red One came out of the breach after the 1st British Armoured Division had attacked through, so we essentially had 4 divisions from north to south, the 1st US Armoured Division, 3rd US Armoured Division, 1st US Infantry Division and the 1st UK Armoured Division, 4 divisions on line as it were, about 8 to 9 brigades, depending on what the units were doing, each one of these considerable, sizeable formations, I think the calculations were if you would line up vehicle

186

to vehicle, end to end, in the 1st UK Armoured Division, you'd stretch about 350 kilometres, so we're talking sizeable numbers of units packed into a frontage of maybe 120 kilometres.

Q: You've got a wall of tanks ..

Franks: That's about correct, a massed fist, smashing into the Republican Guards and destroying them, as was our mission. All throughout the night of Tuesday, into Wednesday morning, Wednesday morning then I wanted to go and do a quick assessment, because my initial calculation was that we could entrap the remaining units in our sector if we could do a double envelopment.

Q: Tell me about the Medina Ridge, what was the significance about that?

Franks: There it was that we ran into the Medina Division of the Republican Guards. I actually went out to visit General Ron Griffith and the 1st US Armoured Division, to talk about moving the 1st Cavalry around to the north, it was at that point that the battle of the Medina Ridge was going on. Again it was an indication of the great skill and toughness and capability of our soldiers and our equipment in that the 1st Armoured Division was able to essentially reduce a brigade of Iraqi vehicles, render them totally combat ineffective and destroyed in lessthan an hour, at great ranges, at ranges in excess of 2 kilometres where you couldn't even see the target with a naked eye, so a tremendous combat victory there by the 1st Armoured Division but also an indication that the line of defence of the Republican Guards had stretched further to the north and what they were trying to do was rapidly get vehicles and units in our way as we were attacking and driving to the east.

Q: As this was going on, General Schwarzkopf was standing up saying that the gates are closed.

Franks: I believe that's correct, I didn't know at the time that there was a briefing going on, I found out later that there was a briefing going on, this fight went on mid-afternoon of Wednesday, the 27th of February.

Q: Had General Schwarzkopf consulted you, did General Schwarzkopf say to you, are the gates closed?

Franks: No, .. most of my communication, except for that one phone call, was through my immediate commander there, General John Yeosock, who was commanding the Third Army.

Q: I suppose what I'm getting at is that here you have the Commander in Chief standing up saying the gates are closed and you're on the ground and you're the guy who knows that they're not closed because you've just had a major engagement and you're doing damned well but the gates aren't closed yet, what do you make of all that?

Franks: I knew we were in the middle of a continuous intensive armoured fight, our troops were doing terrific, we had extended the battlefield so it was not just a fight of tank against tank, our scheme of manoeuvre was to extend to simultaneously attack the Iraqi forces throughout the depth of what are now called battle space, so we were using attack helicopters, we were using Air Force air, rocket and cannon artillery, so we had an extended attack zone and that was moving, that was very lethal and deadly and that was moving due east towards the Gulf.

Q: I accept all that was going on, but General Schwarzkopf said the gates were closed, were they?

Franks: I knew that—actually Wednesday morning—that the 1st Infantry Division and the 1st UK Armoured Division had essentially achieved a breakthrough and they were in essentially pursuit and exploitation, which the Big Red One was. I also wanted to attempt to encircle the remaining Iraqi forces that were in front of 7 Corps and so we came up with a double envelopment scheme of manoeuvre to do that, using 2 divisions.

Q: In very simple terms, what was going to happen the following day, the Thursday, what were you going to do?

Franks: Our scheme of manoeuvre in 7 Corps was to bring the 1st Cavalry Division around to the north of the 1st Armoured Division and around from the south we would bring the 1st Infantry Division and they would link up in front of .. actually just to the south of Basra and encircle any remaining Iraqi forces in our sector.

Q: So the following day, what would have happened to the Iraqis?

Franks: Any forces that were still in the 7 Corps sector would have been caught in this encirclement and then in addition we had the 18th Corps attack in the east with the 101st Airborne, with the 24th Division and then the 3rd Cavalry attacking due east and one of the ..

the ARCENT plan was that they would be the hammer on top of the 7 Corps anvil, right on the Iraqi/Kuwaiti border.

Q: How were you told that the war was going to end and what did you feel?

Franks: We had .. all day on Wednesday I had gone around personally visiting units and assembling commanders out on the battlefield to put into motion this double envelopment scheme which would utilise all the assets, all the combat assets of the Corps. Early in the evening then I got the word from my main command post, which was back in Saudi Arabia, that there would be a possible ceasefire the following day so I called my commander, the Army commander, General Yeosock, and asked what was this all about and he told me, yes, there was a possibility, a very real possibility of a ceasefire, he would confirm it later, and so that meant that the scheme of manoeuvre that we had put into effect certainly would not happen so we had to make some adjustments, plus put a warning order out to cease all offensive operations at that point, at 5 o'clock in the morning.

Q: You travelled across all this desert, hundreds of miles to get to grips with the Republican Guard and destroy them and the following day that would have happened, you would have encircled them—and now someone's ringing up saying, hey, you are never going to really get to grips with them, what did you feel?

Franks: We felt that the purpose of destroying the Republican Guard's forces, in our sector anyway, was the means to achieve the strategic objective and the strategic objective was the liberation of Kuwait and so what we had done to that point had achieved the strategic objective.

Q: Should the war have gone on for a little longer, just military considerations?

Franks: We essentially had achieved our objectives, strategic objectives in the theatre, there was some resistance but not very strong organised resistance in the 7 Corps sector.

Q: So you felt no feeling of frustration that just as you were ..

Franks: Not at that point, no, did not, I felt that we had achieved a great victory, I was very proud of the soldiers, as a matter of fact I assembled the commanders of the corps, all the division commanders at the Corps Tactical CP that morning at .. I believe it was about 10 o'clock and I told them I wanted to be the first one to tell them that they and their soldiers, I was enormously proud of them then and I am even more proud of them today for their extraordinary achievement .. extraordinary achievement, toughness and willingness to take the fight to the enemy day and night in some tough weather, sand storms and then the rain.

Q: It undoubtedly was a great .. it achieved everything you wanted to but there were two divisions worth of Republican Guards, according to the D.I.A. who went over and counted them with some of their funny stuff in the next couple of days, two divisions worth of armour stacked up in that Basra pocket that was allowed to drive out eventually into Iraq, with all this fire power, with you chasing across the desert, with all the air, how could it be there was still two divisions worth of armour left at the end of the war?

Franks: I don't know the exact count, what was there, what left the theatre, I'm not aware of the exact figures on that, there've been a variety of pieces of information on that - I do know we were attacking the Iraqi forces in our sector throughout the depth with attack helicopters, with air, and with ground combat vehicles, and within the attack scenario destroyed almost 4,000 then and after, going around the battlefield, destroyed almost 4,000 essentially armoured vehicles and other pieces of equipment. So I believe that the sensing was in the Corps that the strategic objectives had been achieved, that we were enormously proud of the soldiers and the leaders of the Corps. Could we have gone on had we been asked? Of course, but that certainly wasn't the decision of the Tactical Commander at the time.

Q: Safwan ..how did you become aware that Schwarzkopf was irate, what happened?

Franks: There was a call I got said we need a place to conduct the ceasefire discussions, one proposal was the village of Safwan, another proposal was let's do it at the captured headquarters of the Medina division which 1st Armoured Division had overrun, which was not very accessible, it was out in the middle of the desert, no roads to it or anything, so the site was Safwan which then I informed my commander that we don't own Safwan, we had not been there, I think what happened was that, as I learned later, that a map got erroneously posted at CENTCOM and if you talk about the scale of maps, on a large scale map distances show up as a very small space on a map, so I don't know how it happened but apparently as the C-in-C was looking at the map he was under the impression that we had captured Safwan when in fact we had not, none of our maps showed that, I had no information, I knew we were not in Safwan, everybody in the Corps knew we were not in Safwan - the Big Red One knew they were not in Safwan and so then there was a phone call that asked for an official explanation of this, which I provided in writing—I sat down and wrote out a handwritten explanation to the C-in-C as to what happened and why we were not in Safwan. We eventually got there after the cessation of hostilities, the Big Red One did.

Q: Can you describe, as you took off in that helicopter to Safwan, can you just take us through that helicopter ride, what you did, what you felt, what he said, what you could see.

Franks: From Kuwait City to Safwan is about a 20 minute helicopter, in a B... helicopter. We had arranged for a company of Apaches to accompany us on the way up there - we wanted a show of force to Iraqis who could see all of this that there was plenty of combat power still available if they wouldn't agree to the ceasefire terms, but I wanted to show General Schwarzkopf what I had seen, the destruction, we flew over the 1st British Armoured Division, how far they'd come, the Big Red One, the 1st US Infantry Division, so I wanted him to see what I had been able to see on the battlefield and the destruction of the Iraqi military, at least close to Highway 8, so as we took off I instructed the pilots to fly so we could see a lot of that on the way to Safwan and I told General Schwarzkopf as we were flying along, I didn't want to talk too much, except to point out the units, the 1st UK Armoured Division and the 1st Infantry Division, because I wanted him to be able to look out and see what the forces under his command, in this case 7 Corps, had done and the magnificent achievement, victory that they had achieved.

Q: Describe to me what you could see from the helicopter and what Schwarzkopf said to you.

Franks: I instructed the pilots to see as much of the destruction parallel to Highway 8 that we could see on the way to Safwan, so what we saw north of Kuwait City, we saw the destruction there of mainly civilian vehicles that the Iraqis were attempting to escape with, buses, trucks, cars, in addition to some combat vehicles, an enormous destruction scene there, burning vehicles. North of that then it was mainly military vehicles, mainly military vehicles, military vehicles hit by air, also destroyed by the attack of the coalition forces, then north of that the 1st UK Armoured Division who had successfully attacked all the way east, got Highway 8, and also the lst US Infantry Division. There were smoking, burning tanks, other types of vehicles, infantry fighting vehicles, artillery pieces, damaged and bombed out buildings, vehicles at all sorts of angles destroyed, the Highway 8 was not even .. you could not even drive down Highway 8 for the vehicles destroyed on Highway 8, so there was a tremendous amount of armoured vehicle destruction visible from the air, even with the oil fires burning and all the smoke burning, and I wanted .. General Schwarzkopf had not been able to see that as I had seen that for almost four days on a continuing basis out on the battlefield so I wanted him to see what the coalition forces, ground, air and sea had done to achieve a great victory in the Kuwaiti theatre of operations, so I didn't want to occupy him with a lot of small talk and told him such and instructed the pilots to fly so that he could see all of this, so we didn't .. we didn't talk a lot, I didn't initiate a lot of conversation, he remarked about the damage, he remarked about what a terrible decision it was for the Iraqis to set fire to all the oil fields, all of the oil, .. the tremendous waste, tremendous damage that that would do to the environment and how completely .. how difficult that was to understand how the Iraqis could do that.

Q: And then what did General Schwarzkopf remark?

Franks: Then General Schwarzkopf remarked, as we were flying along, he said hey Fred, just as we planned it, just as we planned it, which to me was just as he had envisioned this whole thing unfolding back at that early briefing in early November and this was the culmination of that operation, as we could witness on the ground.

Q: What do you remember of the Iraqi officers arriving and the look on their faces, what was said at the ceasefire?

Franks: We had arranged a show of force there, we picked up the Iraqis in US vehicles, drove them down a line of combat vehicles that were lined up along the route. I recall the Iraqis being very stone-faced, not much emotion, a lack of emotion in their faces, pretty much agreeing to everything that was said, not having a whole lot to I think they could .. perhaps there was some surprise on their part as to the amount of destruction that they could even see there in the vicinity of Safwan as to their army in the field.

Q: The Iraqis were stony-faced but I remember you saying to me that there was one time when they showed some emotion... What happened when they discovered there was 60,000 Iraqi prisoners?

Franks: I think there was genuine surprise on their part as to the number of Iraqi prisoners that the coalition forces held, that probably surprised them more than anything during the discussions there, that plus the combat power available to the coalition forces and plus the destruction that they could see even there around Safwan that had happened to their army in the field.

Q: Was there ever a day you didn't think about Vietnam when you were out there?

Franks: No .. constantly in my mind. Memories of Vietnam are very sharp, clear to me, I mean with every other step I take I'm reminded of Vietnam and I remember the great soldiers that I was privileged to serve with there, those that I was in the hospital with at Valley Forge General Hospital, I remember those whose names are on the Vietnam memorial here in Washington .. no, never .. never far from my mind and especially during the Gulf War, we didn't say it to each other but I think we all felt that we're going to do it right this time.

Q: Did you feel when you'd won this great victory that you'd re-established the American military in the eyes of the American public?

Franks: I felt that what our soldiers had done certainly was proof of the sustained commitment to excellence that we had seen done in the US military following the Vietnam war, the training in leader development, in equipment, training at our national training centre, that it was a vindication of the wisdom of those decisions and that sustainment to tough, hard, realistic training and that was evident on the battlefield.

Q: You've got a photograph there I want to ask you about, how many of those guys helping you in that picture, and I think you know the picture very well, how many of them came back? Franks: All except one. Q: And when you were in the hospital, there were people around you who were pretending they'd been in car crashes and things.

193

Franks: Well, what happened of course for the Vietnam era, generation, was that for a while .. we couldn't separate the war from the warriors and so the soldiers - and the members of the other services - but soldiers in our case, got caught up in a lot of the anti-war business that was going on in the United States at the time and so there was not a sense of thanks, you went and did what your country asked you to do, and even if one questions the wisdom of the commitment, nonetheless young American men and women went and did what their country asked them to do, at great personal sacrifice, families, friends, and at great personal risk, pain, soldiers I was with in the hospital got so tired of going on convalescent leave back to their home town or out of the hospital and having to explain that they were wounded in Vietnam and people saying to them, oh what a shame, all that for nothing, that they stopped talking about it, they made up stories about they were hurt in a paint factory explosion or an automobile accident so they wouldn't have to talk about service in Vietnam. All of those memories were sharp and clear to me, as they were to many others during the Gulf War.

Q: Did you ever think you'd be able to achieve such a big victory with so few casualties?

Franks: I felt confident in our soldiers .. the soldier who said, don't worry, General, we trust you. They were tough British and American soldiers, I had seen .. I had been out and around them, I felt certainly it was within our grasp to achieve a great victory at least cost, and I felt as if I and the leaders, and we had a great team, division commanders, if we could get the soldiers to the right place at the right time in the right combination, then they would take it from there.

Q: And what do you say to the revisionists now,that if only these soldiers, these 146,000 guys, had moved a bit faster, been a bit more aggressive, we'd have got the Republican Guard?

Franks: I said to the soldiers then that a lot would be written and said and shown about what happened or didn't happen over here, but their willingness to take the fight to the enemy day and night, in sand storms and in the rain, with a sense of toughness and courage, will be forever etched in the desert sands of Iraq and Kuwait - what happened happened and the facts are the facts and so I'm enormously proud of the soldiers and leaders of 7 Corps, US and British, who fought side by side and achieved a great victory.

Chapter XI

Email and Mail to high political figures

On several different occasions I have written email to President Bill Clinton and several Senators and Congressmen. The only thing that I hear over and over again is what and see. One of the reasons I keep writing letters is to let them know that someone out here gives a DAMN. Eventhough that they don't, for some people like you and I it is really sickening to know that they are getting all of the money from all of the lobbyist and people that server their country is considered second class citizens. To date there have been over 9,600 soldiers, sailors and airmen that have died due to their neglect and politics of the Government of the United States. And they don't tell the public the real problems 10 years later that Saddam is still playing TAG on a daily basis with the US and its policies. Clinton is a Real Prick and cant wait until he is out of office and someone with Balls gets in and fixes the problems that we have since all of the Clinton cutbacks to the Military.

Chapter XII

What is coming in the future

I strongly think that Saddam Hussein and Osama Bin Laden and Iran are going to do something in the future and will not stop until they have destroyed the world and the United States of America. We are a strong nation but we cannot handle Terrorism of any sort because as Americans we take everything for granted. But go to another country overseas and watch them carry heavy weapons and do not tolerate any type of these situations. We should follow suit but it will take something really serious to make that America to take the blinders off and face reality as it is. I have been to 13 countries all over the world and as a service member you see a lot but all of the old people and high politicians have no clue what life is about and they think that being a DEMOCRAT everything is OK in the World. Guess what I told myself that the next problem would be in the desert but we did not finish the first battle with SADDAM Hussein in IRAQ. Today the 5th of January, 2002 the Army times said that the Veterans administration finally came to another conclusion that now 11 years later that the Government just found out that some of the ailments are true that some of the soldiers are coming back with and that they intend to help even thought is some what too late and alot of soldier have lost their families like I have and will be compensating those that need it now let just sit back and see how long this takes this time?

Chapter XIII
Short Term Disability

On August 28 2001 I was told for the third time that I was going to be on Short term Disability and now I am thinking that I need to try for 100% disability from the Veterans Administration. But my fear is that it takes too long to get into the system for another evaluation to pay those bills and continue to have a messed up life for me and my daughter since I am a single parent after 6 years of being divorced. And now getting calls from Bill collectors about the 2 cars that I had that were leased and they would not even talk to me until I paid off the leases on both cars. So now FORD motor credit say that I owe them $11,000 and mitsubishi says that I owe them $10,000 which is not more than a scam that people do not realize since they make a lease sound like a good idea. But for them to talk with me I had to come up with the money to pay the lease off then they would talk. All I can figure out that it must really be nice to have money all of the Times then there are no worries in the world. Back to the main problem is the Veterans Administration and the way they treat their veterans, One of the things that I have found out since getting out of the ARMY and that was that you not only need proof of medical problems and then it takes them about 6 months to a year to figure out what your disability is going to be rated at for Compensation. Oh, by the way if you are a retiree then they deduct that much money from your retirement check and turn it into Disability. Another well kept secret from Uncle Sam and something that they tell you when you enlist is that they will take care of you for life but that too is just a rumor from Uncle Sam you have to have proof of you getting hurt in the Service too. Then you send the paperwork to your regional office and see what they have to say about your disability.

Chapter XIV
September 11, 2001

My daughter came home from school and asked me if the government or US Army would call me back if something started and I told her no because I was considered disable rated at 70 % and take 35 pills a day at the current time. But if it were up to me and I would not loose everything that I have worked from over the last 5 years I would volunteer. But knowing what I know now about the way the reserves were treated and the sick too I would not want to endure any of that. But remember what I said earlier is that the politicians are only worried about their health and welfare and not the soldiers that are putting their live in harms way. Send their sons and daughter there when the draft starts since we have some many spoiled kids in todays society we need to come up with a solution and teach them right from wrong and that is not the teachers problems either. This is a parenting issue completely. I always said that the problems in the Middle East were not over due to Saddam Hussein still being in power and having control over things in the world and now comes that Idiot Osama Bin Laden. The support of the terrorist world and having the money to make lives miserable and now striking the United States and its citizens. There is now no more freedom just torture as to where will be his next target and since we have a society that says that you cannot bear arms it is not fair and we should be able to protect what we have worked for all our lives. Since this has happened I have been put on Administrative leave from work due to PTSD (posttraumatic Stress Disorder) and now taking 35 pills a day and changed to 38 a day now. I had a conflict with a person at work since I do not call him a man, a person Named Larry Epperson while working for Alcatel USA, Inc. I was pushed out of a position that I had been working as a project manager while working for Alcatel for almost 4 years and here this guy comes out of the woodwork and and takes the place of a super person named Glenn Estes. Since Larry coming in the picture life has been bad for several of the project mangers in the company.

October 07, 2001 First Day of New Campaign and Bombing

I have been waiting for someone to do something to us here in the United States and now we are trying to pick up the pieces and see what is next. But killing all of the people in New York was not the problem but now we need to take care of our own and send all of the people from the other countries home and we will get all of the jobs back that they took when they came to OUR COUNTRY… And if this stuff continues then we should be able to bear arms and take care of what is ours. But I know deep down that all of the politicians would not agree to this but I am somewhere in the bottom of the pile and I have worked for what I have without hiding behind politics and the protection they have at our expense. As of today the bombings have been going on for 12 days now but my only fear is that we are going to loose a lot of people if there is a ground war in Southwest Asia. What wee should do is clean out all of the prisons and tell all of the prisoners that is they can survive the fighting then they can have peace in any other country EXCEPT the United States. Having said that you probably think that this is totally off of the wall but it makes sense and would save the American people a lot of money in the long run if you look it with an open mind.

October 12, 2001 and still working from the Air.

Still waiting on news about the Ground forces other that the Special Operations soldiers that have been there since this thing started. All that I can say is that I talked with a recruiter and was told that they would not take me due to being a Disabled Veteran. They need to start the draft so that all of these PUNKS will get off of the street and defend the Country that we all love so well. They are so Spoiled no a days that they don't have to do anything other than what mom and dad says and to defend the country is what a lot of them are afraid of today. We all know that have been there that there are going to be a lot of body bags in this conflict and there is nothing that anyone can do about it we are committed and we need to follow through to defend what we love most and that is FREEDOM.

**October 22, 2001 and still working from the Air and Anthrax
scare is starting to work.**

Today the White House has 2 workers that have tested positive for
the first time or at least that is what the media thinks. I strongly feel
that this has been ongoing and is getting worse in the United States of
America. And the Air Campaign and the new Ground troops are
stepping up and today on CNN News channel it is talking about the
Australian Troops are now headed to Afganastain too. Somewhere in
the next 2 weeks we need to send the Ground Troops in country to
make sure that Bin Laden is still there or we are wasting a lot of
Taxpayer money as time goes on. November 23, 2001 my teenage
daughter Brittni for school wrote this

HATE FILLED WORLD

We live in a hate-filled world. One does not need to quote statistics
to support this premise, as news articles and the media cry aloud each
day with horrific stories about groups being harassed, beaten, fired-
upon—the list is endless. Are high school students able to confront
their own biases? I believe so. And at what better age can one start to
allow young people to look inward! Will the unit cure our hate-filled
prejudices? Perhaps not, but it certainly is a start. The organization of
this unit is flexible. One can teach it after reading all three literary
selections, or one can teach it after each novel is read and discussed.
However, my personal preference is to make this into a separate unit
culminating after all works are read and discussed. Therefore, the time
element will probably take place in the spring of the school year, and
will last approximately six to nine weeks. To begin the unit, one must
start with a working definition of the term "stereotype." The text of the
class seminar, *Diversity and Resistance,* is Dr. James Jones' *Prejudice
and Racism.* Jones writes:

A stereotype is a positive or negative set of beliefs held by an
individual about the characteristics of a group of people. It varies in its
accuracy, the extent to which it captures the degree to which the
stereotyped group members possess these traits, and the extent to
which the set of beliefs is shared by others...Stereotyping is the
process by which an individual employs a stereotypical belief in the

evaluation of or behavior toward a member of a stereotyped group (170).

In summary, Jones explains: "Stereotypes are thought by many to be the engine that drives prejudice...Stereotypes are prejudicial because they involve generalization (201)." Milton Kleg, in his book, *Hate Prejudice and Racism,* explains "...when tied to prejudiced attitudes, stereotypes help create a number of behaviors ranging from avoidance to violence. Our review of stereotypes indicates that one's perceived reality is not reality itself, but is a mixture of fact and fiction (155)." Certainly it is difficult to explain the root causes of prejudice and stereotyping. The Rogers and Hammerstein musical, *South Pacific,* gives an almost simplistic reason in the song that Lt. Cable sings. These lyrics state: "You've got to be taught to hate and fear...You've got to be taught to be afraid of people whose eyes are oddly made and people whose skin is a different shade...You've got to be taught before it's too late before you are six or seven or eight, to hate all the people your relatives hate."

Children are born innocent. Their behaviors, it seems to me, as they grow older, are a reflection of the attitudes and belief in stereotypes found in the home. The above lyrics attest to this, as do countless commercials sponsored by various and sundry organizations, pushing this same idea. Interestingly enough, in class discussions, many of my students have alluded to being discriminated against in one way or another. I often share a personal story, when these discussions come up, about an incident which happened to me when I was a newly minted college graduate pursuing teaching employment. Obviously the times were different, and employers could say just about anything to prospective employees.

I was interviewing for a teaching position in a district outside the city of Pittsburgh. My looks had a faint suggestion of being exotic—Italian or perhaps Jewish. My name was a common and rather "safe" name, with no great ethnic connotations. The interviewer commented upon that fact, and asked me pointedly where my ancestors came from. Knowing that this person was fishing to see if I was Jewish, which I was and am, I proudly answered the question by saying that my ancestors came from America, and that I was Jewish. Obviously, I did not take that position nor was it offered me. But the incident has remained with me for my entire teaching career. Today, that question would be prohibited. But then, Jews faced a number of discriminatory practices in the employment field. I first began to think of writing this unit on stereotypes in literature when my scholars' class read the novel, *The Learning Tree.* There are many examples of stereotypical comments about the African-American Winger family in that book, and the focus is on the young Newt Winger's desire to attend college. But it was during the discussion of *All Quiet on the Western Front that* the idea hit home with an impact. As a preliminary activity to reading the novel,

I asked the students to jot down some information about what they knew of the Germans and of the country of Germany. Most responded that they knew little of Germany, and were frightened to visit there, and a majority said that they believed that the country was filled with Nazis and skinheads. As the unit progressed, students were able to see that their views were based on pre-judged stereotypes, and that the German soldiers fighting in World War I, were similar to most fighting men across the world. I would want the students through this unit, to understand that certain feelings and actions are universal. The German soldiers experienced fear, horror, the desire to live—in short, all the emotions that fighting men would experience. Paul Baumer, Remarque's spokesman, experiences a similar awakening, when he finds that the Russian prisoners of war are very similar to the German soldiers. And my students should also experience an epiphany in reading about the German experience, which is, of course, parallel to the experience of any universal soldier.

To Kill A Mockingbird Prejudice has caused the pain and suffering of others for many centuries. Some examples of this include the Holocaust and slavery in the United States. In to Kill a Mockingbird, by Harper Lee racism was the cause of much agony to the blacks of a segregated South. Along with blacks, other groups of people are judged unfairly just because of their difference from others. The prejudice and bigotry of society causes the victimization of people with differences. Some who are discriminated against are those who are born differently than the majority. One person that is treated unfairly is Calpurnia, as you can see when Aunt Alexandra tried to get Atticus to fire Calpurnia, because in her eyes, Calpurnia wasn't a good enough female role model (p.136). This is a prejudice action, because Calpurnia is as good as a role model as Aunt Alexandra, if not better.

Aunt Alexandra is a bigot and doesn't see the character of Calpurnia, just the color of her skin. Another person who is treated like an inferior is Scout by her teacher, because she knew how to read. "She discovered that I was literate and looked at me with more than faint distaste. (p.17)." Scout is treated like it is her fault that she knows more than the average child did. She learned earlier than others so she gets punished unjustly. Tom Robinson is also one who is discriminated by a biased community. Tom is found guilty by the jury in his case against the Ewells (p.211). The guilty verdict is a direct result of a racist community. Tom was never given a fair chance in the trial, even though that the evidence was proving him innocent. People that are born differently often get mistreated and are discriminated against. Another group that is treated poorly in the society based on bigotry, are the people who have chosen to be different. One who chose to be different is Dolphus Raymond. He pretended to be drunk so no one gave him any trouble on the way that he lived his life (p.200). The way a person lives should be there own personal business. He has the right to live differently than others if he feels that is the way he wants to live.

Another person that lives differently is Boo Radley. Boo stayed inside his house for a number of years without ever coming out to interact with others. He didn't want attention that would come from the rumors that were said about him. Stories were made up about him and he felt it was best for him to stay inside. The people who chose to be different took a risk of being made outcasts of the majority of the society. The final group that was made to feel different was the group that defended and protected the minorities and the wrongfully treated people. Atticus was a good example of one who defended the different by defending Tom Robinson in his case. Atticus had integrity that gave him the strength to endure the ridicule that arose from his decision to defend a black man in a segregated area. Atticus was threatened and his children were treated poorly by their peers, because he had the courage to stand up for the oppressed. Sheriff Tate defends the different when he says, "I never heard tell that it's against the law for a citizen t do his utmost to prevent a crime from being committed, which is exactly what he did, but maybe you'll say it's my duty to tell the town all about it and not hush it up. (p.276)." Sheriff Tate is trying to protect Boo from the attention that could frighten him. The sheriff is doing the right thing by hiding the truth from the community. By defending the different, people take a chance of being known as strange or inferiors to the rest of the people that they are around. Throughout the story, people that are unlike the majority, get hurt. They are given obstacles that they have to overcome in order to survive. Some people in the world can survive these obstacles, and there are some that just give up. By fighting for your rights, people start to realize that character is the important attribute to a person. To Kill a Mockingbird, by Harper Lee showed me that the people with differences are not always doing things the wrong way. It is the majority that may be going at it all wrong.

15 January 2001

- John Walker Lindh, the 20-year-old Californian who fought with the Taliban in Afghanistan), will be charged with conspiracy to kill U.S. citizens and could face life in prison if convicted, Attorney General John Ashcroft said Tuesday.

Lindh, who converted to Islam at 16 and is alleged to have trained at an al-Qaida camp in Afghanistan, will be charged in U.S. District Court in Alexandria, Va., rather than a military tribunal. Ashcroft said Lindh admitted in interviews with the FBI that he met Osama bin Laden and knew bin Laden had ordered the Sept. 11 attacks on the United States.

``He chose to embrace fanatics, and his allegiance to those terrorists never faltered,'' said Ashcroft. ``Terrorists did not compel John Walker Lindh to join them. John Walker Lindh chose terrorists.''

Lindh learned in early June that bin Laden had sent people to the United States to carry out suicide operations, according to an FBI affidavit. The document described an odyssey that began with Walker's conversion to Islam in 1997, later training in Pakistan and Afghanistan and a decision last year to join the Taliban.

Friends have described Lindh as an intelligent young man who wore full-length robes to high school and went by the name ``Suleyman'' after his conversion to Islam. After his capture in December, his parents, Marilyn Walker and Frank Lindh, had asked the public to withhold judgment about their son.

James Brosnahan, a lawyer for the separated couple, could not be reached Tuesday. A spokeswoman at his law office in San Francisco said he was ``issuing no statements at this time.''

``We may never know why he turned his back on our country and our values, but we cannot ignore that he did,'' said Ashcroft. ``Youth is not absolution for treachery, and personal self-discovery is not an excuse to take up arms against your country.''

Lindh also is being charged with providing support to terrorist organizations and engaging in prohibited transactions with the Taliban, Ashcroft said.

The Bush administration had considered whether to charge Lindh in a civilian or military court and whether to charge him with treason, which carries the death penalty.

Ashcroft suggested that proving Lindh committed treason would be difficult, but he left open the possibility that other charges could be filed as evidence is developed.

``The Constitution imposes a high evidentiary burden to prove the charge of treason'' - a confession in open court or testimony by two witnesses, said Ashcroft.

White House spokesman Ari Fleischer said President Bush "is supportive of the process put in place. He is confident that the process will end in justice."

The charges were recommended to Bush by the National Security Council, which mediated advice from the Justice Department the Pentagon and the State Department.

The chairman of the Senate Judiciary Committee Sen. Patrick Leahy D-Vt., said he supported the "difficult and complex" decision to place the case in the civilian criminal justice system.

Lindh was captured in November fighting with the Taliban in Afghanistan. He was taken into custody by U.S. forces after a prison uprising at a fortress in the northern Afghan city of Mazar-e-Sharif.

CIA agent John Spann, who had questioned Lindh, was killed in the uprising. There has been no indication that Lindh was involved in Spann's death.

The federal affidavit said that after Spann interviewed him, Lindh was moved to a lawn and tried to run when he heard gunfire. He was shot in the leg. ``Walker claims not to have seen what happened to the two Americans who had interviewed him,'' the affidavit said.

Lindh since then has been held on the amphibious attack ship USS Bataan in the Arabian Sea. He will be transferred to FBI custody, Ashcroft said.

Lindh, who was baptized Roman Catholic and grew up in a liberal San Francisco suburb, told the FBI that after he trained at a paramilitary camp run by the terrorist group Harkat ul-Mujahedeen, he was given a choice of fighting in Kashmir or with the Taliban in Afghanistan.

Ashcroft quoted Lindh as telling Taliban recruiters that ``he was a Muslim who wanted to go to the front lines to fight.''

Lindh was interviewed by the FBI on Dec. 9 and 10 and waived his rights to a lawyer, the affidavit said. He had joined the military training camp in May 2001, it said, and was told by al-Qaida people to pretend that he was Irish and not to admit to anyone that he was American.

On one occasion, the complaint said, Walker and four other trainees met with bin Laden for about five minutes, during which time bin Laden thanked them for helping.

MILL VALLEY, Calif.—Before he became known on battlefields in Afghanistan as the holy warrior Abdul Hamid, or had shocked his doting parents by adopting the Muslim name Suleyman, John Walker Lindh walked into a mosque in this foggy hillside town near the Golden Gate Bridge five years ago eager to learn about a religion that would soon dominate his life. He was shy and studious, a lanky 16-year-old who had a basketball hoop in his driveway but showed little interest in predictable teenage pastimes. And his strange odyssey was about to begin. "He was a good person, a quiet person," said Abdullah Nana, 23, who often prayed with Walker on the red carpet of the Islamic Center of Mill Valley and gave him rides home because he did not have a driver's license. "He was accepted and respected for his dedication. No one like him had ever come here before." As his devotion grew, Walker would get rid of his coarse collection of more than 200 hip-hop and rap CDs and begin wearing an ankle-length white robe. He would forsake an easy path to college to travel alone to remote villages in Yemen and Pakistan. He would try to memorize the Koran. And he would scorn the peace-and-love precepts of his parents to take up arms with the harshly conservative Taliban. "When he left, he just said that he wanted to learn Arabic and follow Islam full time," Nana said. "We thought it would be beneficial for our community, because no one else here had gone to study overseas the way he wanted to. We thought he would be a pioneer." Instead, Walker has become a puzzling prisoner of war, the lone American caught with enemy forces in the aftermath of the Sept. 11 terrorist attacks, dragged filthy and wounded from a medieval fort with other defiant al Qaeda fighters last month. U.S. military officials have Walker in custody, and President Bush is preparing to decide his fate. He could be prosecuted for treason or aiding terrorists, charges that could bring the death penalty or many years in jail. But much of Walker's journey is still a mystery. Was he just an innocent abroad, an impressionable young scholar swept up in a movement he did not fully understand— "brainwashed," as his mother, Marilyn Walker, has suggested? Or was he a teenage rebel with a cause, renouncing the have-it-all, progressive suburban culture from which he came and duping his parents into believing they were supporting, and financing, a purely spiritual quest? His father, Frank Lindh, has said he was astonished to discover that his son had even gone to Afghanistan, much less to help the Taliban. "He never came to his papa to ask for permission," he said. But Frank Lindh's son did not sound clueless or contrite while lying on a hospital bed shortly after his capture. As a doctor tended to his wounds, a CNN correspondent asked him whether he thought he had been fighting on the right side. "Definitely," Walker replied. He seemed dazed. But was he?

'A Birkenstock Family'

Frank Lindh had just received a master's degree in social work when he and Marilyn Walker had their second child in February 1981. They decided to name him John, partly in homage to Beatle John Lennon, who had been murdered by a deranged fan two months earlier. The couple were renting a house in Takoma Park, settling into new roles as middle-class parents after coming of age in the counterculture of the 1960s. Neighbors say they were Sunday regulars at St. Camillus Catholic Church, took an interest in natural foods and medicines, and embraced the People's Republic politics of the community. Both parents declined to be interviewed for this story, but answered a few questions through their lawyer. They also spoke to reporters briefly after their son's capture. "They were kind of a Birkenstock family," said Chris Madison, who lived near them. "Very earnest, very nice, very intellectual." "They were liberal in the classic sense," said Dan Parr, another neighbor. "They said they really wanted to let their children develop by giving them different experiences." John showed promise. By fourth grade, he was among a select group of students in the "gifted and talented" program at Kensington Parkwood Elementary School. His parents appeared to be deeply involved in his life. "They seemed like such a happy family," said Judy Colwell, who had a child attending the same school and became friends with Marilyn Walker. Lindh had decided to pursue a career in law, working as a clerk in the solicitor general's office of the Justice Department by day, attending Georgetown law school at night. But he was the rare father who also found time to attend PTA meetings. Walker, a stay-at-home mom, chaperoned school field trips and earned a little money by taking jobs at retail stores during the holiday season. She was busy raising John and two other children, a boy a few years older than him and a baby girl. She also had become something of a local activist. Neighbors recall her waging a zealous campaign to have a metal slide at a local playground removed, saying it was too dangerous for children. But some old friends of the couple remember thinking that they might be pampering the children a bit too much— like the time, one neighbor recalled, that John told classmates that his parents had taken him to a therapist to cope with the death of a pet. The first big change in John's life came when he was 10. Frank Lindh, who had graduated from Georgetown with honors and was working at a Washington law firm, decided to move his family west. He had accepted a job at the firm's San Francisco office and bought a multi-floor modern home on a narrow, leafy street amid the lush hills and redwood groves of Marin County, another place with a tolerant, liberal creed. "I figured they would fit right in," Dan Parr said.

Home in a California Cliché

The joke about Marin is that it is a California cliché, a hot-tub haven that values nothing as much as self- discovery. It is a community where the local Center for Massage Therapy is celebrating its 25th anniversary and graying lefties in fleece vests walk the streets sipping chai tea. But it also is one of the wealthiest counties in California, a land of $300 strollers, crowded SAT prep classes, and chic cafes crackling with chatter about high-speed modems and ski trips to Tahoe. It is also a place willing to dabble in novel educational trends. So, too, were Frank Lindh and Marilyn Walker. They decided to send John to a small, new public high school that had a rare teaching philosophy: It held no classes. Tamiscal High School, which opened in 1991, was designed for academically elite and creative students, a select group of highly motivated self-starters. John Walker made the cut. He had to take the same courses as any other high school student in California, but the curriculum was more rigorous and far-flung. And he had to show up only once or twice a week for one-on-one meetings with teachers. "The kids here are not flaky or wacky, they're very serious," said Bill Levinson, superintendent of the local school district. "It's not easy. The biggest challenge is that you don't depend on teachers telling you what to do." John had to study world cultures and try his hand at poetry and read "The Autobiography of Malcolm X," the story of an aimless petty criminal whose life is transformed by his conversion to Islam. Lindh has said that the epic tale seemed to captivate his son. The teenager began spending his unscripted days asking questions about Islam in Internet chat rooms and expressing moral doubts about some of the rap musicians he had liked. On one Internet posting under his name, he questioned why one rapper whom someone else in the chat room apparently had called a "god" deserved such adoration. "If this is so," Walker wrote, "then why does he smoke blunts, drink Moet, fornicate and make dukey music? That's a rather pathetic 'god,' if you ask me." His family was changing, too. Frank Lindh had taken a job as a staff attorney for corporate giant Pacific Gas and Electric Co., and Marilyn Walker, once an avid Catholic, began practicing Buddhism. But Jay Murphy, who lived next door, said the family seemed content. "They were kind people, very intelligent," he said. "They were all doing their own thing." In 1997, at 16, John Walker dropped out of Tamiscal. His family says it was because he had an intestinal illness. He took and passed a state proficiency exam to earn a high school diploma. Then he announced that he was changing his name and converting to Islam. Family friends say that both of his parents struggled at first with the decision, then were struck by how committed he seemed to be. Lindh has said that his son reminded him of a "Catholic seminarian." Marilyn Walker worried about some Islamic views on the rights of women but believed local mosques were not militant. "They were very supportive," said Bill Jones, a friend of Frank Lindh. "It was all very spiritual. He wasn't angry, and it had nothing do with politics." The family was not apolitical, however. About that time, Marilyn Walker took their 9-year-old daughter, Naomi, to a small local demonstration denouncing U.S. bombing raids over Iraq. The Marin Independent Journal ran a photo of the girl standing amid a few dozen protesters waving signs at passing traffic that read, "Don't Kill Iraqi Kids." Not long after John Walker converted to Islam, he told his family that he wanted to live and study in Yemen, at a school where he could learn a dialect of Arabic that would allow him to read the Koran in its original language. Again, his parents obliged. But it was no longer a happy household. Frank Lindh and Marilyn Walker separated. She moved into a nearby apartment. He rented a room from Jones. John left home for the first time. He would not return for nearly a year.

First Sign of Trouble

In hindsight, the first sign of trouble may have been an e-mail Frank Lindh has said he received from his son in the fall of 2000, after the USS Cole was bombed while it idled in a port in Yemen. The terrorist attack, which U.S. officials blamed on Osama bin Laden, killed 17 U.S. sailors. Lindh told John how upset he was by the incident. From overseas, the son sent back a surprising message. Lindh has told reporters that his son wrote that the U.S. ship should not have been docked in an Islamic country. By then, the teenager had embarked on his second extended stay in the Middle East. After his first trip to Yemen, he had returned home to Marin for about eight months in 1999. But Nana, his friend at the Mill Valley mosque, remembers that he was restless and said that he no longer felt comfortable in a place where Islam was not a way of life. Walker spent much of his time visiting other mosques in the San Francisco Bay area. Family friends say his parents were not worried. He was talking about going to medical school, then returning to Pakistan to aid the poor— "on a mission of mercy," Jones said. Not long after the Cole bombing, John Walker told his parents he was traveling to Pakistan, to attend another religious school. Accounts from the time that he spent there

210

are sketchy, but a school official has told reporters that Walker was an intense, solitary student. After his capture, Walker told CNN that during his studies his "heart became attached" to the Taliban because the movement had strong support in the region. "I started to read some of the literature of the scholars, the history of the movement," Walker said. "I wanted to help them one way or another." Last April, Walker told his parents in an e-mail that he was still studying the Koran and might travel "someplace cooler" for the summer. Lindh has said that his son did not mention Afghanistan, or hint that he had any other plans but to study. He had not been home in more than a year. But he asked his father for money. Lindh wired $1,200. He did not hear from his son again for eight months.

'Am I in Safe Hands'

20 December 2001

President Bush, referring for the first time to John Walker as a fighter for Osama bin Laden's al Qaeda terrorist network, said yesterday that he hasn't ruled out bringing treason charges that could mean the death penalty for the 20-year-old from Marin County. "Walker's unique in that he's the first American al Qaeda fighter that we have captured," the president said at the White House. The remark represented significantly tougher presidential rhetoric about Walker, who was turned over to U.S. forces in northern Afghanistan this month after being found in a prison with other Taliban or al Qaeda members. Just two weeks ago, the president had described Walker as a "poor boy" who had been "misled, it appears to me." The New York Times reported that unnamed administration officials said there is "growing sentiment" inside the White House to charge Walker with at least one crime that carries the death penalty. Facing a charge that carries a death penalty doesn't mean the government would act to impose it on Walker, one official told the Times. But it would give the government more leverage to negotiate with his lawyers. By referring to Walker as a member of al Qaeda, Bush included him yesterday in a group that the United States has pledged to eradicate and that Washington blames for the Sept. 11 terrorist attacks and such previous assaults as last year's attack on the battleship Cole in Yemen that killed 17 American sailors.

WALKER 'BEING WELL TREATED by the United States Government'

Bush said that Walker, who is now being held aboard a Navy vessel in the Arabian Sea with at least four other detainees, "is being well treated on a ship of ours." "I suspect he's finding his berth a little better than it was when he was placed in the prison in Afghanistan," he added. Bush also said he has ordered the National Security Council to work with the Justice and Defense Departments on a uniform strategy for prosecuting all prisoners seized in Afghanistan that the United States decides to put on trial. Bush will make the final decision on prosecuting Walker. The government disclosed that some 7,000 captured Taliban and al Qaeda members are being held, mostly by Afghan and Pakistani forces. But a few, including Walker, are in U.S. custody. Included among them are some Taliban and al Qaeda leaders, Defense Secretary Donald Rumsfeld said. Positively identifying them and figuring out who the United States wants to prosecute will take some time. In saying he has not ruled out treason charges, Bush was playing down earlier news reports that the Justice Department has recommended prosecuting Walker on charges of lending material support to terrorists. That charge carries a maximum penalty, which was increased after the Sept. 11 attacks, of life in prison, the Justice Department said.

BUSH UNDECIDED ON WALKER

"I have no answer on Walker yet because I want the process to be able to address all the different circumstances that may arise," Bush said. "We've told his lawyer that at the appropriate time we'll let everybody know, including his family, how we're going to proceed with Walker, as well as others that have become captured during this war," Bush said. Walker's lawyer, James Brosnahan of San Francisco, said in a brief written statement that the White House has informed him that it is working on how to proceed in the case. But he denied that a plea bargain is being negotiated. Brosnahan has yet to speak with Walker, who is being held as a "battlefield detainee" under the Geneva Convention on the treatment of prisoners of war. The lawyer repeated his plea for access to his client. "We ask no more than that which the Constitution guarantees to all Americans," he said. Officials told the Times it is likely Walker will land first in Virginia upon his return to the United States. That would allow prosecutors to try him in federal court in the Eastern District of Virginia in Alexandria that is regarded by lawyers as having a relatively conservative jury pool. Moreover, the region was the home of Johnny Micheal "Mike" Spann, the CIA officer who was killed in the prison uprising in Afghanistan where Walker was captured. Anthony Arend, a professor at the Georgetown University law school in Washington, said he was troubled by Bush's characterization of Walker. "He shouldn't have said it, just as he previously shouldn't have called him a 'poor boy.' It can prejudice various people and make selecting a jury more difficult." Arend also said it was unprecedented for the National Security Council to be involved in drafting decisions on prosecuting criminal defendants and said involving several agencies in planning for handling such cases could delay policy formulation. Trying Walker for treason could be tricky because the Constitution requires two witnesses to testify in court about each allegedly treasonous act. Treason charges could also be subject to challenge because Congress did not formally declare war in Afghanistan. Walker could be tried either in U.S. District Court or in a military court- martial. As a U.S. citizen, he is not subject to trial in the secret military tribunals that Bush has authorized. Arend speculated that one result of the continuing administration discussions could be a revised order to allow trying Walker in the closed tribunals.

"Dear Mama and Papa," Walker, a bedraggled new captive of the U.S. military, began in a brief letter to his parents a few weeks ago. "I apologize for not contacting you in such a long time. I realize this must have caused you a lot of grief. I am currently alive and well in Afghanistan and I am in safe hands. I cannot give you many details about my situation but it would be good to hear from you all." He had just survived a bloody uprising of captured al Qaeda fighters in the northern Afghan city of Mazar-e Sharif. Johnny "Mike" Spann, a CIA officer who had been questioning prisoners, including Walker, was killed when the riot erupted. From a hospital bed, Walker told CNN that he did not see or take part in the uprising because he was hiding in a basement of the fort with dozens of other captured Taliban fighters. They did not surrender until Afghan and U.S. forces bombed the compound, then dumped burning oil into the basement, then flooded it with cold water. In a groggy interview, which CNN broadcast last month, he also said that he had been in Afghanistan for six months, had been assigned to a branch of Arab fighters in the Taliban army, and had trained at several camps in the country. With only a faint American accent, a world away from the comforts of his former life and the mild- mannered mosque where his spiritual search began, Walker said that he had volunteered for the fighting. "It's exactly what I thought it would be," he said, softly.

John Walker Lindh bumbled his way through his first trip to the Middle East, unwittingly insulting other Muslims and repeatedly getting into trouble with authorities, say those who encountered the California teen-ager in Yemen. Ultimately, he came to feel that the brand of Islam he encountered in Yemen's capital was not fervent enough - he even objected to having women in his classes, according to students and administrators at the school where he studied Arabic. Lindh, the 20-year-old American who was captured in November fighting with the Taliban in Afghanistan traveled alone to Yemen at 17 in the summer of 1998. A recent Muslim convert, he stepped off the plane full of zeal. He donned white robes and sandals, wore a full beard, and even pretended to speak broken English with an Arabic accent before abandoning the school where his parents had paid thousands of dollars for a year's stay. Lindh instead sought more fundamentalist teachings in the country's dangerous northern mountains, but was repeatedly turned back by Yemen's military, said Steven Hyland, who taught English and studied Arabic at the Yemen Language Center. ``This is an individual whose idealism led to ideology and he lost all ability for pragmatic thought,'' Hyland said by telephone from Texas. It was not the first time he embarrassed the school, situated in the capital of San'a. That came the morning after his arrival, after he exchanged several hundred dollars - a substantial sum in a country where the average civil servant earns about $75 a month. On his way back from the money market, Lindh saw beggars and decided to pay alms to the poor, one of the five pillars of Islam. ``When you give money to beggars in the street, you give them about 10 rials,'' Hyland said. ``He starts passing out 200 rial notes, which is way, way, way too much.'' Lindh was mobbed. A woman who worked at the school had to break up the crowd to protect the young American. ``John is in the middle of this whirlwind of people,'' Hyland recalled. ``He's much taller than the average Yemeni, with a fist full of cash just raised in the air with his left hand and with his right hand just duking the Yemenis away.'' After that incident, Lindh told other students he was disenchanted with aspects of Yemeni culture and began skipping classes at the school, where about 15 language teachers instruct four or five students each in several elegant buildings near the city's center. ``From that point on, Yemenis weren't Muslims and that was the argument that he tried to make,'' Hyland said. Josh Mortensen, another student, said from Cairo that Lindh asked peers to call him Suleiman, affected a ``bogus'' Arabic accent and wore traditional Muslim garb unlike that of most Yemenis. Other foreign students at the school mockingly nicknamed him ``Yusuf Islam,'' the name pop singer Cat Stevens took when he became a Muslim and rejected his music career. ``That whole convert thing just doesn't compute for lifelong Muslims. It's almost like they're being made fun of in a way,'' Mortensen said. ``He was so clueless and so rigid, and it was almost patronizing. He adopts all these ridiculous stereotypes.'' Lindh slipped up again by approaching another student, Rizwan Mawani, who happens to be a Shia Muslim, and asking for directions to a Sunni mosque. Lindh was adamant about not wanting to pray with Shiites, who are part of the other main branch of Islam. ``I wasn't insulted. I found it quite humorous,'' Mawani recalled in a telephone interview from London. In Yemen, Mawani said, Shia and Sunni Muslims typically pray side by side. Lindh was frustrated when he saw some Yemeni Muslims ignoring the calls to prayer, students said. He was particularly bothered when Mawani told Lindh he was more interested in taking a nap, Mawani recalled. Mawani said Lindh considered himself a Salafi, part of a movement whose members believe they are promulgating the true Islamic faith as taught by the prophet Muhammad in seventh-century Arabia. ``Yemenis speak one of the purist forms of Arabic, but it's not a fanatical country,'' said Barbara Bodine, U.S. ambassador at the time. ``Somebody looking for that fire-and-brimstone approach would get to Yemen and be very unhappy. It's simply not there.'' The language center's owner, Sabri Saleem, said Lindh disappeared after complaining that his classes included women and that the secular school did not offer the Islamic studies he craved. Lindh's goal, other students said, was to reach the mountains of northern Yemen, a risky venture for an American teen-ager. Militants there have kidnapped or killed numerous Western tourists. ``John was problematic for the center because he kept trying to steal away to the northern part of the country because there was an Islamic theologian there that he wanted to study under," Hyland said. Saleem, interviewed by telephone recently while visiting the United States, said Lindh did not surface until police caught him at the airport months later. He had overstayed his visa and failed to get an exit visa. Lindh came home to Marin County, north of San Francisco, in the spring of 1999. Eight months later, he returned to Yemen, then went to Pakistan and then Afghanistan, where he fought with the Taliban. Now he is being held by the U.S. military as the Bush administration decides how to deal with him. Lindh's parents referred all questions to their lawyer, James Brosnahan. His spokeswoman had no comment on Lindh's stay in Yemen. Islamic experts said that in his naivete, Lindh, a baptized Roman Catholic who converted to Islam at 16, fell into a trap so common that Muhammad himself predicted it. ``A person who might have been living a typical happy-go-lucky life and then he really gets very much attracted to the teaching of Islam and its ideal, but then he wants to change overnight - that's what the prophet actually was teaching against," said Jamal Badawi of the Islamic Information Foundation in Halifax, Nova Scotia. ``He said, `Go gently.'" American Taliban fighter John Walker Lindh could be tried by a military court-martial in a death-penalty case even though he is not a member of the U.S. armed forces, according to sources close to the Bush administration's deliberations on Walker's fate. The sources say Walker, 20, a former Californian captured in Afghanistan in November, could be charged under a little-known provision of the U.S. military code of justice that prohibits ``aiding the enemy" with ``arms, ammunition, supplies, money or other things." Most provisions of the military justice code apply only to members of the armed services. But part of the code, namely a rarely used provision called Article 104, applies to ``any person." It could be used to help U.S. officials answer the vexing question of how to bring Walker to justice. Because Article 104 charges carry the death penalty, charging Walker with ``aiding the enemy" in a military court-martial would be a way for U.S. authorities to subject him to a potential death sentence while avoiding legal issues that would accompany any plan to try him in a civilian court. A military court-martial is one of several legally complicated options being considered in the Walker case by the

Defense and Justice departments, sources close to the discussions on the case say. U.S. officials have said that Walker, as a U.S. citizen, would not be subject to President Bush's order authorizing military tribunals to try foreigners accused of terrorism. But military law experts say Bush could issue another order to create a tribunal that would deal only with Walker. If Walker were charged in a civilian court, two of the most viable criminal charges that could be brought— treason and murder of a U.S. government employee—would be difficult to prove. Both carry the death penalty. Treason charges are rarely used, largely because of the high standard of proof the Constitution requires for conviction: a "confession in open court" or the testimony of two witnesses to the same treasonous act. Charging Walker with murdering a U.S. government employee also would pose a high hurdle for prosecutors. It would require proof that Walker played a role in the death Nov. 25 of CIA officer Johnny "Mike" Spann during an uprising by Taliban captives at a prison in Afghanistan. Spann tried to interview Walker shortly before the rebellion. U.S. officials have not said whether they believe that Walker had a role in the uprising. H. Wayne Elliott, a retired Army lieutenant colonel who has taught war-crimes courses to Army lawyers, says the laws of war recognize the right of prisoners of war to try to escape. Walker, he says, likely would raise that as a defense if he were charged in the CIA officer's death. Other possible charges Walker could face in a civilian court trial include providing support to terrorists, which carries a maximum punishment of 15 years in prison. Several public opinion polls have indicated that most Americans are outraged by Walker's alleged actions and believe he should be punished more severely. Bush administration officials appear determined to bring serious charges against Walker, or at least to use the threat of such charges to get Walker to tell them everything he knows about Osama bin Laden's al- Qaeda terrorist network. Shortly after his capture, Walker told a CNN crew that he sympathized with al-Qaeda, which U.S. officials say carried out the Sept. 11 attacks on New York and Washington. Walker, who goes by his mother's maiden name, converted to Islam as a teen and traveled to the Middle East in 1998. Legal analysts, citing reports that Walker has told U.S. authorities that he once met bin Laden, say Walker could be valuable to U.S. military intelligence and law enforcement. They say he could be given leniency if he can help identify al-Qaeda members and describe how he became part of the terrorist network. A tribunal, also known as a military commission, would allow prosecutors more leeway in admitting evidence at trial than they would receive in a traditional military or civilian court. To put Walker before a military commission, authorities would have to charge him with a war crime, such as killing civilians, Elliott says. The most logical way Walker could be charged with a war crime, Elliott says, is if he were linked to al-Qaeda. Bush is expected to make the final decision about Walker's prosecution. If he opts for a military court- martial, Elliott says, Walker could argue that he joined the Taliban before the United States went to war in Afghanistan and that he could not leave. Trying a U.S. civilian—even one accused of taking up arms against the United States—in a military setting also raises tough political issues for the White House, analysts say. ''I don't think the administration would want to take the political heat of putting a U.S. citizen before a court-martial or a military tribunal,'' says Michael Nardotti, a retired Army judge advocate general, the military equivalent of a lawyer. ''They may just deal with him in the U.S. (civilian) courts,'' he says. ''But I don't think they will let him walk.''

KABUL (Reuters) - Afghan authorities warned on Saturday the vanquished Taliban movement was regrouping outside the country, while hailing the surrender of a senior Taliban figure as a breakthrough in tracking down other fugitive leaders. Afghan interim Foreign Minister Abdullah Abdullah said some former leaders of the hard-line Islamic Taliban, overthrown as Afghanistan 's rulers by the U.S.-led military campaign, were forming new organizations to oppose the government in Kabul. ''The Taliban leaders ... apparently they are running new organizations,'' Abdullah told reporters in the Afghan capital. ''There are two organizations outside Afghanistan,'' he said. ''We do not have details of the organizations or their structure but on the whole it is not acceptable that the Taliban be able to act either outside or inside Afghanistan in any capacity.'' Most Taliban leaders who fled Afghanistan are thought to be in neighboring Pakistan, which had previously given backing to Taliban rule. Abdullah said he received assurances from Pakistani officials on a visit to Islamabad on Friday with Afghan interim leader Hamid Karzai that Pakistan would take measures to prevent such activities. But distrust has lingered between Pakistan and Afghanistan's Northern Alliance group of military factions, which dominates Karzai's government. Within Afghanistan, U.S. troops continued to track down Taliban officials and remnants of Osama bin Laden 's al Qaeda network, blamed by the United States for the Sept. 11 attacks on New York and Washington. A team of 50 U.S. troops on Saturday investigated the site of a missile strike in southeastern Afghanistan to try to determine who was killed in the attack, a day after U.S. military authorities announced the surrender of former Taliban Foreign Minister Wakil Ahmed Muttawakil. Khalid Pashtoon, spokesman for Kandahar Gov. Gul Agha, told Reuters on Saturday Muttawakil could provide valuable intelligence on the whereabouts of other senior Taliban—including supreme leader Mullah Mohammad Omar. ``Of course he will have important information. He was the foreign minister,'' said Pashtoon, surprised by the sudden detention of Muttawakil by U.S. forces.

MULLAH OMAR'S RIGHT-HAND MAN

Muttawakil was considered Mullah Omar's right-hand man, and Abdullah, the current Afghan foreign minister, said he had been living in the Pakistani city of Quetta with other leaders who had fled Afghanistan. Abdullah was unaware of the circumstances leading to his reappearance, but speculated that Pakistani authorities may have had a hand. ``I don't know how it happened that he finally gave himself up. This might have been with the aid of the Pakistani authorities,'' Abdullah said. Pakistani authorities in Quetta denied any knowledge of Muttawakil's surrender or handover to U.S. forces, and a senior Kandahar political source, who said Muttawakil was a moderate, thought he may have made a deal in return for his safety. A group of 34 prisoners captured during the Afghan war arrived at the U.S. Navy base at Guantanamo Bay, Cuba, on Saturday bringing the total there to 220. The U.S. holds another 237 prisoners in Afghanistan. A senior U.S. Army officer said interrogators were struggling to identify prisoners as Taliban or al Qaeda. ``A large number claim to be Taliban, a smaller number we have been able to confirm as al Qaeda, and a rather large number in the middle we have not been able to determine their status,'' said Brig. Gen. Michael Lehnert. U.S. troops were scouring a remote mountain site struck by a missile fired from a pilotless drone aircraft on Monday at what was believed to be a group of al Qaeda members. The private Afghan Islamic Press said U.S. troops arrived in the Zawar Khili, 20 miles southwest of Khost and 10 miles from the Pakistani border, on board helicopters and spoke with village elders. The AIP said the missile hit a group of young civilians, three of whom were killed. In Kabul, about 270 Afghan Taliban prisoners were released in a ceremony at the presidential palace on Saturday under the watch of Karzai, appointed in December to lead a six-month interim administration. ``We decided some time back we should release everybody who did not have a bad record, who were not terrorists but just ordinary people,'' Karzai said. Pakistani investigators said they were putting pressure on the family of leading suspect Ahmed Omar Saeed Sheikh in the hope it would lead them to U.S. reporter Daniel Pearl, kidnapped in Karachi on Jan. 23

The International Committee of the Red Cross said on Friday it considered Taliban and al Qaeda fighters \ held by U.S. forces to be prisoners of war, despite Washington's latest refusal to accept that. "They were captured in combat (and) we consider them prisoners of war," ICRC spokesman Darcy Christen told Reuters. President Bush (news - web sites) agreed on Thursday to apply the Geneva Conventions to Taliban prisoners but said the al Qaeda network could not be considered a state that is party to the treaty, which guarantees a wide range of rights to captives. Even though acknowledging the Conventions applied to the Taliban, Washington said that group would not be granted full prisoner of war status. Britain, the staunchest ally of the United States in its war against those it considers responsible for the September 11 attacks in New York and Washington, welcomed the move. A spokesman for United Nations (news - web sites) High Commissioner for Human Rights Mary Robinson, who has warned the United States it must treat captives humanely, also said she felt Washington's decision could be a "step forward." But spokesman Jose Luis Diaz added that her legal advisers were still examining the implications of Bush's announcement. A similarly cautious response came from some European capitals, several of which have expressed strong reservations about the way captives from the war in Afghanistan are held. A French Foreign Ministry spokesman said that Paris's view had not changed. "We believe that all the prisoners at Guantanamo should benefit from all the guarantees provided by international law," he said. Washington triggered a storm of international protest after a photograph was released showing some inmates at the Guantanamo Bay prison camp manacled, blindfolded and on their knees. The United States has dismissed all suggestions of mistreatment.

STATUS STILL DISPUTED

Granting prisoner of war status to the captives would have given them sweeping rights, including the right to disclose only their name, rank and serial number under interrogation and to go home as soon as the conflict ended. Both the ICRC and Robinson said that under the Geneva Conventions, to which the United States is a signatory, any dispute over the status of a prisoner must be settled by a tribunal and not the government of one of the sides to the conflict. "You cannot simply decide…what applies to one person and what applies to another. This has to go to court because it is a legal decision not a political one," Christen said. The ICRC spokesman also noted that Article Three of the Third Geneva Convention on captives taken in international combat applied to all fighters. The article sets out minimum standards, including prohibiting cruel treatment and guaranteeing that any trial of prisoners must be carried out before a "regularly constituted" court. Christen said that there was no category under humanitarian law giving more than minimum Article Three protection but falling short of full prisoner of war status—as the U.S. decision implied. "It does not exist," he said. U.S. officials have expressed concern that if Washington gave prisoner of war status to Taliban fighters and members of al Qaeda—the network loyal to Saudi-born militant Osama bin Laden (news - web sites) who Washington says masterminded the September 11 attacks—it would be virtually impossible to interrogate them. Christen noted that former Panamanian dictator Manuel Noriega—overthrown and captured by U.S. troops in 1990—was formally declared a prisoner of war but this did not prevent him being tried and jailed in the United States for drugs offences. The ICRC is visiting prisoners held at the U.S. naval base at Guantanamo Bay, Cuba, as well as inside Afghanistan and will continue to report on their treatment based on standards laid down in the Geneva Convention. From rescue workers who say they have lung problems to business owners who say their shops were damaged, 1,300 people have given notice they may sue the city for a total of $7.18 billion over the aftermath of the World Trade Center attack. The claims involve injuries or damage caused not by the attack itself but by the alleged negligence of the city during the recovery and cleanup. The vast majority are from firefighters who say the city gave them inadequate respiratory protection at the smoldering trade center site. Not all of those who served notice will sue. Some, for example, may instead seek money from the federal victims compensation fund. But the notices preserve their right to bring a lawsuit. The notices show the extent of the health complaints being lodged by hundreds of firefighters, police officers and other recovery workers who fear cancer or other ailments. Asbestos, benzene, dioxin, PCBs and other contaminants have been detected in the twin towers' ruins. In the first few days after the attack, as many as 150 firefighters and police officers were at the scene 24 hours a day. Firefighter Palmer Doyle said he worked two 12-hour days without a respirator at the site. He filed notice of a $10 million claim. ``You run up a couple flights of stairs, which I used to do with no problem, and you find yourself sucking in the air,'' he said. ``What if, five years down the road, we develop lung cancer or something like that?'' Most other notices are from property owners near the trade center. Police officers commandeered Murray's Deli, about four blocks from the twin towers, on the day of the attack, according to Brian Rappaport, the owners' lawyer. They allege the shop was left open by police, robbed and vandalized. The city is self-insured and awards from successful lawsuits would be paid out of the city's general fund. ``We don't believe the city is liable. But we'll obviously have to take a look at the complaints if and when they come in,'' said Corporation Counsel Michael Cardozo, the city's chief lawyer. Notices to sue have to be filed within 90 days, though people can go to court and obtain a waiver of the deadline. An additional 111 notices have been filed with the Port Authority of New York and New Jersey, the owner of the World Trade Center complex. Some city workers could be eligible for benefits from the federal victims' compensation fund. Kenneth Feinberg, the fund's administrator, said workers would have to waive their right to sue if they sought federal compensation, but would get money more quickly and easily through the fund. Yet many firefighters worry that they could develop cancer long after tapping

222

into the federal fund, said Michael Barasch, whose law firm filed notices on behalf of several hundred workers. Fire Department spokesman Frank Gribbon said the department tried to get respirators to firefighters as fast as possible after the attack. ``We know that they were available in a limited capacity in the days that followed Sept. 11,'' Gribbon said. They soon became more plentiful, he said, but even then, ``guys had them around their necks and they weren't wearing them.'' Firefighters may also file for Social Security benefits and receive three-quarters of their last year's pay tax-free for life if a line-of-duty injury forces retirement.

The encrypted jihad

We can't stop terrorists from using uncrackable codes. So we shouldn't even try. - ~ - - ~ - ~ - ~ ~ ~

By Barak Jolish

Feb. 4, 2002 | Here's a tip for Treasury Department agents tracking al-Qaida's finances: You might want to pay a visit to the volume discount department at Dell Computer. Al-Qaida, it seems, has been an avid consumer of computers over the last several years, and is especially fond of laptops. It isn't hard to understand why. With his hectic, on-the-go lifestyle, no self-respecting terrorist can function without a computer that fits comfortably on an airplane tray table. Alleged "20th hijacker" Zacarias Moussaoui, for instance, used his to research crop dusters, quite possibly in preparation for a biological attack on a densely populated American city. Ramsi Yousef used a laptop he accidentally left in a Manila apartment to plan his extensive itinerary, which included assassinating the pope in the Philippines, attacking an Israeli Embassy in Thailand, and bombing the World Trade Center in 1993. It's not surprising, then, that the seizure of computers has become a primary goal for U.S. soldiers scouring Afghan caves and ambushing Taliban and al-Qaida operatives. Ironically, though, winning possession of this equipment on the battlefield may be the easy part; terrorists today have the capacity to protect data with encryption schemes that not even America's high-tech big guns can crack. The number of possible keys in the new 256-bit Advanced Encryption Standard (AES), for example, is 1 followed by 77 zeros—a figure comparable to the total number of atoms in the

223

universe. Luckily, not all encryption is hopelessly secure. Ramsi Yousef was careless in protecting the password to his encrypted files, giving the FBI relatively easy access to their contents. It took the Wall Street Journal only days to decrypt files on two Al-Qaida computers that used a weak version of the Windows 2000 AES cipher in Afghanistan. The U.S. cannot, however, count on such carelessness indefinitely.

But recent changes in U.S. policy have actually reduced restrictions on the spread of sophisticated encryption. In January 2000, for instance, the Clinton administration ruled that "retail products" that undergo a one-time, 30-day government review can be exported to nearly all countries (with the exception of Cuba, Iran, Iraq, Libya, North Korea, Sudan and Syria) without any government licensing requirement. Revisions published later that year relaxed even these limitations for products exported to the 15 nations of the European Union and several of their major trading partners. The practical effect of these reforms has been that the industrial-strength Windows 2000 128-bit High Encryption Pack is now freely available over the Internet to anyone, including Hamburg residents such as presumed.

Since Sept. 11, some commentators and lawmakers have suggested that the U.S. reverse itself once again, and redouble efforts to control encryption. On the surface, this sentiment is understandable—it is difficult to argue against any moves that may prevent future terrorist attacks on the scale of the WTC disaster. This position is, however, dead wrong. Quite simply, the U.S. regime of strict encryption controls didn't make sense before Sept. 11, and it doesn't make sense now. The starkest illustration of this reasoning is the case study of Israel, which is simultaneously a leader in encryption product exports and a major focus of terrorist attacks.

Before President Clinton's 2000 reforms, proponents of encryption export controls were besieged from all sides: on the left and right flanks privacy advocates argued that strong encryption is vital to protecting individual liberty against government intrusion. First Amendment devotees launched a frontal attack in the courts, claiming that encryption code was essentially speech. Most effective, however, was the carpet bombing of lobbyists and campaign contributions from the software industry—the Microsofts, IBMs and Suns of the world— who argued that export controls simply drove customers seeking secure products to companies in other countries—such as Israel. These companies estimated their losses in billions of dollars, and noted the costs to workers as well; even domestic companies were hiring independent overseas software developers to create encryption products.

Though their agendas differed, the above parties were united in their claims that the government's policy stood little chance of significantly controlling criminal use of encryption. First, they noted that producing encryption algorithms takes few resources beyond advanced mathematical training. In fact, sometimes even these skills are not necessary; in early 1999 a 16-year-old Irish high school student named Sarah Flannery developed a new data-encryption algorithm that was 22 times faster than the popular RSA algorithm used in many business transactions today.

Second, reform advocates stressed that there is no practical way to keep encryption within or without the confines of physical borders. For instance, anyone can purchase a copy of the encryption program Crypto II on the streets of Moscow for $5, and then e-mail it to a friend in New York.

Third, legal controls on encryption will bind only those who decide to follow the law. Terrorists who are willing to fly a jet into the side of a building will have no qualms about breaking laws against illegal encryption. Finally, encryption advocates claim that government control stifles development of the strong encryption we need to protect computer networks from attacks by hackers and other criminals, and to secure our systems for air traffic control, electrical distribution, financial markets and telecommunications.

But hasn't Sept. 11 changed the equation? Americans have, after all, now come to accept that they will have to compromise on issues like privacy or economic growth in favor of increased security.

It is specifically in the aftermath of this trauma that where it becomes instructive to look at the policy of Israel, a country defined by its obsession with security. The Israeli predicament is essentially a starker version of that of the U.S. On the one hand, Israel has faced six wars in its first 50 years, and confronts terrorist shootings and suicide bombings virtually every week. Both the Israeli army and the FBI have confirmed that Hamas and other Islamic militants regularly use the Internet to transmit encrypted instructions for terrorist attacks—

including maps, photographs, directions, codes and technical details about how to use bombs. On the other hand, Israel's economy is among the most reliant in the world on high technology exports. In fact, the share of Israel's information technology exports as a percentage of services exports is surpassed only by Japan. All of this has helped earn a country with few natural resources other than potash a per capita GDP of $17,500—higher than that of several members of the European Union.

In this context it is significant that in 1998 Israel, too, revised its rather draconian encryption laws, granting regulators a great deal of flexibility to permit the export of strong encryption products— including a "free means" category for which all license requirements are waived. These changes were prefaced by a government report that noted the futility of limiting "the use of means that can be freely obtained from many public sources," and said that the law should permit Israeli companies to develop and export "competitive products that can be marketed in most of the world's countries as off-the-shelf products." In fact, even before the 1998 liberalization, flexible enforcement had allowed Israeli companies such as Checkpoint Software to dominate the network security field.

The lesson from the Israelis is not how to control terror—they don't seem to have better answers than anyone else—but rather how to live with it and continue to function with as little social and economic disruption as possible. If, as President Bush tells us, we're in this war for the long haul, we simply cannot afford to sap our economic strength to prop up the fantasy that we can control the actions of terrorists by fiat. There are some battles we just shouldn't fight.

A train barreled over Joseph Hewins' body on a wintry evening in 1845 in the Massachusetts Berkshires. Hewins had spent the workday shoveling snow off the tracks, only to be killed on his trip back to town when a switchman got distracted. Hewins left behind a wife and three children, who were poor even before his death. His widow sued but lost at every level. Had the train merely chopped off Hewins' leg, the railroad would have paid. But in the perverse logic of that time, when a man died, he took his legal claims with him. And so the thinking went for most of the century, until something unheard of began to happen. The courts started to put a dollar value on a life— after death. The concept of assigning a price tag to a life has always made people intensely squeamish. After all, isn't it degrading to presume that money can make a family whole again? And what of the disparities? Is a poor man's life worth less than a rich man's? Over the past 100 years, U.S. courts have crafted their answers to these questions. Forensic economists testify on the value of a life every day. They can even tell you the average valuation of an injured knee (about $200,000). But until now, the public at large has not had to reckon with the process and its imperfections. Until the terrorist attacks of Sept. 11 created a small city's worth of grieving families and the government established an unprecedented fund to compensate them, the mathematics of loss was a little-known science. Now the process is on garish display, and it is tempting to avert the eyes.

On the morning of Jan. 18, about 70 family members file into the rows of crimson seats at the Norwalk, Conn., city hall auditorium. They listen quietly to special master Kenneth Feinberg, whom the government has entrusted with dispersing its money to those most affected by the Sept. 11 tragedy. His first job is to persuade them to join the federal Victim Compensation Fund, the country's largest experiment in paying mass victims and their families without placing blame. The effort is being closely watched for the precedents it will set.

Much has been made of the enormous charity funds raised after the attacks. Donations to those groups do funnel thousands of dollars to the victims' families—in particular, the families of fire fighters and police officers. But overall, the nearly $2 billion in charity money is chump change compared with the cash that will flow out of government coffers. There is no limit to the federal fund, but the tab is likely to be triple the size of the charity pot. And while charity funds are doled out to a vast pool of people, including businesses hurt by the attacks, the government money will go exclusively to the injured and to families of the deceased.

Feinberg, in a black-and-white polka-dot tie, speaks in short, punchy sentences and a loud voice. He has already given the speech 32 times up and down the East Coast. The main thrust: The government, for the first time ever, has agreed to write large checks to victims' families without any litigation. The checks will arrive within four months after a claim is filed—no legal fees, no agonizing 10-year lawsuit. But every award will be based on a cold calculus, much the way courts handle wrongful-death claims.

That means different sums for different families. In a TIME/CNN poll taken last month, 86% said all families should receive the same amount. But that's not how it's going to work.

The calculus has several steps, Feinberg explains. First, the government will estimate how much a victim would have earned over his or her lifetime had the planes never crashed. That means a broker's family will qualify for a vastly higher award than a window washer's family. To estimate this amount, each family was handed an easy-to-read chart on the way into the meeting: Find your loved one's age and income and follow your finger to the magic number. Note that the lifetime earnings have been boosted by a flat $250,000 for "pain and suffering"—noneconomic losses, they are called. Tack on an extra $50,000 in pain and suffering for a spouse and for each child. The charts, while functional, are brutal, crystallizing how readily the legal system commodifies life.

Then—and this is crucial—don't get too excited. That first number may be quite high—in the millions for many. But you must, according to the rules of the fund, subtract all the money you are getting from other sources except charities. A court settlement would not be diminished this way, but this is not a court, Feinberg repeatedly points out. Deduct life insurance, pension, Social Security death benefits and workers' compensation. Now you have the total award the government is offering you for your loss.

The deductions have the effect of equalizing the differences in the awards. Critics have called this Feinberg's "Robin Hood strategy." For many people in the room, the number is now at or close to zero. Feinberg says he will make sure no one gets zero. "Leave it to me," he says. But nowhere will that be written into the rules when they are finalized in mid-February. Likewise, many fiances and gay partners will be at the mercy of Feinberg's discretion in seeking awards. Before finding out exactly what they will get—and the rules are complex—families will have to agree never to sue anyone for the attacks. "Normally, that would be a difficult call," says Feinberg. "Not here. The right to sue in this case is simply not a reasonable alternative."

That's because Congress has capped the liability of the airlines, the airport owners, the aircraft manufacturers, the towers' landlord and the city of New York. In the name of the economy, the government severely restricted the victims' rights to sue—whether they join the fund or not. It is this lack of a viable option, even if they would not take it, that galls many families.

Congress created the fund as a safety net for the victims' families, to ensure that they maintain something resembling their current standard of living—whether they get assistance from private insurance or government money. The families see it as so much more. For the traumatized, the charts are like a Rorschach test. Some view the money as a halfhearted apology for the breakdown in security and intelligence that made the attacks possible. Others can't help seeing the award as a callous measure of their loved one's value. Many regard it as a substitute for the millions they think they may have got in court, had the liability not been capped. When the total comes out to be underwhelming, these families take it personally. There's a fundamental clash between the way they interpret the purpose of the fund and the way the government sees it.

After Feinberg speaks, he stands back and braces himself for an artillery of angry rhetorical questions. Gerry Sweeney, whose brother died in Tower 2, Floor 105, points at Feinberg and explains why $250,000 is not enough for pain and suffering in the case of her now fatherless nephew. "Have you ever seen a 12-year-old have a nervous breakdown?" she asks. Another woman concocts an analogy to illustrate for Feinberg what it was like to talk to loved ones as they came to accept their imminent, violent deaths and to watch the towers collapse on live TV. "If your wife was brutally raped and murdered and you had to watch and listen to it happen, what would you think the right amount would be?" Finally, Maureen Halvorson, who lost her husband and her brother, speaks up from the front row in a quiet, bewildered voice. "I just can't accept the fact that the Federal Government is saying my husband and my brother are worth nothing." Feinberg is silent.

The more than 3,000 victims of the Sept. 11 attacks are frozen in snapshots, wide-smiling men and women in crisp suits and uniforms who liked to build birdhouses on weekends and play practical jokes. In the literature of grief, they have become hardworking innocents, heroes and saints. But those they left behind are decidedly human. Some compete with others for most bereaved status; others demand an apology even when no one is listening. Some are popping pills, and others cannot leave the house. Most days, they are inconsolable. And as the rest of the country begins to ease back into normalcy, these families stand, indignant, in the way.

Already, some Americans have lost patience with them. "My tax money should not be given to someone with a $750,000 mortgage to pay who needs a set of fresh, matching towels in her bathroom every season," one person wrote anonymously to the Department of Justice's Web page on victim compensation. "I'm shocked and appalled and very disappointed," wrote a Florida resident, "that some individuals are living in such a rare and well-gilded ivory tower that they feel $250,000 is not sufficient compensation. Most of us, the working people of America, make $20,000 to $40,000 per year. Where do these wealthy, spoiled, greedy folks in New York get off, pretending that what happened to them was so uniquely horrible? I'm over it. Yeah, it was unique. Yeah, it was horrible. Yeah, I sent money to help. And after reading about them suing for more money, I begin to regret it."

It's true that some families' behavior has been less than dignified. The divorced parents of a woman killed in the Pentagon, who are eligible for money because their daughter left no dependents, have filed competing claims. Lawyers are now involved. Says her father: "I guarantee she loved her daddy as much as she loved her mom. I feel that I'm entitled to something."

And it's also a fact that these families will get more money from charities and the government combined than anyone has so far received after the Oklahoma City bombing or the 1998 bombing of the Nairobi embassy. For that matter, if these victims had been killed in a drive-by shooting, they probably would not have received more than a few thousand dollars from state victim-compensation funds.

WTC Aftermath: What Is A Life Worth?

That fact is not lost on the public, particularly people whose relatives have died in everyday tragedies. At the Wichita Eagle in Kansas, editorial-page director Phil Brownlee has received calls and letters from locals disgusted by the families' complaints, and he agrees. "It's just frustrating that the goodwill demonstrated by the government seems to be deteriorating," he says. "Now you've got families who are upset with what most Americans deem to be generous contributions. It's the loss of the spirit of Sept. 11, the souring of that sense of solidarity."

But it may not be fair to compare Sept. 11 with a street crime or even Oklahoma City. After all, these recent attacks involved an orchestrated, simultaneous security breach on four airplanes, carried out by 19 men who had been living and training on our soil. A better comparison might be past international terrorist attacks and plane crashes. Those that have been resolved—and that's a major distinction—do show higher payouts than the average amount likely to come out of the Sept. 11 federal fund.

In 25 major aviation accidents between 1970 and 1984, the average compensation for victims who went to trial was $1 million in current dollars, according to a Rand Corp. analysis. Average compensation for cases settled without a lawsuit was $415,000. The biggest aviation payout in history followed the crash of Pan Am Flight 103 over Lockerbie, Scotland, in 1988. Settlements ranged all over the spectrum, with a couple dozen exceeding $10 million, according to Manhattan attorney Lee Kreindler, who acted as lead counsel. Dividing the total $500 million payout over the 270 victims yields an average award of $1.85 million. However, the families had to hand about a third of their awards to their lawyers, and they waited seven to eight years to see any money. And the families of the six people killed in the 1993 World Trade Center bombing are still waiting for their day in civil court.

In the end, most families will probably choose the fund over litigation. The Lockerbie millions are simply not a realistic possibility. It is always extremely difficult to sue the government. And the liability for the Sept. 11 attacks was capped by Congress at about $1.5 billion per plane. So while the families of those killed in the Pennsylvania and Pentagon crashes may have enough to go around, there are far too many victims in New York. "The court model works perfectly when you don't have $50 billion in damages or 3,000 deaths," says Leo Boyle, a Boston lawyer and president of the Association of Trial Lawyers of America, which supports the fund option and has lined up more than 2,000 attorneys to offer free help navigating its rules. Even without the caps, Boyle insists, victims could not have extracted more money by putting United and American Airlines through bankruptcy. So far, only a handful of suits have been filed.

In any event, there was no talking Congress out of the liability caps when it drafted the airline-bailout package 10 days after the attacks. The airlines could not fly without insurance, and their coverage was far short of what it would take to pay the damages. Federal Reserve Chairman Alan Greenspan privately told congressional leaders that getting the planes up again was the single biggest "multiplier" that could revive the economy on every level. So the Democrats, who usually balk at limiting the ability to sue, accepted the idea of an airline bailout—as long as it came with a mechanism to compensate victims. Oklahoma Senator Don Nickles, the No. 2 Republican in the Senate and a longtime proponent of tort reform, pushed hard to limit how much the victims' families could claim, but he did not prevail.

But once the interim rules were drawn up by Feinberg's office—in conjunction with the Department of Justice and the Office of Management and Budget—there were some surprises. In particular, the figures for pain and suffering astonished some who had backed the fund. "The numbers are low by any measure," says Boyle. Feinberg says he chose the $250,000 figure because that's how much beneficiaries receive from the Federal Government when fire fighters and police die on the job. The additional $50,000 for the spouse and each child is, he admits, "just some rough approximation of what I thought was fair." He calls the fund "rough justice."

The American Tort Reform Association, backed mostly by Republicans, has been lobbying since 1986 to limit noneconomic damages in some suits to $250,000. John Ashcroft, head of the Justice Department, pushed for such a cap on punitive damages when he was a Senator. But Feinberg, a Democrat, insists he was not pressured by the Administration to keep the numbers low.

No matter how many times tearful widows accuse him of protecting the airlines, Feinberg does not blush. A lawyer with decades of experience in the messy art of compromise (Feinberg was special master for the $180 million distributed to veterans exposed to Agent Orange), he is accustomed to rage. "On Tuesday I get whacked for this or that in New Jersey. The next day it's New York. It goes with the job." But he rejects the theory that greed is a factor. "People have had a loved one wrenched from them suddenly, without warning, and we are only five months beyond that disaster. It was nearly yesterday. And they are desperately seeking, from what I've seen, to place as much of a value on that lost loved one as they can. So here is where they seek to amplify the value of that memory. They do it by saying we want more, as a validation of the loss. That's not greed. That's human nature."

Susan and Harvey Blomberg of Fairfield County, Conn., have been to three meetings on the victim-compensation fund, even though, as parents of a victim who has left a wife and kids behind, they are not in line for compensation. The rules give preference to the victim's spouse and children. But the Blombergs come to these meetings to be part of something, to be counted. And they linger after everyone else has left. "My daughter-in-law was upset when we went to the meetings," Susan says. "She said, 'It's not really about you. It's about the widows and children.' And I said, 'I want more information.' You can't compare grief, because nobody can get inside you. But I feel like an orphan. When they did this formula, why didn't they consider the parents? My daughter-in-law was married for five years. We had Jonathan for 33 years."

"It's a horrible thing that this is where our energies need to be pulled," says Cheri Sparacio, 37, the widow of Thomas Sparacio, a currency trader at Euro Brokers who died in Tower 2. In their modest house in Staten Island, littered with the toys of her twin two-year-olds, she explains why she sees the estimated $138,000 she would get from the fund as a cheap bribe. "The government is not taking any responsibility for what it's done. This was just one screw-up after another." She is also worried about her financial stability; in less than a month, she will have their third child. Thomas was the primary wage earner, although Cheri worked as a part-time school psychologist until Sept. 11. She doesn't see how she can go back to work with an infant and two toddlers unless she hires full-time help. "Please, come step into my shoes for a minute," she says, her eyes flat and unblinking. "I am not looking to go to Tahiti."

But uptown in the apartment where Samuel Fields once lived, the fund acts like a quiet equalizer, a way for the government to guarantee that victims with less insurance emerge with basic support. Fields was a security guard for six years in Tower 1. He made $22,000 a year and lived with his family in a housing project in Harlem. On Sept. 11, he helped people evacuate the building and then went back inside to help some more. Fields never came home. Next month his widow Angela will give birth to their fifth child. Because Fields made a small salary, his family's preliminary award is less than Sparacio's. But his family's deductions are also smaller. In the end, Angela's estimated $444,010 award will probably be three times the size of Cheri's.

In valuing different lives differently—the first part of the equation—the fund follows common legal practice. Courts always grant money on the basis of a person's earning power in life. That's because the courts are not attempting to replace "souls," says Philip Bobbitt, a law professor at the University of Texas who has written about the allocation of scarce resources in times of tragedy. "We're not trying to make you psychologically whole. Where we can calculate the loss is in economic loss." The Feinberg plan differs from legal norms in deducting the value of life insurance and pensions. Also, it allows no flexibility in determining noneconomic damages. In court, pain and suffering would be weighed individually.

Money aside, a lawsuit can be an investigative device like no other, forcing answers about what led to a death. Some Sept. 11 families say they might file suit for that reason alone, even if they never get a dime. And for other families, there is enormous value in no lawsuits at all. David Gordenstein lost his wife, Lisa Fenn Gordenstein, on American Flight 11. "Am I sad? I've had my heart torn out," he says. But he would rather devote his life to raising his two young daughters than pursuing a lawsuit. He will probably file a claim with the federal fund, which he acknowledges is not perfect. "I am proud of what my country tried to do. I think the intention is noble."

The night before Lisa died, she slipped a clipping under the door of David's home office, something she often did. It was a saying from theologian Charles Swindoll that read, "Attitude, to me, is more important than facts. It is more important than the past, than education, than money, than circumstances, than failures, than successes, than what other people think or say or do...It will make or break a company, a church, a home." David read it at her memorial. And while he jokes that it's kind of cliched—"typical Lisa"—he says he thinks its message might help carry his family through this.

For a moment last week it looked as if George W. Bush was about to declare war on three enemies at once. During his State of the Union speech, when the President asserted that Iran, Iraq and North Korea "constitute an axis of evil," he fired a shot that had been months in the making. Since the fall, Bush had been worrying that terrorists might get their hands on nuclear, biological or chemical weapons—and he wanted to warn rogue states not to help them do it. So in January the Defense Department drew up an assessment of the danger and channeled it back to the White House, where two speechwriters, Michael Gerson and David Frum, came up with what they thought was the perfect rallying cry.

Bush liked their phrase—"axis of evil"—from the start, catching the historical reference to the World War II alliance among Germany, Italy and Japan. So after 11 drafts circulated among his top advisers, he stood before Congress, the country and the world last Tuesday, clenched his fist and delivered the line with gusto, then made a vow. "I will not wait on events while the dangers gather," he said. "I will not stand by as peril draws closer and closer. The United States of America will not permit the world's most dangerous regimes to threaten us with the world's most destructive weapons." He drew a rousing cheer from the crowd; but as people caught their breath, they had to wonder precisely what Bush had in mind.

As those questions mounted the next day—allies wondered if Bush was moving toward some sort of unilateral, pre-emptive strike—the Administration scaled back its rhetoric. A senior White House official cautioned reporters not to read too much into the President's remarks. But on Thursday Bush and his team cranked it up again. The President warned Iran, Iraq and North Korea that they are on his "watch list" and that "they better get their house in order." National Security Adviser Condoleezza Rice vowed that the U.S. would "use every tool at our disposal" to turn back the threat.

If the stop-and-go saber rattling was a sign of disagreement among senior Bush officials, there was no doubt that the hard-liners had won again. The "axis of evil" line was in many ways a repudiation of policies that the Administration's lonely moderate, Secretary of State Colin Powell, has championed since the early days of the current presidency. Powell's first major conflict with the White House came last year, when he expressed a desire to continue talks with North Korea begun during the Clinton years. Bush's rhetoric last week made that almost unthinkable for now. Powell was stone-faced during and after the speech, and the moderates at State were stunned. Most of the top officials there had not seen the tough language before it was delivered. Powell had seen it, but he is not a natural infighter, and in recent weeks he has lost ground on a series of debates with hard-liners like Vice President Dick Cheney and Defense Secretary Donald Rumsfeld over Administration policy toward the Middle East (Powell wanted greater engagement) and treatment of al-Qaeda detainees at Guantanamo Bay (Powell wanted to be more faithful to the Geneva Convention). But Bush himself had pushed for linking the three countries, and Powell appears not to have contested it. At his morning meeting on Thursday, he told senior staff members "not to take the edge off" Bush's message. On Friday at the World Economic Forum in New York City, he stuck to the party line.

As a phrase, "axis of evil" is misleading. There is no alliance among the three countries Bush chose to label. In fact, Iran and Iraq fought a war from 1980 to 1988 in which a million people died. Moreover, the connection between weapons of mass destruction and terrorism is not as straightforward as Bush made it seem. Administration experts admit that North Korea has been out of the terrorism business for more than a decade and that it remains on the State Department's list of state sponsors of terrorism largely as a form of diplomatic pressure. Iraq's support for terrorism has centered mainly on groups that attack Iran.

The one area in which the three countries do cooperate is missiles, and it is there that the true logic of the speech may lie. Iran financed North Korea's missile program in exchange for shipments of the finished product. Administration officials claim that Iraq has bought missile equipment from North Korea, one of the most prolific of blatant weapons producers. But terrorists have little interest in missiles—they would rather get their hands on a small nuclear or biological device that could be smuggled into the U.S. Critics say Bush blurred the two threats—terrorism and missile attacks—with an eye to his $200 billion missile-defense program. Linking the two, says Ivo Daalder of the Brookings Institution, "gives you a rationale for building missile defense that terrorism alone does not."

Even if they are not an axis, Iran, Iraq and North Korea pose real threats. Tehran may have helped senior Taliban and al-Qaeda members escape from Afghanistan. All three are trying to obtain nuclear weapons and have—or have had—chemical and biological weapons stockpiles; any of them could provide a weapon of mass destruction to a terrorist if one came shopping. For that reason, the Administration argues, it must be prepared to act pre-emptively—and put the bad guys on warning. A senior Administration official says the message is, "You have a choice. That doesn't mean military action is imminent, but it does mean the President is serious about the campaign."

The response from the so-called axis, not surprisingly, was hostile. Iran's religious leader, Ayatullah Ali Khamenei, joining Bush in a name-calling standoff, said it is the U.S. that is "evil." North Korea said the speech was "little short of declaring war." And Iraq said, "Such threats do not scare us."

America's closest allies offered a muted response while they tried to figure out what would come next. But even top Bush aides could not agree on that. Some said relations with the axis states would actually be helped by the speech. "We do have this willingness to engage if North Korea is prepared to get serious," an official said Friday. But others crowed that engagement was dead. "How are you going to negotiate with a member of the axis of evil?" said a Bush hard-liner.

That has been the question for years, as one Administration after another has tried to deal with the problems posed by Iran, Iraq and North Korea. All three have at times survived as much isolation as the rest of the world could muster and still succeeded in stockpiling their weapons. And while Western diplomacy has brought somewhat better behavior—increased contact with Iran, easing of tensions on the Korean peninsula—it has not diminished each country's fervent search for weapons of mass destruction. Pentagon brass still wince at the memory of Bill Clinton's 1998 speech warning that the world must come up with "a genuine solution" to the Saddam problem and "not simply one that glosses over" it. Bush may not be glossing over the problem, but a genuine solution will require more than tough talk.

With Reporting by John F. Dickerson, Mark Thompson and Douglas Waller/Washington, Tim Larimer/Tokyo and Azadeh Moaveni/Tehran Saddam Hussein

"Iraq continues to flaunt its hostility toward America. This is a regime that has something to hide."—BUSH

- THE CHARGE Iraq hid large parts of its chemical and biological weapons from U.N. inspectors. It is the only country to use chemical weapons in recent history, killing thousands of Iranians and its own Kurdish citizens. Believed to have been close to building a primitive nuclear weapon before the Gulf War, it may be close to nuclear success now. Saddam has given sanctuary to several terrorist groups and is suspected of sponsoring some terrorist attacks.

- IS IT REALLY THAT BAD? There is widespread sympathy for the suffering of Iraqi people. Even most Arab leaders would like to see Saddam go—though they would surely not welcome a U.S. invasion.
- WILL THE U.S. TAKE ACTION? The Pentagon is still developing its options. To invade, the U.S. would need months to organize a coalition and find a staging area in a neighboring country. For now, the U.S. has restored funding (suspended for a few weeks early this year) to the opposition Iraqi National Congress and is looking for other dissenters to support.

Ayatullah Ali Khamenei

"Iraq continues to flaunt its hostility toward America. This is a regime that has something to hide."—BUSH

- THE CHARGE Iraq hid large parts of its chemical and biological weapons from U.N. inspectors. It is the only country to use chemical weapons in recent history, killing thousands of Iranians and its own Kurdish citizens. Believed to have been close to building a primitive nuclear weapon before the Gulf War, it may be close to nuclear success now. Saddam has given sanctuary to several terrorist groups and is suspected of sponsoring some terrorist attacks.
- IS IT REALLY THAT BAD? There is widespread sympathy for the suffering of Iraqi people. Even most Arab leaders would like to see Saddam go—though they would surely not welcome a U.S. invasion.
- WILL THE U.S. TAKE ACTION? The Pentagon is still developing its options. To invade, the U.S. would need months to organize a coalition and find a staging area in a neighboring country. For now, the U.S. has restored funding (suspended for a

few weeks early this year) to the opposition Iraqi National Congress and is looking for other dissenters to support.

Ayatullah Ali Khamenei

"Iran pursues these weapons and exports terror, while an unelected few repress the people."—BUSH

- THE CHARGE Most active state-terror sponsor. Believed to be behind that boatload of weapons to Arafat, it has chemical and biological stockpiles and is thought to be less than a decade away from building nuclear weapons.
- IS IT REALLY THAT BAD? Moderate President Mohammed Khatami has tried to rein in terror activity and offered support during the U.S. campaign in Afghanistan.
- WILL THE U.S. TAKE ACTION? Not yet; this was merely a warning.

Kim Jong Ii

"North Korea is a regime arming with weapons of mass destruction, while starving its citizens."—BUSH

- THE CHARGE Thought to have made enough plutonium for at least one nuclear weapon before freezing its program in 1994. Has chemical and biological weapons; missile program could threaten the U.S. Has sold missile technology to Iran and Pakistan.
- IS IT REALLY THAT BAD? Experts agree NoKo hasn't been in the terror game for years. Relations with South Korea had been thawing.
- WILL THE U.S. TAKE ACTION? No, at least for now.

An American who fought with the Taliban in Afghanistan is expected to plead innocent to a 10-count indictment, as prosecutors and defense lawyers agree the trial should start no earlier than mid-November.

From this time forward our government needs to hold john walker accountable for his actions as a act of Terrorism. This by no means is over it is just starting and will continue to until we bring our soldiers, sailors and airman and women home and worry about this in this country since we are in a recession.

With John Walker Lindh's lawyers vigorously fighting the charges, the former California resident was being arraigned Wednesday before U.S. District Judge T.S. Ellis III. He was moved from the Alexandria jail to the federal courthouse two hours before his scheduled appearance.

Before months of legal squabbling is to begin, the defense and federal prosecutors filed a rare, joint motion Tuesday agreeing to put off the trial for at least nine months.

The defense said it would need time to conduct overseas investigations, handle classified information, argue for suppression of evidence and allow the effects of prejudicial publicity to fade.

Federal prosecutors said they disagreed with a delay due to publicity, but accepted the other reasons for a November date.

Until now the two sides have agreed on little, with prosecutors portraying Lindh as a cold-blooded killer who hated America, and the defense contending he signed up to fight the anti-Taliban northern alliance, not the United States.

Lindh, who just turned 21, could face life imprisonment if convicted of the major charges.

The defense said in the motion that "due to the high level of prejudicial publicity, passage of time will be necessary in order that the defendant receive a fair and impartial trial."

The federal courthouse in Alexandria is just a few miles from the Pentagon where suicide hijackers crashed one of the four airliners they commandeered on Sept. 11.

Pointing out that the indictment describes Lindh's conduct in Yemen, Pakistan and Afghanistan, the defense said it would conduct interviews abroad. Lindh's lawyers also served notice that pretrial hearings would be required on the handling of classified information.

Lindh trained in an Osama bin Laden camp in Pakistan and stayed after he was told bin Laden "had sent forth some fifty people to carry out twenty suicide terrorist operations against the United States and Israel," the indictment charges.

Bin Laden is the No. 1 suspect in the Sept. 11 attacks.

Lindh's lawyers have argued in court and to the news media that the government is relying on a tainted FBI interview of Lindh in Afghanistan, conducted without a lawyer present. The government countered that Lindh signed a paper waiving his right to an attorney.

Virginia (CNN)—John Walker Lindh pleaded not guilty Wednesday to 10 charges filed against him in federal court, including conspiracy to kill Americans overseas while fighting with the Taliban in Afghanistan.

The judge asked defense and prosecuting attorneys to return to court in Alexandria, Virginia, on Friday to set a trial date.

Walker Lindh is accused of joining al Qaeda fighters in the Afghan war. The grand jury indictment against him also includes charges of providing support to al Qaeda and other terrorist groups; and using firearms and destructive devices, including hand grenades, in crimes of violence, in addition to conspiracy to kill Americans overseas.

Walker Lindh, wearing a green prison jumpsuit, replied "not guilty, sir," to the charges.

U.S. District Court Judge T. S. Ellis rejected an agreement between prosecutors and defense attorneys to delay the trial until November, saying the date was "too far, it's not appropriate."

Instead, Ellis asked attorneys to return to court Friday with an agreement to start in August or September, suggesting they consider starting jury selection on August 26.

Defense attorneys had been concerned about pretrial publicity and hoped for a delay to allow emotions to settle. Federal attorneys said pretrial publicity would not dissipate, but cited the need to collect evidence from three countries, including a war zone, in their request for a delay.

Walker Lindh's parents were in the courtroom, as were the parents and widow of CIA operative Micheal (Johnny) Spann, who was killed in an uprising at the Mazar e-Sharif prison where Walker Lindh was held. Spann, the first American killed in combat in Afghanistan, interrogated the 21-year-old Californian about 30 minutes before the start of the uprising.

"We expect Mr. Walker to be held personally responsible for all the things that he's done," said Spann's widow, Shannon, after the arraignment.

Spann would not comment on whether she thought Walker Lindh should be charged with treason, but her late husband's mother unequivocally said Walker Lindh's actions were "treasonous."

Walker Lindh is not charged with, nor is he believed involved directly in, Spann's death.

241

ROCHELLE RILEY: U.S. Taliban's parents let him down

February 13, 2002
BY ROCHELLE RILEY FREE PRESS COLUMNIST

I don't know Marilyn Walker. But I can't help but sympathize with her grief.

I can't help but wonder how she's handling the what-if's that she surely is asking herself, the woulda-coulda-shouldas that must be haunting her about her son, John, who's sitting in a northern Virginia detention center, indicted on everything but treason.

I can't help but feel her pain, knowing she cannot hug him, cannot take back the years she and her ex-husband, Frank Lindh, let him have total freedom instead of guiding him with stronger hands. I can't help but admire the unconditional love she has declared for him at press conferences.

But what I can't understand is how a parent could let go so easily of a son just because he's becoming a man.

It's just too easy to say Marilyn Walker and Frank Lindh weren't parenting their son, John, but only financing his fantasies and misguided exploration of Islam. It's harder to understand why.

A long leash

When John rejected his family's Catholicism, they weren't bothered. When he needed more freedom, they sent him to an alternative high school where, according to Newsweek, students shape their own studies and check in with their teacher once a week.

When he embraced hip-hop at 14 and occasionally posed as an African American online, his parents were not the ones he turned to with questions; he asked his online friends.

When he converted to Islam, walking around Marin County, Calif., in long flowing robes and quitting school, his parents did not object.

And when he wanted to move to Yemen to be closer to Islamic purity, his parents paid for it, his father later telling Newsweek he supported his son's "commitment to learning."

But there was more, according to Newsweek. When he e-mailed his father defending the October 2000 attack on the USS Cole that killed 17 sailors because, he said, it was "an act of war" for the

242

destroyer to enter a Yemeni harbor, his father didn't stop funding his descent into hate.

When John came home in 1999, his parents, despite their worries, didn't make the 18-year-old stay home. They let him return to Yemen, which he later left for Afghanistan.

Belated lessons

His parents were committed to his learning, but what has John Walker Lindh—I mean, Suleyman al-Faris—I mean, Abdul Hamid (the name he took when he joined the Taliban)—learned?

For one thing, he has learned that his parents cannot buy his way out of that detention center.

He also has learned that taking up arms with Islamic terrorists against America is serious business.

Some Americans want Lindh tried for treason, something that is not likely to happen to the son of upper-middle class California parents who only wanted to find himself. Others want a trial only if he fought against Americans.

What can a young Islamic convert who bit off more than he could chew do now? He can stand as an example to other teens to be careful of what you search for and what you do with what you find. He is a reminder to parents of all backgrounds that you must parent your children, not just finance their delusions.

If we ever forget, there's a young man who can remind us. He's sitting in a northern Virginia detention center facing a 10-count indictment accusing him, among several things, of conspiring to kill Americans and providing resources to terrorists.

He's only 20 years old. But he'll go to jail like a man.

Exceptional answer but he will prevail like all other in his situation and his parents money like all other rich kids the parent will pull him out of this situation. This will happen due to some fault of the soldiers or our government between religion and politics... Same thing that happened with Saddam still in power. But my opinion is that he should FRY just like any other traitor.

DEPARTMENT OF VETERANS AFFAIRS
Regional Office
One Veterans Plaza
701 Clay Avenue
Waco, Texas 76799

April 8, 2002

In Reply Refer To: 349/213C

RANDY L STAMM
APT 203
901 W BRUTON
MESQUITE TX 75149

Dear Mr. Stamm:

This is to certify that records maintained by the Department of Veterans Affairs (VA) certify that **RANDY L STAMM**, social security number **465-21-1583**, has a compensable service-connected disability of **100%** percent due to Individual Unemployability. This disability was in effect **JANUARY 1, 2002**.

The appropriate Tax Collector's Office will determine your eligibility for tax exemption upon presentation of this letter.

Sincerely yours,

Maribeth Cully

MARIBETH CULLY
Veterans Service Center Manager

213C/098   SSZ:ssz

fl27-8

244

MAR 2 5 2002

DEPARTMENT OF VETERANS AFFAIRS
VA Regional Office
One Veterans Plaza
701 Clay Avenue
Waco TX 76799

In Reply Refer To: 349/211E
C▬▬▬▬
STAMM, R L

RANDY L STAMM
APT 203
901 W BRUTON RD
MESQUITE TX 75149

Dear Mr. Stamm:

We made a decision on your claim for an increase in your service connected compensation received on November 30, 2001.

This letter tells you about your entitlement amount and payment start date and what we decided. It includes a copy of our rating decision that gives the evidence used and reasons for our decision. We have also included information about additional benefits, what to do if you disagree with our decision, and who to contact if you have questions or need assistance.

What Is Your Entitlement Amount And Payment Start Date?

Your monthly entitlement amount is shown below:

Monthly Entitlement Amount	Payment Start Date	Reason For Change
▬▬▬	Apr 1, 2002	Increased Evaluation
▬▬▬	Aug 7, 2004	Brittni Will Attain Age 18

When Can You Expect Payment?

Your payment begins the first day of the month following your effective date. You will receive a payment covering the initial amount due under this award, minus any withholdings, in approximately 15 days. Payment will then be made at the beginning of each month for the prior month. For example, benefits due for May are paid on or about June 1.

What Did We Decide?

We granted entitlement to the 100% rate effective March 2, 2002, because you are unable to work due to your service connected disability/disabilities.

245

Stamm, R L

No examination will be scheduled in the future.

Your overall or combined rating is 70% plus entitlement to individual unemployability. We do not add the individual percentages of each condition to determine your combined rating. We use a combined rating table that considers the effect from the most serious to the least serious conditions.

We have enclosed a copy of our Rating Decision for your review. It provides a detailed explanation of our decision, the evidence considered and the reasons for our decision. You can find the decision discussed in the section titled *"Decision."* The evidence we considered is discussed in the section titled *"Evidence."* The reasons for our decision can be found in the portion of the rating titled *"Reasons for Decision"* or *"Reasons and Bases."*

We enclosed a VA Form 21-8760, "Additional Information for Veterans with Service-Connected Permanent and Total Disability," which explains certain factors concerning your benefits.

We enclosed a VA Form 21-8764, "Disability Compensation Award Attachment-Important Information," which explains certain factors concerning your benefits.

Are You Entitled To Additional Benefits?

Your dependents may be eligible for Dependents' Educational Assistance. We are enclosing a VA pamphlet 22-73-3, "Summary of Education Benefits," which explains the program. To make a claim, complete and return the enclosed VA Form 22-5490.

You are entitled to medical care by the VA health care system for any service connected disability. You may apply for medical care or treatment at the nearest medical facility. If you apply in person, present a copy of this letter. If you apply by writing a letter, include your VA file number and a copy of this letter.

What You Should Do If You Disagree With Our Decision.

If you do not agree with our decision, you should write and tell us why. You have *one year from the date of this letter to appeal the decision.* The enclosed *VA Form 4107, "Your Rights to Appeal Our Decision,"* explains your right to appeal.

Do You Have Questions Or Need Assistance?

If you have any questions or need assistance with this claim, please call us at 1-800-827-1000. If you use a Telecommunications Device for the Deaf (TDD), the number is 1-800-829-4833.

Stamm, R L

If you call, please refer to your VA file number 465 21 1583. If you write to us, put your full name and VA file number on the letter. Please send all correspondence to the address at the top of this letter. You can visit our web site at www.va.gov for more information about veterans' benefits.

We sent a copy of this letter to Disabled American Veterans (254) 299-9932 because you appointed them as your representative. If you have questions or need assistance, you can also contact them.

Sincerely yours,

Maribeth Cully

MARIBETH CULLY
Veterans Service Center Manager

Enclosure(s): Rating Decision
              VA Form 21-8760
              VA Form 21-8764
              VA Form 22-5490
              VA pamphlet 22-73-3
              VA Form 4107

cc: DAV

212/083   DPSTAMM   DP:dp

DEPARTMENT OF VETERANS AFFAIRS
VA Regional Office
One Veterans Plaza
701 Clay Avenue
Waco, Texas 76799

Randy L. Stamm

VA File Number
████████

Represented by:
DISABLED AMERICAN VETERANS

Rating Decision
March 21, 2002

INTRODUCTION

Randy Stamm is a Peacetime and Gulf War veteran. He served in the Army from February 14, 1980 to April 30, 1995.

DECISION

1 . Entitlement to individual unemployability is granted effective March 2, 2002.

2 . Basic eligibility to Dependents' Educational Assistance is established from March 2, 2002

EVIDENCE

- Treatment Reports, North Texas Health Care System (VAMC Dallas, Bonham and Outpatient Clinic Ft. Worth), from July 15, 1999 through March 13, 2002
- Statement from, veteran, dated October 26, 2001
- VA Form 119, Report of Contact, dated March 21, 2002

REASONS FOR DECISION

1. Entitlement to individual unemployability.

FACTS: Treatment Reports, North Texas Health Care System (VAMC Dallas, Bonham and Outpatient Clinic Ft. Worth) from July 15, 1999 through March 13, 2002 show the veteran on treatment for fibromyalgia. The veteran has insomnia. A report in February 2002 shows the veteran has been up for four days. The records also show that on February 28, 2002 the veteran reported he wanted to return back to work and a statement to return to work was provided. A report dated March 5, 2002 shows the veteran stating he was laid off from work.

Statement from, veteran, dated October 26, 2001 shows the veteran stating that he has lost two jobs since leaving the military due to his medical problems. The veteran further states that he is on medical leave for the second time in four years with the chance of loosing another job because of his medical problems and medications.

VA Form 119, Report of Contact, dated March 21, 2002 shows the veteran stating that he lost his job on March 1, 2002. The veteran further reported that he was told he was no longer needed. The veteran reports missing significant time from work due to his disabilities.

ANALYSIS: Entitlement to individual unemployability is granted because the claimant is unable to secure or follow a substantially gainful occupation as a result of service-connected disabilities.

The evidence of record shows the veteran missing work because of his service-connected disabilities. The records also show the veteran with a loss of jobs because of his medical conditions. The records further show the veteran recently lost employment again. Since the veteran is unable to maintain a substantially gainful occupation due to service connected disabilities, entitlement to individual unemployability is warranted. Entitlement to unemployability is granted from the first day following loss of employment.

2. Eligibility to Dependents' Educational Assistance under 38 U.S.C. chapter 35.

FACTS: The evidence of records shows the veteran permanently and totally disabled due to service- connected disabilities.

ANALYSIS: Eligibility to Dependents' Educational Assistance is derived from a veteran who was discharged under other than dishonorable conditions and has a permanent and

Randy L. Stamm
Page 3

total service-connected disability; or a permanent and total disability was in existence at the time of death; or the veteran died as a result of a service-connected disability.

Randy L. Stamm
Page 4

REFERENCES:

Title 38 of the Code of Federal Regulations, Pensions, Bonuses and Veterans' Relief contains the regulations of the Department of Veterans Affairs which govern entitlement to all veteran benefits. For additional information regarding applicable laws and regulations, please consult your local library, or visit us at our web site, www.va.gov.

 **Department of
Veterans Affairs**

R L Stamm

**ADDITIONAL INFORMATION FOR VETERANS WITH SERVICE-CONNECTED
PERMANENT AND TOTAL DISABILITY**

BENEFITS FOR VETERANS
SPECIALLY ADAPTED HOUSING

Veterans who have a service-connected disability entitling them to compensation for permanent and total disability due to:

(1) the loss, or loss of use of both lower extremities, such as to preclude locomotion without the aid of braces, crutches, canes, or a wheelchair, or

(2) disability which includes (a) blindness in both eyes, having only light perception, plus (b) loss or loss of use of one lower extremity, or

(3) the loss or loss of use of one lower extremity together with residuals of organic disease or injury or the loss or loss of use of one lower and one upper extremity which so affect the functions of balance or propulsion as to preclude locomotion without resort to braces, crutches, canes or a wheelchair;

may be entitled to a VA grant of not more than 50 percent, or up to a maximum of $43,000, to pay part of the cost of building, buying or remodeling a specially adapted house or to pay indebtedness on such homes already acquired. Apply to the nearest VA office.

SPECIAL HOME ADAPTATION GRANT

Veterans who have a service-connected disability entitling them to compensation due to:

(1) blindness in both eyes with 5/200 visual acuity or less, or

(2) the anatomical loss or loss of use of both hands may be entitled to a VA grant of not more than $8,250 to pay the cost of remodeling a house in which they reside. Apply to the nearest VA office.

SOCIAL SECURITY CREDITS

Monthly retirement, disability, and survivors benefits under Social Security are payable to a veteran and his/her family if he/she has earned enough work credits under the program. In addition, the veterans may qualify at 65 for Medicare's hospital insurance and medical insurance. Since July 1, 1973, Medicare also has been available to people under 65 who have been entitled to Social Security disability checks for 2 years or more and to insured people and their dependents with severe kidney disease who need dialysis or kidney transplants.

Service personnel and veterans may be entitled to Social Security work credits for active service performed after September 15, 1940.

Further information about Social Security credits and benefits is available from any Social Security office. For the address and telephone number, look in the telephone directory under Social Security Administration.

VA FORM
AUG 1998 **21-8760 (JF)** SUPERSEDES VA FORM 21-8790, OCT 1992, WHICH WILL NOT BE USED.

BENEFITS FOR VETERANS *Continued*
COMMISSARY AND EXCHANGE PRIVILEGES

Honorably discharged veterans with 100 percent service-connected disability, their dependents and unremarried surviving spouses are entitled to unlimited exchange and commissary store privileges. Certification of total disability will be given by the Department of Veterans Affairs. Assistance in completing DD Form 1172 (Application for Uniformed Services Identification and Privilege Card) may be provided by the nearest VA office. If you have questions or need more information call toll-free 1-800-827-1000 or for the hearing impaired - TDD 1-800-829-4833.

BENEFITS FOR DEPENDENTS
EDUCATIONAL ASSISTANCE

Generally surviving spouses of deceased veterans, spouses of living veterans and children of either, between 18 and 26 years old, when the death or permanent and total disability was the result of service in the Armed Forces, are entitled to benefits.

If eligible children under 18 have (a) graduated from high school or (b) are above the age of compulsory school attendance, VA benefits may begin for this schooling before the children reach age 18.

CHAMPVA (Civilian Health and Medical Program of the Department of Veterans Affairs)

VA is authorized to provide medical care for the spouse or child of a veteran who has total disability, permanent in nature, resulting from a service-connected disability, and the surviving spouse or child of a veteran who has died of a service-connected disability, providing they do not have entitlement to care under **CHAMPUS (Civilian Health and Medical Program of the Uniformed Services)** or Medicare. Normally, this care will be provided in non-VA facilities under the CHAMPVA program. VA facilities however, may be utilized for specialized treatment when (1) they are uniquely equipped to provide the most effective care and (2) use of these facilities does not interfere with the care and treatment of veterans.

JOB COUNSELING AND EMPLOYMENT SERVICES

A job and job training counseling service program, employment placement service program, and job training placement service program are available to a spouse of any veteran who has a total disability permanent in nature resulting from a service-connected disability or the spouse of a veteran who dies while a disability so evaluated was in existence.

Information concerning other Department of Veterans Affairs, Federal, State or local benefits may be obtained from your nearest VA office or from any national service organization representative.

**Department of
Veterans Affairs**

R L Stamm

DISABILITY COMPENSATION AWARD ATTACHMENT
IMPORTANT INFORMATION

WHEN IS YOUR VA CHECK DELIVERED?
A check covering the initial amount due under this award will be mailed within 15 days. Thereafter, checks will be delivered at the beginning of each month for the prior month.

HOW CAN YOU RECEIVE HOSPITALIZATION AND OUTPATIENT TREATMENT?
Veterans who have one or more service-connected disabilities as determined by the Veterans Benefits Administration are eligible for medical care through the VA health care system. If you are interested in obtaining VA medical care, you may contact your nearest VA health care facility or the VA Enrollment Service Center at 1-877-222-8387.

HOW CAN YOU RECEIVE DENTAL TREATMENT
If you are evaluated as 100% disabled for service-connected disabilities or as 100% disabled because of Individual Unemployability, you may be eligible for VA dental treatment. For additional information, contact your nearest VA Medical Center or Outpatient Clinic.

HOW CAN YOU RECEIVE ADDITIONAL COMPENSATION FOR DEPENDENTS?
Veterans having a 30% or more service-connected condition may be entitled to additional compensation for a spouse, dependent parents, or unmarried children under 18 (or under 23 if attending an approved school) or when prior to age 18 the child has become permanently incapable of self-support because of mental or physical defect. The additional benefitfit for a spouse is payable in a higher amount upon receipt of evidence establishing that the spouse is a patient in a nursing home or so disabled as to require the aid and attendance of another person.

HOW CAN YOU RECEIVE INDIVIDUAL UNEMPLOYABILITY?
If your service-connected disabilities are seriously disabling and you are unable to secure and hold steady work/employment because of your disabilities, you may apply to receive total disability. To apply for this benefit, you should contact the nearest VA office and complete 21-8940, Veteran's Application for Increased Compensation Based on Unemployability.

HOW CAN YOU RECEIVE EDUCATIONAL BENEFITS?
A monthly educational assistance allowance is payable to veterans who qualify for one of VA's educational assistance programs. Each program has unique eligibility specified by law, and only one program can be used at any given time. If you need help with your VA education benefits, you can call toll-free by dialing 1-888-442-4551 or visit the VA national education web site at www.gibill.va.gov.

HOW CAN YOU RECEIVE GOVERNMENT LIFE INSURANCE
If you are paying premiums on Government life insurance (GI insurance) and are unable to work, you may be entitled to certain benefits as provided for in your policy. For complete information contact the VA regional office where you pay premiums.

ARE YOUR BENEFITS EXEMPT FROM CLAIMS OR CREDITORS?
Compensation payments are exempt from claims of creditors. With certain exceptions the payments are not assignable and are not subject to attachment, levy or seizure except as to claims of the United States.

HOW DO YOU REPORT A CHANGE OF ADDRESS?
Please notify this office immediately of any change of address.

HOW DO I RECEIVE MORE INFORMATION?
Telephone: You can call toll-free by dialing 1-800-827-1000 or for the hearing impaired TDD 1-800-829-4833.
Internet: Visit VBA web site at htt://www.vba.va.gov.

VA FORM
FEB 2001 **21-8764**

SUPERSEDES VA FORM 21-8764, MAY 1999,
WHICH WILL NOT BE USED.

(See Reverse)

Disabled American Veterans
National Service Office
VA Medical Center • 4500 South Lancaster • Dallas, TX 75216
(214) 857-1119

MEMORANDUM

TO: Adjudication Division-211 E
             VARO; Waco, Texas

FROM: Brian Bible
             National Service Officer

RE: **Stamm, Randy L.**
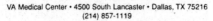

DATE: March 14, 2002

ISSUE: The above named veteran would like to submit his original application for Individual Unemployability.

We submit the attached information on behalf of the above captioned.

VA form 21-8940
VA form 21-4192

Your attention to this matter is greatly appreciated. Thanking you in advance for your cooperation.

Brian Bible
National Service Officer

BB/ bb

cc: Randy L. Stamm
901 West Bruton Rd # 203
Mesquite, TX 75149

PROTECT YOUR BENEFITS - REGISTER AND VOTE!

**Department of
Veterans Affairs**

701 CLAY AVE   83   February 1, 2002
WACO TX 76799

                                                    In Reply Refer To:

RANDY L STAMM   File Number:
APT 203
901 W BRUTON RD   PAYEE NO 00
MESQUITE TX 75149   R L STAMM

We are still processing your application for COMPENSATION.
We apologize for the delay. You will
be notified upon completion of processing. If you need to
contact us, be sure to show the file number and full name of
the veteran.

If your mailing address is different than that shown above,
please advise us of your new mailing address. You should
notify us immediately of any changes in your mailing address.

IF YOU RESIDE IN THE CONTINENTAL UNITED STATES, ALASKA, HAWAII
OR PUERTO RICO, YOU MAY CONTACT VA WITH QUESTIONS AND RECEIVE
FREE HELP BY CALLING OUR TOLL-FREE NUMBER 1-800-827-1000 (FOR
HEARING IMPAIRED TDD 1-800-829-4833).

                        MARIBETH G. CULLY
                        VETERANS SERVICE CENTER MANAGER

Disabled American Veterans
National Service Office

VA Regional Office • One Veterans Plaza • 701 Clay • Waco, TX 76799
(254) 299-9932

March 26, 2002

Randy L. Stamm
901 W. Bruton Rd. #203
Mesquite, TX. 75149

RE:

Dear Mr. Stamm:

This letter is to advise you unofficially that I have appeared on your behalf before the Veterans Administration Rating Board. The Rating Board has advised me informally of their decision and the following results.

The VA has determined that your service connected disability(ies) are of such severity as to prevent you from seeking and maintaining gainful employment. This award will remain in effect only as long as you continue to be unemployable. You may be required to complete the VA Employment Questionnaire (VA Form 21-4140) annually.

This award of individual unemployability is effective 3/2/02.

Entitlement to Dependents' Educational Assistance is established effective 3/2/02.

If you are not satisfied with the VA decision, you have one year from the date of notification to enter an appeal or the decision will become final.

If you have any questions relative to the action described in this letter, please contact me after you receive the VA letter that will <u>officially</u> notify you of this decision.

Sincerely,

Felecia Weston

Felecia P. Weston
National Service Officer

anp   **<u>PROTECT YOUR BENEFITS—REGISTER AND VOTE!</u>**

255

PITTS & ASSOCIATES

Attorneys at Law

8866 Gulf Freeway, Suite 117
Houston, Texas 77017-6528
(713) 910-0555
(713) 910-0594 (Fax)

CONFIDENTIAL ATTORNEY-CLIENT COMMUNICATION

ANNUAL STATUS REPORT

April 9, 2002

Dear Gulf War Veteran Client:

National Gulf War Veteran Conference May 3-5, 2002

The National Gulf War Resource Center, a coalition of grassroots groups advocating for research, compensation, and treatment for Gulf War vets who have been ill since the war, invites you to attend their Seventh Annual Conference in Atlanta, Georgia.

The three day conference, May 3, 4 & 5, 2002 will be held at the Holiday Inn-Airport North, near Atlanta airport. Government and independent scientists, including the leading researcher, Robert Haley, M.D., will present information on recent research into Gulf War Illness. I will also speak on the legal status, and answer questions. V.A. and Pentagon officials will attend to report on various programs which may provide assistance to Gulf vets.

Mr. Ross Perot, former Presidential candidate, veteran's advocate and contributor of significant amounts of money and time to Gulf War Illness research from the beginning through today, will be the keynote speaker at the NGWRC's annual banquet on May 4.

A special room rate of $69 per night is available to all conference participants. Call (404) 762-8411 to reserve, and mention "NGWRC conference" to obtain this rate (free airport shuttle).

For general information on the conference call: 800-882-1315, ext. 162 or go to: www.ngwrc.org I recommend attending the conference if you have a chance to.

Veterans Administration Recognizes ALS (Lou Gehrig's Disease)
as Caused by Gulf War Exposure

Recently, statistics showed that there is an elevated number of Gulf War veterans with ALS (Lou Gehrig's Disease), compared to nondeployed service members during the Gulf War period. In the wake of this research, the new Secretary of the Veterans Administration, Anthony Principi, decided to grant service connection disability as a result of Gulf War exposures, to Gulf War veterans with ALS. This decision will directly help four of your named co-plaintiffs, in this lawsuit, Major Michael Donnelly, Major Randy Hebert, Sergeant Thomas Oliver and Sergeant Montana Rickett, Jr. The March, 2002 edition of VFW Magazine, and an upcoming edition of People magazine, profiled Major Donnelly and this recent development.

V.A. Secretary Creates the Research Advisory Committee on
Gulf War Veterans' Illnesses

Though a 12-member Research Advisory Committee on Gulf War Veterans' Illnesses was authorized by law on November 11, 1998, the Clinton administration never appointed anyone to it. On January 23, 2002, V.A. Secretary

256

Administration is going to take this on. They've brought in some guys with some real guts."

V.A. Investigates Gulf Veteran Death Rates in Relation to Change in Khamisiyah Chemical Agent Plume Maps

About 100,000 Gulf veterans received letters in 1997 or 1998 from the OSAGWI department of the Pentagon saying that they were within the nerve gas plume from the Khamisiyah explosions. In 2000, the OSAGWI department of the Pentagon said a revised computer model showed the vapor cloud went a little differently than they first calculated. New letters went out. About 34,000 who received the previous letter were told it was believed that they were not in the cloud. About 34,000 new veterans were told that they might have been in this cloud. About 65,000 were told they were still thought to be have been in the cloud.

Recently, a V.A. analysis showed puzzling facts: among the 65,000, the death rate was 3.38 per 1000. Among the 34,000 added to the cloud projection in 2000, the death rate was 3.03 per 1,000. Among the 34,000 dropped from the cloud projection in 2000, the death rate was 29.37 per 1,000, however roughly ten (10) times that of the 34,000 added by shifting the nerve gas cloud coverage. This has given rise to some questions and skepticism over the motivation for shifting the nerve gas cloud's alleged coverage in 2000. The V.A. has promised to investigate the matter further.

V.A. Releases Gulf Veteran Cancer Statistics

The V.A. recently released Gulf War veterans' cancer diagnosis statistics, at my request. For the 696,759 deployed to the Gulf area between August 2, 1990 and July 31, 1991, there have been 2,208 individuals diagnosed with cancer, 1,843 of which were held to be service-connected and 527 held to be non-service connected. These are only statistics from the V.A. system, and do not include Gulf War veterans who have been treated for cancer in active military or civilian medical facilities since the war. If you, or any other Gulf veteran that you know of, have been treated for any form of cancer only in a civilian or active military medical facility, and never used a V.A. medical facility, please contact my office and let us know about it, so that we can get some idea of the frequency of that happening.

I am also asking the V.A. to refine the cancer diagnosis statistics to those deployed between January 17, 1991 and March 30, 1991, and to obtain a number of the total deployed during the that time. This was the period in which the low-level mustard gas (and nerve gas) fallout from the air campaign bombings and post-war detonation of Iraqi ammunition dumps occurred. Mustard gas is a known carcinogen. I am also asking for the V.A. cancer diagnosis statistics for service members that were not deployed, to compare the frequency.

Statistics for Miscarriage and Birth Defects Among Gulf Veterans' Families Published

The October, 2001 edition of Annals of Epidemiology published a V.A. study of pregnancy outcomes of a sample of 15,000 Gulf War veterans, from four military branches and three unit components (active, reserve and National Guard), compared to those of 15,000 non-Gulf War veteran controls. The results showed that male Gulf War veterans reported a significantly higher rate of miscarriage among their wives' pregnancies. The ratio of incidence was 1.62 deployed, compared to 1.00 for non-deployed.

Both men and women deployed to the Gulf theater also reported significant excesses of birth defects among their liveborn infants. The rate in the subset of "moderate to severe" birth defects was 1.78 for deployed males and 2.80 for deployed females, compared to 1.00 for non-deployed veterans. Thankfully, no significant differences were found by deployment status for stillbirths, pre-term deliveries or infant mortality.

symptoms and signs, that share features such as fatigue, pain, disability out of proportion to physical findings, and inconsistent demonstration of laboratory abnormalities.

In evaluating chronic multisymptom illnesses, the Committees expect that VA will develop a schedule for rating disabilities based on severity of symptoms and the degree to which these impair a veteran's ability to obtain and retain substantially gainful employment. The ratings schedule already established by VA in section 4.88b of 38 CFR (6354) for chronic fatigue syndrome bases the degree of disability on the veteran's incapacitation rather than specific medical findings. This schedule can be used as a model for rating disabilities stemming from chronic multisymptom illnesses in general.

The long and short of this new law is that if you have been seriously disabled from Gulf War Illness symptoms, and you were previously turned away for compensation for this disability by the V.A., you should reapply under this new law.

Any claim that you have with the V.A. is separate and apart and unaffected by: 1.) your claim against the Iraqi funds, when congress passes implementing legislation; and 2.) any recovery that you may eventually obtain through the litigation against the bio/chem suppliers to Iraq.

Because of constrains of time with other responsibilities, my law firm is not representing individuals in their V.A. claims. I generally recommend that you contact your local veterans' service organizations for their advice and assistance regarding your claim, and obtaining legal counsel in your area.

Iraqi Asset Claim Status

Senator Helms is no longer Chairman of the Senate Foreign Relations Committee. He will be leaving the Committee entirely when he retires at the end of this year.

Congressman Lloyd Doggett filed and championed the Gulf War Veterans' Iraqi Claims Protection Act of 1999 (H.R. 618 in the 106th Congress), which would allow Gulf War veterans who have been ill since the war to file claims with the Justice Department's Foreign Claims Settlement Commission against the Iraqi funds that was frozen when it invaded Kuwait in August, 1990. The funds that are subject to U.S. jurisdiction are now about $1.7 billion. On July 21, 1999, Congressman Doggett's bill passed the House of Representatives unanimously as an amendment to H.R. 2415. but stalled in the Senate Foreign Relations Committee. Senator Helms killed the bill in the Senate by not letting it out of his Committee.

About 158 former hostages in Iraq have also filed suit in District Court in D.C. recently. They are seeking to quantify their damages, and to also make a claim against the frozen Iraqi assets.

Congressman Doggett will be resubmitting the bill to Congress, before the Gulf veterans' convention next month. With the change in the Senate, the matter will hopefully be passed and signed into law this year. Once that is done, the Justice Department will set up a claims process, which we will handle with your help. The Justice Department would assign a value to each veteran's case based on the individual facts. The Foreign Claims Settlement Commission has estimated that the claims process will take about two years from the time that they get the money, before checks could start going out.

Please Send Letters of Appreciation

If you have the opportunity, it would be helpful if you would write a couple of thank you letters. You do not need to spend much time on them, but a show of support and thanks can help the morale and focus of those who deal with the pressure of contrary political currents in D.C.

KAY BAILEY HUTCHISON
TEXAS

COMMITTEES:
APPROPRIATIONS
COMMERCE, SCIENCE,
AND TRANSPORTATION
RULES AND ADMINISTRATION

United States Senate

WASHINGTON, DC 20510–4304

April 8, 2002

Mr. Randy L. Stamm
901 W. Bruton Rd., #203
Mesquite, Texas 75149

Dear Mr. Stamm:

Thank you for contacting Senator Hutchison regarding the difficulties you are experiencing. In order to make an inquiry on your behalf we will need you to complete the enclosed Information and Privacy Act Form and mail it to my attention at our Dallas Office at 10440 N. Central Expressway, Suite 1160, Dallas, Texas 75231-2223.

Please feel free to contact me at 214/361-3500 with any questions you might have.

Sincerely,

Brenda Davis
Constituent Liaison

Enclosure

KAY BAILEY HUTCHISON
TEXAS

COMMITTEES:
APPROPRIATIONS
COMMERCE, SCIENCE,
AND TRANSPORTATION
RULES AND ADMINISTRATION
ENVIRONMENT AND PUBLIC WORKS

United States Senate
WASHINGTON, DC 20510-4304

The Information and Privacy Act Form

I hereby authorize SENATOR KAY BAILEY HUTCHISON to request on my behalf, pertinent to the Freedom of Information and Privacy Act of 1974, access to information concerning me in the files of the Department of _____. In addition, SENATOR HUTCHISON is also authorized to see any materials that may be disclosed pertinent to that request.

NAME: _____

STREET/APT: _____

CITY/STATE/ZIP: _____

HOME PHONE #: _____

WORK PHONE #: _____

SOC SEC #: _____

VA CLAIM #: _____

ALIEN REGISTRATION #: _____

OTHER ID #: _____

DATE OF BIRTH
(mm/dd/yy): _____

SIGNATURE: _____

DATE: _____

INSTRUCTIONS:
Please write a brief letter outlining the nature of your problem. Be as specific as possible, particularly include the names of the public officials you have communicated with in the past and the dates these communications occurred. Also, please attach any relevant correspondence that you have initiated or received concerning your problem.

_____

_____

_____

_____

_____

Return to:

U.S. Senator Kay Bailey Hutchison
10440 N. Central Expressway
Suite 1160; LB 606
Dallas, TX 75231
(214) 361-3500
(214) 361-3502 FAX

SUBJECT: Denial of Social Security Benefits

Senator Hutchison,

In March ,01 2002 I was laid off for the 3rd time in 6 years after getting out of the Armed Services US Army in May 1995 due to medical reasons. In March I was given the status of 100% disable and applied for Social Security and was denied by the office in Dallas Texas and the address and number are below,

Social Security
Suite 156 1st Floor
10325 Lake June Road
Dallas Texas 75217
(214) 655-2900

And the person that I talked to was Mary and she seemed at the time that there would be no problem with this until I received a letter on April 5, 2002 stating that Based on our talk they have made a informal decision that I was not eligible for SSI. Since I have worked for the last 20 something years and paid into Social Security and paid my due to our Nation now to find out that I am not eligible? This does not make sense to me since I am a Tax payer and have done all that my Country has asked of me and now this. maybe you can find out why I am not eligible in the Governments Eyes?

Lastly, since I am a taxpayer and I have done all that the country has asked of me and become sick due to Gulf War Illnesses, is it that the Veterans get SCREWED AGAIN.

Regards,

Randy Stamm
901 W. Bruton Rd, Apt 203
Mesquite Texas 75149
972-288-4415 home
469-774-3510 cell

JOE BARTON
6TH DISTRICT, TEXAS

2264 RAYBURN HOUSE OFFICE BUILDING
WASHINGTON, DC 20515-4306
(202) 225-2002

REPUBLICAN STEERING COMMITTEE
REGIONAL REPRESENTATIVE

COMMITTEE ON
ENERGY AND COMMERCE

SUBCOMMITTEES:
CHAIRMAN, ENERGY AND AIR QUALITY
TELECOMMUNICATIONS AND THE INTERNET
HEALTH

COMMITTEE ON SCIENCE

SUBCOMMITTEE:
SPACE AND AERONAUTICS

Congress of the United States
House of Representatives
Washington, DC 20515-4306

April 10, 2002

Mr. Randy L. Stamm
901 West Bruton Road, Apt 203
Mesquite, Texas 75149-5715

Dear Mr. Stamm:

Thank you for contacting my office regarding Social Security disability benefits.

I have determined by your address that you are a resident of the 5th Congressional District of Texas. It is a custom and a courtesy in the United States House of Representatives to allow each Member of Congress the opportunity to assist his or her own constituents.

I have taken the liberty of forwarding your letter to the Honorable Pete Sessions. I feel certain that Congressman Sessions will be in touch with you shortly.

Again, thank you for contacting me.

Sincerely,

Joe Barton
Member of Congress

JB/sd
xc:

ARLINGTON OFFICE:
805 WASHINGTON DRIVE, SUITE F
ARLINGTON, TX 76011

ENNIS OFFICE:
303 WEST KNOX, SUITE 201
ENNIS, TX 75119-3942
817-543-1000 (main number for all offices)
Homepage: http://www.house.gov/barton/welcome.html
PRINTED ON RECYCLED PAPER

FORT WORTH OFFICE:
4521 SOUTH HULEN STREET,
SUITE 216
FORT WORTH, TX 76109

INFORMATION AND INSTRUCTIONS FOR COMPLETING THE APPLICATION FOR EDUCATION BENEFITS

PRIVACY ACT INFORMATION: No benefits can be paid unless a completed application has been received (38 U.S.C. 3513). The information requested on this form is necessary to determine your eligibility to education benefits. The responses you submit are considered confidential (38 U.S.C. 5701) and may be disclosed outside VA only if the disclosure is authorized under the Privacy Act, including routine uses identified in VA system of records, 58VA21/22, Compensation, Pension, Education and Rehabilitation Records-VA, published in the Federal Register.

RESPONDENT BURDEN: Public reporting burden for this collection of information is estimated to average 30 minutes per response, including the time for reviewing instructions, searching existing data sources, gathering and maintaining the data needed, and completing and reviewing the collection of information. Send comments regarding this burden estimate or any other aspect of this collection of information, including suggestions for reducing this burden, to the VA Clearance Officer (045A4), 810 Vermont Ave., NW, Washington, DC 20420. ONLY SEND COMMENTS ONLY, NOT THIS FORM OR REQUESTS FOR BENEFITS TO THIS ADDRESS.

1. GENERAL - Read this information and instruction sheet carefully and then complete Items 1 thru 32 on the application fully and accurately. Show "N/A" (not applicable) where appropriate.

2. ELIGIBILITY

a. To qualify for educational assistance you must be either:

(1) The son, daughter or spouse of a veteran who is permanently and totally disabled as the result of a service-connected disability, or the son, daughter or spouse of an individual on active duty who has been listed for a total of more than 90 days as missing in action, captured in line of duty by a hostile force, or forcibly detained or interned in line of duty by a hostile force, or forcibly detained or interned in line of duty by a foreign government or power; or

(2) The son, daughter or surviving spouse of a veteran who died of a service-connected disability or who died while a service-connected disability was rated total and permanent in nature.

b. Eligibility for educational assistance will be terminated in the event VA determines that the person on whose account benefits are claimed is no longer totally disabled, or VA is notified that the person is no longer listed as captured, missing in action or forcibly detained.

c. Generally, the period of eligibility for a son or daughter is between the ages of 18 and 26 years. In certain instances, it is possible to begin training before age 18, and to continue after age 26. The marriage of a son or daughter is not a bar to this benefit.

d. A spouse may use educational benefits during the 10-year period after eligibility is found. A surviving spouse may use these benefits during a 10-year period after the veteran's death, or 10 years after VA determines the veteran's death was caused by a service-connected disability. Eligibility will terminate in the event a spouse is divorced from the veteran or in the event of remarriage by a surviving spouse.

NOTE: "Son" or "daughter" includes stepson or stepdaughter.

3. ENTITLEMENT

a. The Departments' Educational Assistance program offers eligible persons up to 45 months of full-time training benefits.

b. Entitlement is reduced by 1 month for each month of full-time training. Proportionate reductions are made if training is less than full-time.

c. Persons who are entitled to benefits under more than one of the VA educational assistance programs may receive an overall maximum of 48 months of benefits.

4. COUNSELING - VA will provide you with educational or vocational counseling if you request it. VA counseling can help you: find out more about your abilities and interests; learn about opportunities in different fields of work; and determine the type of training or employment that is best for you. To request counseling, contact your nearest VA office. There is no charge for VA counseling. However, you must pay for the cost of traveling from your home to the counseling session. If you are required to receive counseling (see paragraphs 5b and 5c below), VA will provide assistance to cover the cost of travel. EXCEPT FOR THE REPUBLIC OF THE PHILIPPINES, VA COUNSELING IS NOT AVAILABLE IN FOREIGN COUNTRIES.

5. COURSES AND PROGRAMS YOU MAY PURSUE

a. Any eligible person may pursue postsecondary courses approved by the State approving agency at a vocational or technical school, business college, college or university. Benefits are also payable while pursuing an approved apprenticeship, on-the-job training, cooperative of farm cooperative program. Courses may be taken in a foreign country if they lead to a standard college degree or its equivalent, and vocational courses may also be taken in the Republic of the Philippines.

b. A son and daughter who is under 18 and who has not completed high school must have his or her program of education or training approved by a VA counselor before educational assistance benefits can be authorized.

c. Specialized restorative training can be approved for a son or daughter, and specialized vocational training can be approved for any eligible person, if it is determined through VA counseling that a specialized program is needed to overcome the effects of a physical or mental handicap.

d. An eligible person who has not received a high school diploma or equivalent can pursue approved secondary-level programs. An eligible person can also pursue refresher, remedial, or deficiency courses that are needed for admission into an education program.

e. A spouse or surviving spouse may pursue an approved home study course. Information on home study courses is available at the nearest VA regional office.

(1) If you are considering enrollment in a home study course or combination correspondence-residence course, be sure that the field of study is suitable to your abilities and interests before signing a contract with the school. You should consider your decision carefully since the contract you sign may require you to pay for all or the majority of the course even though you complete only a portion of it.

(2) The law provides that a contract for enrollment in a home study course must be affirmed by a student after more than 10 days have elapsed following the date the contract was signed. No payments of VA benefits will be authorized for any lessons serviced by the school prior to the date of affirmation of the contract. If you decide not to enroll in a correspondence course after signing a contract, but before you sign the affirmation, you are entitled to receive a full refund from the school of any payment made for the course.

6. EDUCATIONAL ASSISTANCE ALLOWANCE

a. If you attend school at the rate of one-half time or more, you will be entitled to receive a monthly allowance to help you with the cost of tuition, fees, books, supplies, and other costs of school attendance. If you pursue courses at less than one-half time, you will generally receive a single payment based on the tuition and fees charged for your course(s), not to exceed the maximum rate established for quarter-time or half-time training, as applicable.

b. You will generally be paid through breaks between standard terms if the break does not span a full calendar month. However, you may wish to save entitlement by asking VA not to make payments for any breaks. Except for advance payments, checks are normally sent at the first of each month for the previous month's training.

c. Payments for on-the-job or apprenticeship training are not released until after a monthly report of hours worked is received. If less than 120 hours are worked in a month, less than a full benefit payment is made.

d. Payments for correspondence courses are made each calendar quarter after a certification of lessons completed is processed.

NOTE: Sons and daughters are not eligible for correspondence training.

263

VA Department of Veterans Affairs

APPLICATION FOR SURVIVORS' AND DEPENDENTS' EDUCATIONAL ASSISTANCE
(Under provisions of Chapter 35, Title 38, U.S.C.)

1. VA FILE NUMBER *(If known)*
► **465 21 1583**

IMPORTANT: Before completing this form, read the instructions on the attached sheet. Type or print answers in ink. If additional space is needed use Item 29, "Remarks" or blank paper and key answers to item numbers. Return this application to the VA office serving the area where the veteran's records are located, if known; or, if not known, to the VA office serving the area where you live.

PART I - GENERAL INFORMATION REGARDING APPLICANT

2. FIRST NAME - MIDDLE NAME - LAST NAME OF APPLICANT
►

3. SOCIAL SECURITY NUMBER

4. DATE OF BIRTH

5. MAILING ADDRESS OF APPLICANT *(Number and street or rural route, city or P.O. Box, State and ZIP Code)*
►

6. RELATIONSHIP OF APPLICANT TO VETERAN
☐ SPOUSE   ☐ SURVIVING SPOUSE   ☐ CHILD

PART II - INFORMATION CONCERNING DISABLED OR DECEASED VETERAN OR INDIVIDUAL ON ACTIVE DUTY

7. FIRST - MIDDLE - LAST NAME OF VETERAN, OR INDIVIDUAL ON ACTIVE DUTY WHOSE ACCOUNT BENEFITS ARE CLAIMED
► **R L Stamm**

8. SOCIAL SECURITY NUMBER
►

VA DATE STAMP
(For VA Use Only)

9. DATE OF BIRTH

10. BRANCH OF SERVICE

11. SERVICE NUMBER

12. DATE OF DEATH OR DATE LISTED AS MISSING IN ACTION OR P.O.W.

13. VA OFFICE WHERE RECORDS ARE LOCATED

PART III - SPECIAL INFORMATION CONCERNING APPLICANT

14. IF YOU ARE THE SPOUSE OF A DISABLED VETERAN, IS A DIVORCE OR ANNULMENT PENDING?
☐ YES   ☐ NO

15. IF YOU ARE THE SURVIVING SPOUSE OF A VETERAN ON WHOSE ACCOUNT BENEFITS ARE CLAIMED, HAVE YOU REMARRIED SINCE HIS OR HER DEATH?
☐ YES   ☐ NO

16. HAVE YOU EVER SERVED ON ACTIVE DUTY IN THE ARMED SERVICES?
☐ YES   ☐ NO *(If "Yes," complete Items 16B, 16C and 16D)*

16B. BRANCH OF SERVICE

16C. ACTIVE DUTY DATES
FROM   TO

16D. TYPE OF SEPARATION OR DISCHARGE

17. WILL YOU RECEIVE EDUCATIONAL ASSISTANCE BENEFITS FOR YOUR TRAINING UNDER EITHER THE FEDERAL EMPLOYEES' COMPENSATION ACT OR THE GOVERNMENT EMPLOYEES TRAINING ACT?
☐ YES   ☐ NO *(If "Yes," give details in Item 29 "Remarks" or on a separate sheet)*

PART IV - VA BENEFITS AND EDUCATION OF TRAINING PREVIOUSLY APPLIED FOR

18. TYPE OF BENEFITS *(Check applicable box(es))*

A. ☐ NONE

B. ☐ HOSPITALIZATION OR MEDICAL CARE

C. ☐ DISABILITY COMPENSATION OR PENSION

D. ☐ SURVIVORS' AND DEPENDENTS' EDUCATIONAL ASSISTANCE *(Complete Items 18H and 18I)*

E. ☐ EDUCATION OR TRAINING BASED ON YOUR OWN SERVICE *(Complete Items 19A and 19B)*

F. ☐ DENTAL OR OUTPATIENT TREATMENT

G. ☐ OTHER *(Specify below)*

Complete only if Item 18D is checked ►

18H. NAME OF PARENT

18I. PARENT'S FILE NUMBER *(If known)*

19A. YOUR OWN VA FILE NUMBER

19B. VA OFFICE WHERE YOUR RECORDS ARE LOCATED *(City and State)*

PART V - PREVIOUS EDUCATION AND TRAINING

20A. TYPE OF SCHOOL	20B. NO. OF YEARS COMPLETED	DATES ATTENDED		20E. NAME OR DESCRIPTION OF COURSE	20F. NAME AND LOCATION OF SCHOOL *(City and State)*
		20C. FROM	20D. TO		
ELEMENTARY SCHOOL					
HIGH SCHOOL					
COLLEGE					
VOCATIONAL OR TRADE					

20G. CHECK APPROPRIATE BOX AND ENTER DATE IN ITEM 20H
☐ GRADUATE FROM HIGH SCHOOL   ☐ EXPECT TO GRADUATE   ☐ DISCONTINUED HIGH SCHOOL   ☐ PLAN TO DISCONTINUE

20H. DATE

21A. NAME OF APPRENTICESHIP OR OTHER ON-THE-JOB TRAINING COURSE *(If any)*

21B. DATES OF TRAINING
FROM   TO

21C. PLACE OF TRAINING

22A. HAVE YOU EVER HELD A LIENCE TO PRACTICE A PROFESSION OR JOURNEYMAN RATING TO WORK AT A TRADE? *(Examples - electrician, radio operator, teacher, lawyer, CPA, bricklayer, carpenter, etc.)*
☐ YES   ☐ NO *(If "Yes," complete Items 22B, and 22C)*

22B. NAME OF LICENSE OR JOURNEYMAN RATING

22C. STATE IN WHICH HELD

23A. HAVE YOU EVER BEEN EMPLOYED?
☐ YES   ☐ NO *(If "Yes," complete Items 23B, and 23C)*

23B. PRINCIPAL OCCUPATION

23C. NUMBER OF MONTHS EMPLOYED IN THIS OCCUPATION

VA FORM APR 1995 **22-5490 (JF)**

SUPERSEDES VA FORM 22-5490, MAR 1994, WHICH WILL NOT BE USED.

BE SURE TO COMPLETE REVERSE SIDE

264

Randy Lynn Stamm

R L Stamm   465 21 1583

VA Department of Veterans Affairs	YOUR RIGHTS TO APPEAL OUR DECISION

After careful and compassionate consideration, a decision has been reached on your claim. If we weren't able to grant some or all of the VA benefits you asked for, this form will explain what you can do if you disagree with our decision. If you don't agree with our decision, you may:

- appeal to the Board of Veterans' Appeals (the Board) by telling us you disagree with our decision
- give us evidence we don't already have that may lead us to change our decision

This form will tell you how to appeal to the Board and how to send us more evidence. You can do either one or both of these things.

WHAT IS AN APPEAL TO THE BOARD OF VETERANS' APPEALS?

An appeal is your formal request that the Board review the evidence in your VA file and review the law that applies to your appeal. The Board can either agree with our decision or change it. The Board can also send your file back to us for more processing before the Board makes its decision.

HOW CAN I APPEAL THE DECISION?

How do I start my appeal? To begin your appeal, write us a letter telling us you disagree with our decision. This letter is called your "Notice of Disagreement." If we denied more than one claim for a benefit (for example, if you claimed compensation for three disabilities and we denied two of them), please tell us in your letter which claims you are appealing. Send your Notice of Disagreement to the address at the top of our letter.

What happens after VA receives my Notice of Disagreement? We will either grant your claim or send you a Statement of the Case. A Statement of the Case describes the facts, laws, regulations, and reasons that we used to make our decision. We'll also send you a VA Form 9, "Appeal to Board of Veterans' Appeals," with the Statement of the Case. You must complete this VA Form 9 and return it to us if you want to continue your appeal.

How long do I have to start my appeal? You have one year to appeal our decision. *Your* letter saying that you disagree with our decision must be postmarked (or received by us) within one year from the date of *our* letter denying you the benefit. In most cases, you can't appeal a decision after this one-year period has ended.

What happens if I don't start my appeal on time? If you don't start your appeal on time, our decision will become final. Once our decision is final, you can't get the VA benefit we denied unless you either:

- show that we were clearly wrong to deny the benefit **or**
- send us new evidence that relates to the reason we denied your claim

Can I get a hearing with the Board? Yes. If you decide to appeal, the Board will give you a hearing if you want one. The VA Form 9 we'll send you with the Statement of the Case has complete information about the kinds of hearings the Board offers and convenient check boxes for requesting a Board hearing. The Board doesn't require you to have a hearing. It's your choice.

Where can I find out more about appealing to the Board?

- You can find a "plain language" pamphlet, called "Understanding the Appeal Process," on the Internet at: **http://www.va.gov/vbs/bva/pamphlet.htm**. The Board will send you a printed copy of this pamphlet after you file your Notice of Disagreement. You can also write to the following address and ask for a copy of "Understanding the Appeal Process": Chief Bailiff (011), Board of Veterans' Appeals, 810 Vermont Avenue, NW, Washington, DC 20420.

You can find the formal rules for appealing to the Board in the Board's Rules of Practice at title 38, Code of Federal Regulations, Part 20. You can find the complete Code of Federal Regulations on the Internet at: **http://www.access.gpo.gov/nara/cfr**. A printed copy of the Code of Federal Regulations may be available at your local law library.

VA FORM MAY 2001 (RS) **4107**   *(Please continue reading on the other side.)*   JetForm

265

DEPARTMENT OF VETERANS AFFAIRS
REGIONAL OFFICE
111 WEST HURON STREET
BUFFALO NEW YORK 14202

JUL 7 2000

MR RANDY STAMM
901 W BRUTON RD
APT 202
MESQUITE TX 75149

In Reply Refer To: 307/21/kep

STAMM, Randy L.
CSS

Dear Mr. Stamm:

This letter is in response to your inquiry to President Clinton concerning disability benefits for Gulf War veterans. Your inquiry was referred to the Department of Veterans Affairs Buffalo Regional Office because you expressed concern over the status of claims for a veteran in a nursing home in upstate New York, which is in our jurisdiction, as well as another veteran by the name of David Kagels who is unemployed and has five children to support.

While we appreciate your concern for your fellow servicemen, we are unable to discuss either of their claims because your inquiry did not include a release from each of the individuals involved. The Privacy Act of 1974 does not permit us to release information from a veteran's records, or discuss the status of his case, without written authorization, over the claimant's signature, allowing us to disclose information to a third party.

You indicated in your inquiry that you served in the Gulf War and are disabled. A review of our records shows you currently receive compensation for several service connected conditions whose combined effects are 70% disabling. We are referring your inquiry to our Regional Office in Waco, where your claims file is located, so they can explain the actions that have been taken on your behalf, and fully address the issues you have raised. You may expect a reply from them shortly.

If you have additional questions or concerns please feel free to visit the nearest VA Regional Office, or telephone us toll free at: 1-800-827-1000. A Veterans Service Representative will be happy to assist you.

Sincerely yours,

GREGORY L. MASON
Director

By the Direction of the
Under Secretary for Benefits

266

Patient Medication Instruction Sheet

STAMM, RANDY LYNN 21-1583

===

Rx# 4927455 (#12) GABAPENTIN 300MG CAP

===

[ ] Gabapentin (ga-ba-PEN-tin) is used to help control some types of seizures in the treatment of epilepsy. This medicine cannot cure epilepsy and will only work to help to control seizures for as long as you continue to take it.

[ ] If any of the information in this leaflet causes you special concern or if you want additional information about your medicine and its use, check with your doctor, nurse, or pharmacist. Remember, keep this and all other medicines out of the reach of children and never share your medicines with others

BEFORE USING Tell your doctor, nurse, and pharmacist if you...

* are allergic to any medicine, either prescription or nonprescription (over-the-counter [OTC]);

* are pregnant or intend to become pregnant while using this medicine;

* are breast-feeding;

* are using any other prescription or nonprescription (over-the-counter [OTC] medicine, especially antacids;

* have any other medical problems, especially kidney disease.

HOW TO TAKE AND STORE Take this medicine only as directed by your doctor in order to improve your condition as much as possible. Do not take more or less of it, and do not take it more or less of it, and do not take it more or less often than your doctor ordered.

[ ] Gabapentin may be taken with or without food. Take it as directed.

[ ] When taking gabapentin 3 times a day, do not allow more than 12 hours to pass between any 2 doses.

[ ] If you have trouble swallowing capsules, you may open the gabapentin capsule and mix the medicine with applesauce or juice. Mix only one dose at a time just before taking it. Do not mix any doses to save for later, because the medicine may change over time and may not work properly.

[ ] If you miss a dose of this medicine, take it as soon as possible. However, if it is less than 2 hours until your next dose, take the missed dose right away, and take the next dose 1 to 2 hours later. Do not double doses.

[ ] To store this medicine:

[ ] Keep it out the reach of children. Store away from heat and direct light. Do not store in the bathroom, near the kitchen sink, or in other damp places. Heat or moisture may cause the medicine to break down. Do not keep outdated medicine or medicine no longer needed. Be sure that any discarded medicine is out of the reach of children.

WARNINGS It is important that your doctor check your progress sat regular visits, especially for the first few months you take gabapentin. This is necessary to allow dose adjustment and to reduce any unwanted effects.

[ ] This medicine will add to the effects of alcohol and other CNS depressants (medicines that make you drowsy or less alert). Check with your medical doctor or dentist before taking any such depressants while you are using this medicine.

[ ] This medicine may cause blurred vision, double vision, clumsiness, unsteadiness, dizziness, drowsiness, or trouble in thinking.

[ ] Make sore you know how to react to this medicine before you drive, use machines, or to do other jobs that require you to be alert, well-coordinated, or able to think or see well.

[ ] If these reactions are especially bothersome, check with your doctor.

[ ] Before you have any medical tests, tell the person in charge that you are using this medicine. The results of dipstick tests for protein in the urine may be affected by this medicine.

[ ] Do not stop using this medicine without first checking with your doctor. Stopping the medicine suddenly may cause your seizures to return or occur more often. Your doctor may want you to reduce gradually the amount you are using before stopping completely.

POSSIBLY SIDE EFFECTS Side Effects That Should Be Reported To Your Doctor.

[ ] More Common — Clumsiness or unsteadiness; continuous, uncontrolled back-and-forth or rolling eye movements.

[ ] Less common – Depression; irritability, or other mood or mental changes; loose of memory.

[ ] Rare – Cough or hoarseness; fever or chills; lower back or side pain; difficult or painful urination

[ ] Signs of overdose – Diarrhea; dizziness; double vision; drowsiness; sluggishness; slurred speech

[ ] Side Effects That Usually Do Not Require Medical Attention

[ ] These possible side effects may go away during treatment; however, if they continue or are bothersome, check with your doctor, nurse, or pharmacists.

[ ] More common – Blurred or double vision; dizziness; drowsiness; muscle ache or pain; swelling of hands and feet, or lower legs; trembling or shaking; unusual tiredness or weakness

[ ] Less common – Back pain; constipation; decrease in sexual desire or ability; diarrhea; dryness of mouth or throat; frequent urination; headache; indigestion; low blood pressure; nausea; noise in ears; runny nose; slurred speech; twitching; trouble in sleeping; trouble in thinking; vomiting; weakness or loss of strength; weight gain

[ ] Other side effects not listed above may also occur in some patients. If you notice any other effects, check with your doctor, nurse, or pharmacist.

Patient Medication Instruction Sheet
STAMM, RANDY LYNN 21 – 1583

===

Rx# 4927456 (#12) LITHIUM CARBONATE 300MG CAP

===

[ ] Lithium (LITH-ee-um) is used to treat the manic stage of bipolar disorder (manic-depressive illness). It may also help reduce the frequency and severity of depression in bipolar disorder. Lithium may also be used for other conditions as determined by your doctor.

[ ] It is important that you and your family understand the effects of lithium. These depend on your individual condition and response and the amount of lithium you use. You also must know when to contact your doctor if there are problems

[ ] If any of the information in this leaflet causes you special concern or if you want additional information about your medicine and its use, check with your doctor, nurse, or pharmacist. Remember, keep this and all other medicines out of the reach of children and never share your medicines with others.

BEFORE USING Tell your doctor, nurse, and pharmacist if you...

* are allergic to any medicine, either prescription or nonprescription (over- the-counter [OTC]);
* are pregnant or intend to become pregnant while using this medicine;
* are breast-feeding
* are taking any other prescription or nonprescription (over-the-counter [OTC] medicine;
* have any other medical problems, especially epilepsy, heart disease, kidney disease, leukemia (history of), Parkinson's disease, problems with urination, severe infections, or severe water loss.

HOW TO TAKE AND STORE During treatment with lithium, drink 2 or 3 quarts of water or other fluids each day, and use a normal amount of salt, unless otherwise directed.

[ ] Take this medicine exactly as directed. Do not take more or less of it, do not take it more or less often, and do not take it for a longer time than your doctor ordered. To do so may increase the chance

of unwanted effects. Sometimes lithium must be taken for 1 to several weeks before you begin to feel better.

[ ] In order for lithium to work properly, it must be taken everyday in regularly spaced doses as ordered by your doctor. This is necessary to keep a constant amount of lithium in your blood. Do not miss any doses and do not stop taking the medicine even if you feel better.

[ ] If you do miss a dose of this medicine, take it as soon as possible. However, if it is within 2 hours (6 hours for the long-acting tablets or capsules) of your next dose, skip the missed dose and go back to your regular schedule. Do not double doses.

[ ] To store this medicine:

[ ] Keep it out the reach of children. Store away from heat and direct light. Do not store in the bathroom, near the kitchen sink, or in other damp places. Heat or moisture may cause the medicine to break down. Keep the syrup form of this medicine from freezing. Do not keep outdated medicine or medicine no longer needed. Be sure that any discarded medicine is out of the reach of children.

WARNINGS Your doctor should check your progress at regular visits to make sure that the medicine is working properly and to check for unwanted effects. Laboratory tests may be needed.

[ ] Lithium may not work properly if you drink large amount of caffeine-containing coffee, tea, or colas.

[ ] Lithium may cause some people to become dizzy, drowsy, or less alert than they are not normally.

[ ] Make sure you know how you react to this medicine before you drive, use machines, or to do other jobs that require you to be alert.

[ ] The loss of too much water and salt from your body may lead to serious side effects from lithium.

[ ] Use extra care in hot weather and during activities that cause you to sweat heavily, such as hot baths, saunas, or exercising. Also, check with your doctor before going on a diet to lose weight, or if you have an illness that causes sweating, vomiting, or diarrhea.

POSSIBLY SIDE EFFECTS Side Effects That Should Be Reported T o Your Doctor immediately

[ ] Early signs of overdose or toxicity – diarrhea; drowsiness; loss of appetite; muscle weakness; nausea or vomiting; slurred speech; trembling

[ ] Late signs of overdose or toxicity – blurred vision; clumsiness or unsteadiness; confusion; convulsions (seizures); dizziness; trembling (severe); unusual increase in amount of urine

[ ] Other Side Effects That Should Be Reported To Your Doctor

[ ] Less common – fainting, fast, slow, or irregular heartbeat; troubled breathing (especially during hard work or exercise); unusual tiredness or weakness; weight gain

[ ] Rare – blue color and pain in fingers and toes; cold arms and kegs; dizziness; eye pain; headache; unusual noises in the ears; vision problems

[ ] Sign of low thyroid function – dry, rough skin; hair loss; hoarseness; mental depression; sensitivity to cold; swelling of feet or lower legs; swelling of neck; unusual excitement

[ ] Side Effects That Usually Do Not Require Medical Attention

[ ] These possible side effects may go away during treatment; however, if they continue or are bothersome, check with your doctor, nurse, or pharmacist.

[ ] More common – increased frequency of urination or loss of bladder control usually beginning 2 To 7 Years after start of treatment more common in women; increased thirst; nausea (mild); trembling of hands (slight)

[ ] Other side effects not listed above may also occur in some patients. If you notice any other effects, check with your doctor, nurse, or pharmacist.

Patient Medication Instruction Sheet

STAMM, RANDY LYNN 21 –C 1583

===

Rx# 4927458 (#4) TRAZODONE HCL 50MG TAB

===

[ ] Trazodone (TRAZ-oh-done) belongs to the group of medicines know as antidepressants or "mood elevators." It is used to relieve mental depression that sometimes occurs within anxiety.

[ ] If any of the information in this leaflet causes you special concern or if you want additional information about your medicine and its use, check with your doctor, nurse, or pharmacist. Remember, keep, this and all other medicines out of the reach of children and never share your medicine with others.

BEFORE USING Tell your doctor, nurse, and pharmacist if you…

* are allergic to any medicine, either prescription or nonprescription (over- the-counter [OTC]);

* are pregnant or intend to become pregnant while using this medicine;

* are breast-feeding

* are taking any other prescription or nonprescription (over-the-counter [OTC] medicine;

* have any other medical problems, especially, heart, kidney or liver disease.

HOW TO TAKE AND STORE Take this medicine exactly as directed by your doctor.

[ ] To lessen stomach upset and to reduce dizziness and lightheadedness, take this medicine with or shortly after a meal or light snack, even for a daily bedtime dose, unless your doctor has told you to take it on an empty stomach.

[ ] Sometimes trazodone must be t5aken for up to 4 weeks before you begin to feel better, although most people notice improvement within 2 weeks.

[ ] If you miss a dose of this medicine, take it as soon as possible. However, if it is within 4 hours of your next dose, skip the missed dose and go back to your regular dosing schedule. Do not double doses.

[ ] To store this medicine:

273

[ ] Keep it out the reach of children. Store away from heat and direct light. Do not store in the bathroom, near the kitchen sink, or in other damp places. Heat or moisture may cause the medicine to break down. Keep the syrup form of this medicine from freezing. Do not keep outdated medicine or medicine no longer needed. Be sure that any discarded medicine is out of the reach of children.

WARNINGS It is very important that your doctor should check your progress at regular visits. This will allow your doctor to check the medicine's effects and to change the dose if needed.

[ ] Do not stop using this medicine without first checking with your doctor. Your doctor may want you to reduce gradually the amount you are using before stopping completely.

[ ] Before having any kind of surgery or dental or emergency treatment, tell the medical doctor or dentist in charge that you are using this medicine.

[ ] This medicine will add to the effects of alcohol and other CNS depressants (medicines that slow down the nervous system, possibly causing drowsiness). Check with your doctor before taking any such depressants while using this medicine.

[ ] This medicine may cause some people to become drowsy or less alert than they are normally.

[ ] Make sure you know how you react to this medicine before you drive, use machines, or do other jobs that require you to be alert.

[ ] Dizziness, lightheadedness, or fainting may occur, especially when you get up from a lying or sitting position.

[ ] Getting up slowly may help. If this problem continues or gets worse, check with your doctor.

[ ] This medicine may cause dryness of the mouth. For temporary relief, use sugarless gum or candy, melt bits of ice in your mouth, or use a saliva substitute. However, if your mouth continues to feel dry for more than 2 weeks, check with your medical doctor or dentist. Continuing dryness of the mouth may increase the chance of dental disease, including tooth decay, gum disease, and fungus infections.

POSSIBLE SIDE EFFECTS Side Effects That Should B e Reported To Your Doctor immediately

[ ] Stop taking this medicine and check with your doctor immediately if the following side effect occurs:

[ ] Rare – Painful, inappropriate erection of penis (continuing)
[ ] Side Effects That Should Be Reported T Your Doctor
[ ] Less common – Confusion; muscle tremors
[ ] Rare – Fainting; fast or slow heartbeat; skin rash; unusual excitement
[ ] Side Effects That Usually Do Not Require Medical Attention
[ ] These possible side effects may go away during treatment; however, if they continue or are bothersome, check with your doctor, nurse, or pharmacist.
[ ] More common – Dizziness or lightheadedness; drowsiness; dry mouth (usually mild); headache; nausea or vomiting; unpleasant taste
[ ] Other side effects not listed above may also occur in some patients. If you notice any other effects, check with your doctor, nurse, or pharmacist.

Patient Medication Instruction Sheet
STAMM, RANDY LYNN 21 –C 1583

==

Rx# 4927457 (#4) LORAZEPAM 2MG TAB

==

[ ] Benzodiazepines (ben-zoh-dye-AZ-e-peens) are used to relieve anxiety, and to treat insomnia (trouble in sleeping). However, benzodiazepines should not be used for anxiety, nervousness, or tensions caused by the stress of everyday life. Some benzodiazepines may also be used to relax muscle or relieve muscle spasm, and to treat panic disorders and certain convulsive disorders, such as epilepsy. Benzodiazepines may also be used for other conditions as determined by your doctor.

[ ] If any of the information in this leaflet causes you special concern or if you want additional information about your medicine and its use, check with your doctor, nurse, or pharmacist. Remember, keep, this and all other medicines out of the reach of children and never share your medicine with others.

BEFORE USING Tell your doctor, nurse, and pharmacist if you…

* are allergic to any medicine, either prescription or nonprescription (over- the-counter [OTC]);
* are pregnant or intend to become pregnant while using this medicine;
* are breast-feeding
* are using any other prescription or nonprescription (over-the-counter [OTC]) medicine especially fluvoxamine, itraconazole, ketoconazole, nefazodone, or other CNS depressants;
* have any other medical problems, especially asthma, bronchitis, emphysema, or other chronic lung disease;
* glaucoma;
* or myasthenia gravis.

HOW TO TAKE AND STORE Take this medicine exactly as directed by your doctor. Do not take more of it, do not take it more often, and do not take it for a longer time than directed. If too much is taken, it may become habit-forming.

[ ] If you think this medicine is not working properly after you have taken it for a few weeks, do not increase the dose. Instead, check with your doctor.

[ ] If you are taking this medicine for epilepsy, it must be taken everyday in regularly spaced keep a constant amount of medicine in the blood.

[ ] If you are taking this medicine for insomia, do not take it if you cannot get a full night's sleep (7 to 8 hours). Otherwise, you may feel drowsy and have memory problems when you wake because the effects of the medicine have not worn off.

[ ] If you miss a dose of this medicine, take it as soon as possible. However, if it is almost time for your next dose, skip the missed dose. Do not double dose.

[ ] To store this medicine:

[ ] Keep it out the reach of children. Store away from heat and direct light. Do not store in the bathroom, near the kitchen sink, or in other damp places. Heat or moisture may cause the medicine to break down. Keep the syrup form of this medicine from freezing. Do not keep outdated medicine or medicine no longer needed. Be sure that any discarded medicine is out of the reach of children.

WARNINGS Do not suddenly stop taking this medicine without first checking with your doctor. You may need to reduce the dose gradually to prevent withdrawal effects.

[ ] Benzidiazepines may be a habit-forming (cause mental or physical dependence). If you think you may have become mentally or physically dependent on this medicine, check with your doctor.

[ ] This medicine will add to the effects of alcohol and other and other CNS depressants (medicines that slow down the nervous system, possibly causing drowsiness). Check with your doctor before taking any such depressants while using these medicines.

[ ] Benzodiazepines may cause some people to become drowsy, dizzy, or clumsy.

[ ] Make sure you know how to react to this medicine before you drive, use machines, or do other jobs that require you to be alert and have good muscle control.

[ ] If you think you or someone else may have taken an overdose, get emergency help at once.

[ ] Some signs of an overdose are continuing slurred speech or confusion, severe drowsiness, severe weakness, and staggering.

POSSIBLE SIDE EFFECTS Side Effects That Should Be Reported To Your Doctor Immediately

[ ] Less common – Anxiety; confusion (may be more common with in older adults); fast, pounding, or irregular heartbeat; memory problems (more common with triazolam); mental depression

[ ] Rare – Abnormal thinking, including disorientation, delusions (holding false beliefs that cannot be changed by facts), or loss of sense of reality; agitation; behavior changes, including aggressive behavior, bizarre behavior, decreased inhibition, or outburst of anger; convulsions (seizures); fever, chills, or sore throat; hallucinations; muscle weakness; skin rash or itching; sore throat, fever, and chills; trouble in sleeping; ulcers or sores in mouth or throat (continuing); uncontrolled movements of body, including the eyes; unusual bleeding or bruising; unusual excitement, or nervousness, or irritability; unusual tiredness or weakness (severe); yellow eyes or skin

[ ] Signs of overdose – Confusion (continuing); drowsiness (severe); coma; shakiness; slow heartbeat; slow reflexes; slurred speech (continuing); staggering; troubled breathing; weakness (severe)

[ ] Side Effect That Usually D o Not Require Medical Attention

[ ] These possible side effects may go away during treatment; however, if they continue or are bothersome, check with your doctor, nurse, or pharmacist.

[ ] More common – Clumsiness or unsteadiness; dizziness or lightheadedness; drowsiness; slurred speech

[ ] Other side effects not listed above may also occur in some patients. If you notice any other effects, check with your doctor, nurse, or pharmacist.

[ ] After you stop using this medicine, your body may need time to adjust. During this time, check with your doctor if you experience fast or pounding heartbeat; increased sensitivity to light, sound, touch, or pain; increased sweating; loss of sense of reality; mental depression; muscle or stomach cramps; nausea or vomiting; tingling, burning, or prickly sensations; trembling or shaking; trouble in sleeping; or if you are unusually irritable, nervous, or confused.

Patient Medication Instruction Sheet

STAMM, RANDY LYNN 21 – 1583

==

**Rx# 4297454 (#4) CITALOPRAM HYDROBROMIDE 20MG
TAB**

==

[ ] Citalopram (si-TAL-oh-pram) is used to treat mental depression.
[ ] If any of the information in this leaflet causes you special concern or if you want additional information about your medicine and its use, check with your doctor, nurse, or pharmacist. Remember, keep this and all other medicines out of the reach of children and never share your medicines with others.

BEFORE USING Tell your doctor, nurse, or pharmacist if you…

* are allergic to any medicine, either prescription or nonprescription (over- the-counter [OTC]);
* are pregnant or intend to become pregnant while using this medicine;
* are breast-feeding
* are using any other prescription or nonprescription (over-the-counter [OTC]) medicine especially fluvoxamine, MAO inhibitors, paroxetine, sertraline, or venlafaxine;
* have any other medical problems, especially liver disease.
* **HOW TO TAKE AND STORE** Take this medicine only as directed by your doctor in order to improve your condition as much as possible. Do not take more of it, do not take it more often, and do not take it for a much longer time than directed.

[ ] This medicine may be taken on a full or an empty stomach. However, if your doctor tells you to take it a certain way, take it exactly as directed.
[ ] You may have to take citalopram for 4 weeks or longer before you begin to feel better. Your doctor should check your progress at regular visits during this time. Also, you will probably need to keep taking this medicine for at least 6 months, even if you feel better, to help prevent the depression from returning.
[ ] If you miss a dose of this medicine, check with your doctor.
[ ] To store this medicine:

[ ] Keep it out the reach of children. Store away from heat and direct light. Do not store in the bathroom, near the kitchen sink, or in other damp places. Heat or moisture may cause the medicine to break down. Keep the syrup form of this medicine from freezing. Do not keep outdated medicine or medicine no longer needed. Be sure that any discarded medicine is out of the reach of children.

WARNINGS It is important that your doctor progress at regular visits, to allow for changes in your dose and help reduce any side effects.

[ ] Do not take this medicine with a monoamine oxidase (MAO inhibitor (e.g., furazolidone, isocarboxazid, phenelzine, procarbazine or tranylcypromine). Also, do not take this medicine less than 2 weeks after taking an MAO and do not take MAO inhibitor for at least 2 weeks after taking this medicine. To do so may cause you to have extremely high blood pressure or convulsions.

[ ] Avoid drinking alcoholic beverages while you are taking this medicine.

[ ] This medicine may cause some people to become drowsy. It may also cause problems with coordination and one's ability to think.

[ ] Make sure you know how to react to this medicine before you drive, use machines, or do other jobs that require you to be alert, well — coordinated, or able to think clearly.

POSSIBLE SIDE EFFECTS Side Effects That Should Be Reported To Your Doctor

[ ] More common – Decrease in sexual activity or interest in sex

[ ] Less common – Agitation; blurred vision; confusion; fever; increase in amount of urine or frequency of urination; lack of emotion; loss of memory; menstrual changes; skin rash or itching; troubled breathing

[ ] Rare – Bleeding gums; breast tenderness or enlargement (in females); chills; difficulty in urinating or in holding urine; dizziness or fainting; incomplete, sudden, or unusual movements of the body or face; irregular heartbeat; mood or mental changes; nosebleeds; painful urination; purple or red spots on skin; irritated or red eyes; redness, tenderness, itching, burning, or peeling of skin; sore throat; unusual secretion of milk (in females)

[ ] Signs of low blood sodium—Rare – Confusion; convulsions (seizure); drowsiness; dryness of mouth; increased thirst; lack of energy

[ ] Rare – Signs of serotonin syndrome – Agitation; confusion; diarrhea; fever; overactive reflexes; restlessness; shivering; sweating; talking; feeling, and acting with excitement and activity you cannot control; trembling or shaking; trouble with coordination; twitching

[ ] Side Effects That Usually Do Not Require Medical Treatment; however, if they continue or are bothersome, check with your doctor, nurse, or pharmacist.

[ ] More common – Drowsiness; dryness of mouth; nausea; trouble in sleeping

[ ] Less common – Abdominal pain; anxiety; change in taste; diarrhea; gas; headache; heartburn; increased sweating; increased yawning; loss of appetite; pain in joints or muscles; runny or stuffy nose; tingling, burning, or prickly sensations; tooth grinding; trembling or shaking; unusual tiredness or weakness; unusual weight loss or gain; vomiting; watering of mouth

[ ] Other side effects not listed above may also occur in some patients. If you notice any notice any other effects, check with your doctor, nurse, or pharmacist.

[ ] After you stop using this medicine, your body may need time to adjust. During this time, check with your doctor if you notice any of the following side effects: Anxiety dizziness nervousness trembling or shaking.

Patient Medication Instruction Sheet
STAMM, RANDY LYNN 21 – 1583

===

Rx# 4297454 (#4) Cimetidine 400MG TAB

===

[ ] H2-blockers are used in the treatment and prevention of duodenal ulcers. Some of the H2-blockers are used to treat gastric ulcers. In addition, H2-blockers are used in some conditions in which the stomach produces too much acid. These medicines may also be used for other conditions as determined by your doctor.

[ ] If any of the information in this leaflet causes you special concern or if you want additional information about your medicine and its use, check with your doctor, nurse, or pharmacist. Remember, keep this and all other medicines out of the reach of children and never share your medicines with others.

BEFORE USING If you are using this medicine without a prescription, carefully read and follow any precautions on the label.

[ ] You should be especially careful if you...

* are allergic to any medicine, either prescription (over-the-counter [OTC]);

* are pregnant or intend to become pregnant while using this medicine;

* are breast-feeding;

* are using any other prescription or nonprescription (over-the-counter [OTC]) medicine, especially itraconazole or ketoconazole;

* are taking cimetidine and are also using aminophylline, amitrityline, amoxapine, anticoagulants (blood thinners), caffeine, clomipramine, desipramine, doxepin, imipramine, metoprolol, nortriptyline, oxtriphylline, phenytoin, propranolol

* protriptyline, theophylline, or trimipramine;

* have any other medicinal problems

* especially kidney diseases.

[ ] If you have any questions about any of this, check with your doctor, nurses, or pharmacist.

HOW TO TAKE AND STORE It may take several days for this medicine to begin to relieve stomach pain. To help relieve pain, antacids may be taken with this medicine, unless your doctor has told you not to use them. However, you should wait one-half to one hour between taking the antacid and this medicine.

[ ] Take this medicine for the full time with your doctor so that he or she will be better able to tell you when to stop taking this medicine.

[ ] For patients taking an over-the-counter (nonprescription) medicine for heartburn, acid indigestion, or sour stomach:

[ ] Do not take this medicine everyday for more than 2 weeks, unless your doctor tells you to do so.

[ ] If you have trouble in swallowing or abdominal pain that does not go away, call your doctor. This may be a sign of a serious medical problem.

[ ] For patients taking a prescription form of this medicine for a more serious problem:

[ ] One dose a day

[ ] Take it at bedtime, unless otherwise directed.

[ ] Two doses a day

[ ] Take them with meals and at bedtime for best results.

[ ] For patients taking famotidine chewable tablets:

[ ] Chew the tablets completely before swallowing.

[ ] If you miss a dose of this medicine, take it as soon as possible. However, if it is almost time for your next dose, skip the missed dose and go back to your regular dosing schedule. Do not double doses.

[ ] To store this medicine

[ ] Keep it out the reach of children. Store away from heat and direct light. Do not store in the bathroom, near the kitchen sink, or in other damp places. Heat or moisture may cause the medicine to break down. Keep the syrup form of this medicine from freezing. Do not keep outdated medicine or medicine no longer needed. Be sure that any discarded medicine is out of the reach of children.

WARNINGS Some test may be affected by this medicine. Tell the doctor in charge that you are taking this medicine before:

[ ] You have any skin tests for allergies.

[ ] You have any tests to determine how much acid your stomach produces.

[ ] Remember that certain medicines, such as aspirin, as well as certain foods and drinks (e.g., citrus products, carbonated drinks, etc.), irritate the stomach and may make your problem worse.

[ ] Cigarette smoking tends to decrease the effect of H2-blockers by increasing the amount of acid produce by the stomach. This is more likely to affect the stomach's nighttime production of acid. While taking this medicine, stop smoking completely, or at least do not smoke after the last dose of the day.

[ ] Be careful of the amount of alcohol you drink while taking this medicine. H2-blockers have been shown to increase alcohol levels you in the blood. Ask your doctor, nurse, or pharmacist for guidance.

[ ] Check with your doctor if your ulcer pain continues or gets worse.

POSSIBLE SIDE EFFECTS Side Effects That Should Be Reported To Your Doctor

[ ] Rare – burning, redness, skin rash, or swelling; confusion, fast, pounding, or irregular bruising; unusual tiredness or weakness

[ ] Other side effects not listed above may also occur in some patients. If you notice any other effects, check with your doctor nurse, or pharmacist.

Patient Medication Instruction Sheet

STAMM, RANDY LYNN 21 – 1583

==

Rx# 4927452 (#12) CARISOPRODOL 350MG TAB

==

[ ] Skeletal muscle relaxants are used to relax certain muscles in your body and relieve the stiffness, pain, and discomfort caused by strains, or other injury to your muscles. However, these medicines do not take the place of rest, exercise or physical therapy, or other treatment that your doctor may recommend.

[ ] If any of the information in this leaflet causes you special concern or if you want additional information about your medicine and its use, check with your doctor, nurse, or pharmacist.

[ ] Remember, keep this and all other medicines out of the reach of children and never share your medicines with others.

BEFORE USING If you are using this medicine without a prescription, carefully read and follow any precautions on the label.

[ ] You should be especially careful if you...

*   are allergic to any medicine, either prescription (over-the-counter [OTC]);

*   are pregnant or intend to become pregnant while using this medicine;

*   are breast-feeding;

*   are using any other prescription or nonprescription (over-the-counter [OTC]) medicine, especially narcotics or other CNS depressants;

HOW TO TAKE AND STORE If you miss a dose of this medicine, and remember within an hour or so of the missed dose, take it right away. However, if you do not remember until later, skip the missed dose and go back to your regular dosing schedule. Do not double doses.

[ ] To store this medicine:

[ ] Keep it out the reach of children. Store away from heat and direct light. Do not store in the bathroom, near the kitchen sink, or in other damp places. Heat or moisture may cause the medicine to

break down. Keep the syrup form of this medicine from freezing. Do not keep outdated medicine or medicine no longer needed. Be sure that any discarded medicine is out of the reach of children.

WARNINGS If you will be taking this medicine for a longtime (for example, more than a few weeks), your doctor should check your progress at regular visits.

[ ] This medicine will add to the effects of alcohol and others CNS depressants (medicines that slow down the nervous system, possibly causing drowsiness). Check with your doctor before taking any such depressants while using this medicine.

[ ] Skeletal muscle relaxants may cause blurred vision, or clumsiness or unsteadiness in some people. They may also cause some people to feel drowsy, dizzy, lightheaded, faint, or less alert than they are normally.

[ ] Make sure you know how to react to this medicine before you drive, use machines, or do other jobs that require you to be alert, well coordinated, and able to see well.

POSSIBLE SIDE EFFECTS Side Effects That Should Be Reported To Your Doctor

[ ] Less common – Fainting, fast heartbeat; fever; hive-like swellings (large) on eyelids, face, lips, or tongue; mental depression; shortness of breath, troubled breathing, tightness in chest, or wheezing; skin rash, hives, itching, or redness; burning or stinging of eyes; stuffy nose and red or bloodshot eyes.

[ ] Rare – Blood in urine; bloody or black, tarry stools; cough or hoarseness; fast or irregular breathing; lower back or side pain; muscle cramps or pain (not present before treatment or more painful than before treatment); difficult or painful urination; pinpoint red spots on skin; puffiness or swelling of the eyelids around the eyes; sores, ulcers, or white spots in mouth or on lips; sore throat and fever with or without chills; swollen or painful glands; unusual bleeding or bruising; unusual tiredness or weakness; vomiting of blood or material that looks like coffee grounds; yellow eyes or skin

[ ] Side Effects That Usually Do Not Require Medical Attention

[ ] These possible side effects may go away during treatment; however, if they continue or are bothersome, check with your doctor, nurse, or pharmacist.

Patient Medication Instruction Sheet

STAMM, RANDY LYNN 21 – 1583

==

Rx# 4927451 (#12) BUSPIRONE 10MG TAB

==

[ ] Buspirone (byoo-SPYE-rone) is used to treat certain anxiety disorders or to relieve the symptoms of anxiety. However, buspirone is usually not used for anxiety or tension caused by the stress of everyday life.

[ ] If any of the information in this leaflet causes you special concern or if you want additional information about your medicine and its use, check with your doctor, nurse, or pharmacist.

[ ] Remember, keep this and all other medicines out of the reach of children and never share your medicines with others.

BEFORE USING Tell your doctor, nurse, or pharmacist if you…

* are allergic to any medicine, either prescription (over-the-counter [OTC]);

* are pregnant or intend to become pregnant while using this medicine;

* are breast-feeding;

* are using any other prescription or nonprescription (over-the-counter [OTC]) medicine, especially erythromycin, itraconazole, or MAO inhibitors;

* have any other medical problems, especially liver disease.

HOW TO TAKE AND STORE Take this medicine exactly as directed by your doctor. Do not take it more often, and do not take it for a longer time than directed. To do so may increase the chance of unwanted effects.

[ ] After you begin taking buspirone, 1 to 2 weeks may pass before you begin to feel the side effects of the medicine.

[ ] If you miss a dose of this medicine, take it as soon as possible. However, if it is almost time for your next dose, skip the missed dose and go back to your regular dosing schedule. Do not double doses.

[ ] To store this medicine

[ ] Keep it out the reach of children. Store away from heat and direct light. Do not store in the bathroom, near the kitchen sink, or in

other damp places. Heat or moisture may cause the medicine to break down. Keep the syrup form of this medicine from freezing. Do not keep outdated medicine or medicine no longer needed. Be sure that any discarded medicine is out of the reach of children.

WARNINGS If you will be using buspirone regularly for a long time, your doctor should check your progress at regular visits to make sure the medicine does not cause unwanted effects.

[ ] Buspirone may cause some people to become dizzy, lightheaded, drowsy, or less alert than they are normally.

[ ] Make sure you know how to react to this medicine before you drive, use machines, or do anything else that could be dangerous if you are dizzy or not alert.

[ ] If you think you or anyone else may have taken an overdose of this medicine, get emergency help at once.

[ ] Some signs of an overdose are dizziness or lightheadedness severe drowsiness or loss of consciousness stomach upset, including nausea or vomiting or very small pupils of the eyes.

POSSIBLE SIDE EFFECTS Side Effects That Should Be Reported TO Your Doctor

[ ] Rare – Chest pain; confusion; fast or pounding heartbeat; fever; mental depression; muscle weakness; numbness, tingling, pain, or weakness of hands or feet; skin rash or hives; sore throat; stiff arms or legs; trouble with coordination; uncontrolled movements of the body

[ ] Side Effects That Usually Do Not Require Medical Attention

[ ] These possible side effects may go away during treatment; however, if they continue or are bothersome, check with your doctor, nurse, or pharmacist.

[ ] More common – Dizziness or lightheadedness, especially when getting up from a lying or sitting position; headache; nausea; restlessness, nervousness, or unusual excitement

[ ] Less common or rare – Blurred vision; clamminess or sweating; decrease in concentration; diarrhea; drowsiness; dry mouth; muscle pain, spasm, cramps, or stiffness; ringing in the ears; trouble in sleeping, nightmares, or vivid dreams; unusual tiredness or weakness

[ ] Other side effects not listed above may also occur in some patients. If you notice any other effects, check with your doctor, nurse or pharmacist.

Patient Medication Instruction Sheet
STAMM, RANDY LYNN 21 – 1583

===

Rx# 4927450 (#4) ATENOL 50MG TAB

===

[ ] ATENOL (a-TEN-oh-lol) belongs to the group of medicines known as beta-blockers. It is used to treat high blood pressure (hypertension). It is also help to prevent additional heart attacks. It may also be used for other conditions as determined by your doctor.

[ ] If any of the information in this leaflet causes you special concern or if you want additional information about your medicine and its use, check with your doctor, nurse, or pharmacist.

[ ] Remember, keep this and all other medicines out of the reach of children and never share your medicines with others.

BEFORE USING Tell your doctor, nurse, or pharmacist if you...

*   are allergic to any medicine, either prescription (over-the-counter [OTC]);

*   are pregnant or intend to become pregnant while using this medicine;

*   are breast-feeding;

*   are using any other prescription or nonprescription (over-the-counter [OTC]) medicine, especially allergy shots or allergy skin testing; aminophylline; caffeine; calcium channel blockers; clonide; diabetes medicine; dyphylline; guanabenz; MAO inhibitors; oxtriphylline; theophylline; or medicines for appetite control, asthma, colds, cough, hay fever, or sinus;

*   have any other medical problems, especially allergy, asthma or other lung disease, diabetes, heart or blood vessel disease, mental depression, or overactive thyroid;

*   use cocaine.

HOW TO TAKE AND STORE Even if you feel well, take this medicine exactly as directed.

[ ] Ask your doctor about your pulse rate. If your doctor tells you to check your pulse regularly while you are taking this medicine, and it is much slower than the rate your doctor has said is best, check

with your doctor. A pulse rate that is too slow may cause circulation problems.

[ ] If you are taking this medicine for high blood pressure, remember that it will not cure your high blood pressure, but it does help control it. You must continue to take it —even if you feel well — if you expect to keep your blood pressure down. You may have to take high blood pressure medicine for the rest of your life.

[ ] Do not miss any doses, especially if you are taking only one dose a day. Some conditions may become worse when this medicine, is not taken regularly.

[ ] If you do miss a dose of this medicine, take it as soon as possible. However, if it is within 8 hours of your next dose, skip the missed dose and go back to your regular dosing schedule. Do not double doses.

[ ] To store this medicine:

[ ] Keep it out the reach of children. Store away from heat and direct light. Do not store in the bathroom, near the kitchen sink, or in other damp places. Heat or moisture may cause the medicine to break down. Keep the syrup form of this medicine from freezing. Do not keep outdated medicine or medicine no longer needed. Be sure that any discarded medicine is out of the reach of children.

WARNINGS Do not stop using this medicine without first checking with your doctor.

[ ] Before having any kind of surgery or dental emergency treatment, tell the medical doctor or dentist in charge that you are using this medicine

[ ] For diabetic patients:

[ ] This medicine may cause your blood sugar levels to fall. Also, this medicine may cover up signs of hypoglycemia (low blood sugar).

[ ] This medicine may cause some people to become drowsy, dizzy, or lightheaded.

[ ] Make sure you know how to react to this medicine before you drive, use machines, or do other jobs that require you to be alert.

[ ] Chest pain resulting from exercise or exertion is usually reduced or prevented by this medicine.

[ ] This may tempt you to be overly active. Make sure you discuss with your doctor a safe amount of exercise for your medical problem.

POSSIBLE SIDE EFFECTS Side Effects That Should Be Reported
To Your Doctor
[ ] Less common – Difficulty in breathing; cold hands and feet;
mental depression; shortness of breath; slow heartbeat; swelling of
ankles, feet, or lower legs
[ ] Rare – Back or joint pain; chest pain; confusion (especially in
older adults); dizziness or lightheadedness, especially when getting
up from a lying or sitting position; fever or sore throat;
hallucinations; irregular heartbeat; red, scaling, or crusted skin;
skin rash; unusual bleeding or bruising
[ ] Side Effects That Usually Do Not Require Medical Attention
[ ] These possible side effects may go away during treatment;
however, if they continue or are bothersome, check with your
doctor, nurse or pharmacist.
[ ] More common – Decreased sexual ability; dizziness or
lightheadedness; drowsiness (mild); trouble in sleeping; unusual
tiredness or weakness
[ ] After you have been taking this medicine for a while, it may cause
unpleasant or even harmful effects if you stop taking it suddenly.
Check with your doctor right away if you notice chest pain, fast or
irregular heartbeat, general feeling of body discomfort or
weakness, headache, shortness of breath (sudden), sweating, or
trembling.
[ ] Other side effects not listed above may also occur in some patients.
If you notice any other effects, check with your doctor, nurse, or
pharmacist.

Patient Medication Instruction Sheet

STAMM, RANDY LYNN 2 – 1583

==

Rx# 4927449 (#4) ALLOPURINOL 300MG TAB

==

[ ] Allopurinol (al-oh-PURE-I-nole) is used to treat chronic gout. It helps to prevent gout attacks, but will not relieve an attack that has already started. Allopurinol is also used to prevent or treat medical problems caused by too much uric acid in the body, including certain kinds of kidney stones or other problems.

[ ] If any of the information in this leaflet causes you special concern or if you want additional information about your medicine and its use, check with your doctor, nurse, or pharmacist.

[ ] Remember, keep this and all other medicines out of the reach of children and never share your medicines with others.

BEFORE USING Tell your doctor, nurse, or pharmacist if you…

* are allergic to any medicine, either prescription (over-the-counter [OTC]);

* are pregnant or intend to become pregnant while using this medicine;

* are breast-feeding;

* are using any other prescription or nonprescription (over-the-counter [OTC]) medicine, especially anticoagulants (blood thinners), azathioprine, or mercaptopurine;

* have any other medical problems.

HOW TO TAKE AND STORE If this medicine upsets your stomach, take it after meals. If stomach upset (nausea, vomiting, diarrhea, or stomach pain) continues, check with your doctor.

[ ] In order for this medicine to help you, it must be taken regularly as ordered.

[ ] To help prevent kidney stones while taking allopurinol, adults should drink at least 10 to 12 full glasses (8 ounces each) of fluids each day unless otherwise directed by their doctor. Check with your doctor about the amount of fluids to be taken each day by children being treated with this medicine. Also, your doctor may want you to take another medicine to make your urine less acid.

[ ] For patients taking allopurinol for chronic gout:

[ ] Your gout attacks may continue for a while after you begin to take allopurinol. However, if you take this medicine regularly as directed by your doctor, the attacks will gradually become less frequent and less painful and may stop completely after several months.

[ ] If you are taking allopurinol to prevent gout attacks and they continue, keep taking this medicine, even if you are taking another medicine for the attacks.

[ ] If you miss a dose of this medicine, take it as soon as possible. However, if it is almost time for your next dose, skip the missed dose and go back to your regular dosing schedule. Do not double doses.

[ ] To store this medicine:

[ ] Keep it out the reach of children. Store away from heat and direct light. Do not store in the bathroom, near the kitchen sink, or in other damp places. Heat or moisture may cause the medicine to break down. Keep the syrup form of this medicine from freezing. Do not keep outdated medicine or medicine no longer needed. Be sure that any discarded medicine is out of the reach of children.

WARNINGS It is important that your doctor check your progress at regular visits. Blood test may be needed to make this medicine is working properly and is not causing unwanted effects.

[ ] Drinking too much alcohol may increase the amount of uric acid in the blood and lessen the effects of allopurinol. Therefore, people with gout and other people with to much uric acid in the body should be careful to limit the amount of alcohol they drink.

[ ] Taking too much vitamin C may make the urine more acidic and increase the possibility of kidney stones. Check with your doctor before you take vitamin C while taking allopurinol.

[ ] Check with your doctor immediately if you notice a skin rash, hives, or itching while taking allopurinol or if chills, fever, and joint pain, muscle aches or pains, sore throat, or nausea or vomiting occur, especially if they occur together with or shortly after a skin rash. Very rarely, these effects may be the first signs of a serious reaction to the medicine.

[ ] This medicine may cause some people to become drowsy or less alert than they are normally.

[ ] Make sure you know how to react to this medicine before you drive, use machines, or do other jobs that require you to be alert.

POSSIBLY SIDE EFFECTS Side Effects That Should Be Reported To Your Doctor Immediately

[ ] Stop taking this medicine and check with your doctor immediately if you notice;

[ ] More common – Skin rash, hives, or itching

[ ] Rare – Black, tarry stools; bleeding sores on lips; blood in urine or stools; chills, fever, muscle aches or pains, nausea, or vomiting, especially if occurring with or shortly after a skin rash; difficult or painful urination; pinpoint red spots on skin; red or irritated eyes; redness, tenderness, burning, or peeling of skin; red, thickened, or scaly skin; shortness of breath; sores, ulcers, or white spots in mouth or in lips; sore throat and fever; sudden decrease in urine; swelling of abdomen or stomach; swelling of face, feet, fingers, or lower legs; swollen or painful glands; troubled breathing, tightness in chest, or wheezing; unusual bleeding or bruising; unusual tiredness or weakness; weight gain (rapid); yellow eyes or skin

[ ] Other Side Effects That Should Be Reported To Your Doctor

[ ] Rare – Loosening of fingernails; lower back or side pain; numbness, tingling, pain, or weakness of hands or feet; unexplained nosebleeds

[ ] Side Effects That Usually Do Not Require Medical Attention

[ ] These possible side effects may go away during treatment; however, if they continue or are bothersome, check with your doctor, nurse, or pharmacist.

[ ] Less common or rare – Diarrhea; drowsiness; headache; indigestion; nausea or vomiting occurring without a skin rash or other side effects; stomach pain occurring without other side effects, check with your doctor, nurse, or pharmacist

Web sites that could not be used due to Copy write clauses and the censorship:

These sites can be accessed via the Internet since all of this information could not be added to the book from the publisher. At least this way I can give you the information and you can look up what is missing in the book and you can see the re4al thing for your selves. If you have any Questions you can send me an email to harely2001sport@aol.com anytime and I will help you to view these sites but you must have a computer to view them.

http://dailynews.yahoo/h/nm/200000914/wl iraq usa dc 1.html
U.S. Says Ready to use Force against IRAQ 14 Sept.

http://www.gulflink.osd.mil/org.html
Office of the Special Assistant for Gulf War Illnesses

Http://sg.dailynews.yahoo.com/headlines/…al measures against iraq threats.html
Kuwait seeks international "measures" against Iraqi threats

http://news.bbc.co.uk/hi/english/world/middle east/newsid 929000/929131.stm
Mortar Attacks in Baghdad

http://www.news.bbc.co.uk/hi/english/world/middle east/newsid 92700/92704.htm
US Warns Saddam

http://dailynews.yahoo.com/h/nm/20000917/iraq kuwait dc 6.html
Kuwait asks World for Measures Against Iraq

http://dailynews.yahoo.com/h/ap/20000916/w1/iraq military training 1.html
Iraq Boost Military Training

http://members.aol.com/desertstormmom/vetcenter/taps.htm
Memorial Room

http://www.ngwrc.org/facts/index.htm
1999 Gulf War statistics

http://www.ngwrc.org/aboutboardfiles/bombing.htm
National Gulf War Resource Center. Inc

http://dailynews.yahoo.com/h/ap/20000406/pl/gulg war ilness 2.html
Gulf War Vets Awaits Benefits

http://www.alsa.org/news/news032700.html
Department of Veterans Affairs News Release

http://www.ngwrc.org
Gulf War Vets Die Awaiting Benefits

http://www.ngwrc.org/dulink/du fact sheet.html
NATO Yugoslav War Depleted uranium Fact Sheet

http://pbs.org/wgpbh/pages/frontline/gulf/script a.hmtl
Discussion from military in high positions about some of the problems during the Gulf War

http://www.pbs.org/wgbh/pages/frontline/gulf/maps/4.html
Maps of the Gulf War and the moves during Desert Shield/Storm

http://www.ctnow.com/script...eetype=article&render=y&ck=&v
er=hbl.2.20
Debate Rages on War Illnesses

http://www.gulfwarvets.com/death.htm
Death ruling raises issue of Gulf War Ills

http://www.gulfwarvets.com/treat.htm
Desert Storm Syndrome Treatment Study
http://www.gulfwarvets.com/records.htm
Lost Medical Records on Viet Nam and Gulf War Vets

http://www.gulfwarvets.com/hr2697.htm
Persian Gulf War Syndrome Compensation Act of 1999(Introduced into the house)

http://www.gulfwarvets.com/news7.htm
Gulf War vet study has first evidence of Britain Damage

http://www.gulflink.osd.mil/medical.htm
Gulf Link Medical Information Site

http://www.tricare.osd.mil/gulfrpt.html
Federal Activities related to health of Persian Gulf Veterans

http://www.gulflink.osd.mil/news/na.owf ii 28ser00.html
DOD Re-Examines Oli Well Fire Contaminants

http://www.gulflink.osd.mil
An Nasiriyah Southwest Ammunition Storage Point (Final Report) 1-800-497-6261

http://www.gulflink.osd.mil/news/na cement ii 28sep00.html
Final Version Concludes Investigation into Cement Factory

http://www.gulflink.osd.mil/medical/med eval prgm.html
Medical Evaluation Programs

http://www.gulflink.osd.mil/medical/gwillness defining.html
Gulf War Illnesses-related Medical Research & Publications Epidemiology

http://http://www.gulflink.osd.mil/medical/gwillness exposure.html
Exposure &Exposure/Response Relationships

http://www.gulflink.osd.mil/medical/gwillness other outcomes.html
Other health outcomes

http://www.nap.edu/catalog/4904.html
Health Consequences of Service Duringf the Persan Gulf War

http://www.gulflink.osd.mil
Topical Bibliography of Published Works Regarding the Health of Veterans of the Persian Gulf War

http://www.va.gov/publ/direc/benefits/m2116ch7.htm
Disability compensation and unemployability

http://www.vba.va.gov/pubs/forms/21-8940.pdf
Forms to file under the Veterans Administration System

http://laws.lp.findlaw.com/fed/007009.html
Robertson v Principi (case vs VA)

http://story.news yahoo.com/news?tmpl=story&u=/ap/20020811/ap on re mi ea/iraq saddam s cubs 2
Saddam's Camp seeks youth camps

http://story.news.yahoo.com/news?tmpl=story&u=ap/20020809/ap wo en po/us iraq 18
Iraqi opposition groups claims to have unified stand against Saddam Hussein

http://story.news.yahoo.com/news?tmpl=story&u=ap/20020808/ap to po/us iraq maneuvering 3
Saddam Hussein may be trying to avert an attack with alternative moves on weapons inspections

http://story.news.yahoo.com/news?tmpl=story&u=ap/20020808/ap wo en po/un iraq 33
Saddam Hussein's speech didn't give "an inch" in meeting Security Council demands on return of inspectors

http://top-biography.com/9004-Saddam%20Hussein/
Saddam Biography

http://www.home.earthlink.net/~arison/gws.html
Gulf War Syndrome Defined Evidence and Conclusions

http://news.bbc.co.uk/hi/english/sci/newsid 708000/708379.stm
Blood poisoning, antibodies could be linked to Gulf War Illnesses

http://www.Sunday-times.co...pages/tim/2000/04/25timnwsnw01031
US Test should confirm Gulf War syndrome
Administration so this includes research to help other Gulf War Veterans.

About the Author

Randy Lynn Stamm is a forty-two-year-old retired Army Sergeant and a Gulf War Veteran. Randy was born in March of 1960 and went to Mesquite High School from 1975 to 1978 in Mesquite Texas and now holds a Graduate Degree in Information Systems Engineering with a Minor in Plan and Design. Sergeant First Class Stamm served in the Army from 14 February 1980 to 01 May 1995 in various positions and the highest being a Platoon Sergeant. Sergeant First Class Stamm took the early retirement in May of 1995 due to having major medical problems from the Gulf War and that is what prompted this creation. Randy dedicates his military service to his parents Larry and Wanda Logan on Gun Barrel City, Texas and Grandfather Shawlver (Pappy) Reeda Lewis of Quitman, Texas. Every time he was on leave during his military career he always had to go visit just to get counseling and told to stay in the Army until retirement. Since retiring for the Army in May of 1995 and having joined Corporate America and not knowing that the politics were too much and having lost three jobs due to medical problems from the three different corporations, GTE, ARIS Corporation, and Alcatel USA, Inc.

Now he is rated at 100% from the Veterans Administration after a seven-year battle with the Waco Texas Regional Office. Now Mr. Stamm has filed a claim with the Social Security Administration in Austin Texas and is currently getting Social Security Disability and their process only took about three months with all of the correct documentation being submitted the first time. The key is to have all your documentation from the time you leave the service and back up everything that you say and do, then remember to hurry up and wait. One of the main things now is that he is a single parent of a teenage Daughter Brittni Lynn trying to raise her. Life has really changed since he lost his last job from Alcatel USA, Inc. in Plano, Texas. He says that raising a daughter alone is one of the biggest challenges that he has ever taken in his life. But to this day he still will do anything for her because the love is there *even if its tough love* and always will be no matter what. He is a member of both Sergeant Audie Murphy Club in the United States Army CONCU and Sergeant Morales Club in United States Army Europe, the most prominent clubs in the United States Army.

Lastly, one thing to remember is that you only live once and that there might not be a tomorrow. So enjoy life to the fullest every day of the rest of your life. GOOD LUCK AND GODS SPEED.

Printed in the United States
148696LV00001B/102/A

9 781403 364876